PANTONE

by

G. LUCI

Text copyright © 2012 G. Lucifer
All Rights Reserved.

ISBN Number 978-1-291-08673-7

For legal reasons, this book should be considered a work of fiction.

Any resemblance to characters living or dead is simply a coincidence, or a product of your own overactive imagination.

It is dedicated to those people who believe in me.

Table of Contents

The Repro Trap
The Bog Wanker
"I'm gonna fuck some sense into you…"
Torquay or Bust.
Does that turn you on?
Safe Cracker
Snow White
My Best Friend's Girl
Ring of Fire.
Biscuits
Duck
Torquay 1 York City 0
What was in the wardrobe, Coffin Nail?
Treacle's Teeth
Bacon. Boxes.
View from the Closet.
Sticky back? Drastic…
The Fuddle
The Show
Sid's Snake
The Whistle
A Big Fat One
Pot Poo Ree
Minty Throne
Cum Dancing
Chariots of Liar
Lemon Squeezy
Devil in Disguise
The Shadow

A Moth and a Rat
Statue of Fucking Liberty
Tellingbone
Own Goal
Meet The Parents.
Mutual Mastication.
The Fib Four
The Wander
Squirrel Ripper
Ringleader of the Midnight Zoo
Winkle Picker
Strawberry Fields for Trevor
Amateur Photographer
Cabbage Patch Kid
Animal Crackers
This Time it's Personal(ised)
Cornish Nasty
Bummery Justice
Womb Raider
Davey Donkeydangle and Mister Frisky
Breaking Up is Hard to Do
Feeling Remote.
Smooth Gloss Criminal
Baccy Warehouse
Porn Cracker
Roadkiller Heels
A Little Romance
Operation Superlesbian
Who Dares Whinnies
Smell a Rat
Bedhead
I Know What You've Been Doing!
Beauty and the Yeast

The Love Hammer
Blazing Saddles
The Car Chase
Brief Encounter
Work Experience
Puppet on a Thing
A Doffer you can't Refuse…
Good Lost Cause.
Do You Like Sausages?
A Shadow of his Former Self.
Dead Head
Oracle of the Follicle
The Big Man
One Night Stand
Blog Roll
Three's a Crowd.
Weasily Forgotten.
A Place in the Sun
Porn Free
Local Bike
Help The Aged.
What's The Big Flap?
Office Politics
Coffin Todger
Yosser Hughes Eat your Heart Out.
Dead Wood
A Strife Aquatic
Double Drunk Friday
Twinkle Twinkle Little Star…
Guilty Pleasures
Epilogue.

Foreword

I always assumed the stories I heard at work were normal, everyday.

I was wrong.

I started work in the studio of a Yorkshire print works in 1989 at the age of sixteen, after failing in spectacular fashion in my GCSEs, and although work came as one hell of a shock to me I soon acclimatised.

It was only later, when I started telling other people outside the factory the things that I heard and witnessed that I realised something strange was happening.

The people I work with are not normal.

Far from it.

Don't get me wrong, I'm sure some pretty bizarre things happen in factories across England, across the world, but nobody writes those stories down.

That's where I come in.

I wrote these stories as I remembered them, and as such they are in no particular order. I decided to leave it that way because a timeline is irrelevant – a lot of this stuff could have happened at any time over the past two or three decades.

The Lucifer name is, of course, a pseudonym.

I used the name for some years on an Internet forum, adopting it from an old French bicycle manufacturer, Genial Lucifer. I liked that name.

I also like that Lucifer, the Light Bearer or Bringer of Light, was given the shittiest job in the world and he's had to stick at it for a fuck of a long time.

The Repro Trap

reprographer re·prog'ra·pher n.

reprographic re'pro·graph'ic (rē'prə-grăf'ĭk, rĕp'rə-) adj.

The process of reproducing, reprinting, or copying graphic material especially by mechanical, photographic, or electronic means.

What did you want to be when you grew up?

Astronaut?

Nurse?

Teacher?

Stunt man?

Maybe.

Lithographic reprographer?

No.

Nobody did.

Nobody ever walked into their careers office and loudly declared in a bold voice;

"No lecture for me, Mister Careers Adviser! I already know my destiny.

A Lithographic reprographer I will be!"

Nobody.

Ever.

Me, I wanted to be an artist.

Correction.

I knew I was going to be an artist.

I just knew it.

There was no question.

It was so nailed on that I didn't even need to try at school.

All I needed was my art GCSE.

Everybody said I was good at art.

"I wish I could draw like that, Lucifer! It's ace!"

Yes. Yes it is.

Imagine my surprise when I didn't get that 'C' pass.

As it happened, I didn't get anything.

"Lucifer, your grades are D, D, E, E, Unclassified, etc… Now get out."

That was a bit of a wake up call.

What next?

There was a job going at a print works.

I applied, and got the job.

Any port in a storm...

"I'll give it a go..."

... Untill my art career takes off.

I took the bait.

I got the job.

It was nailed on, to be honest.

I didn't have to do a thing.

I was trapped.

I was in a studio.

That's a bit like being an artist, isn't it?

No. Not in the slightest.

That's the thing with repro.

There's a lot to learn, a whole shit load of knowledge you have to remember.

But there is no skill.

Or passion.

Or creativity.

Or soul.

It was here that I discovered I was pretty shit at art.

I can draw.

I can cook, but that doesn't make me Raymond fucking Blanc.

I wasn't going to be an artist.

I took this little revelation pretty hard for a while.

That and the fact I was stuck in reprographics.

It would have to do, for a while...

I work in direct mail. The most loathed print medium imaginable.

You look at the finished product, and you can never be satisfied.

Ah! That shiny brochure pedalling credit cards to the desperate is finished!

Let's pop it in the post and fuck up somebody's day.

While fucking up the environment at the same time.

Mmmm! I feel all warm and satisfied!

Not.

I remember asking my manager, Soulless Boss, what to do with a big barrel of evil smelling chemical from the film processors.

He said, "Chuck it down the sink."

"But..."

"I said chuck it down the sink!"

I chucked it down the sink.

You really would be shocked at what goes down the sink in a factory.

But I'm not going to go on about reprography.

I've endured twenty years of it.

Why should you suffer?

It's the other stuff that caught my eye.

The things that happen in between the work.

The stuff that fills the cracks in the boredom.

Stories.

Anecdotes.

Rumours.

Bullshit.

People in factories talk and I listen.

 Now I've written those things down.

The factory where I work is owned by God.

God is a rich man, a man who likes the money the factory makes.

He does not like the people who work in the factory.

I don't honestly blame him.

God leaves the everyday running of the factory to Cardboard Supervisor, a weak willed shell of a man, a man who gave up any hope of success years ago.

Cardboard Supervisor is treading water until he gets his gold watch, his fat cheque, his pick of the white goods from a crappy catalogue.

Below Cardboard Supervisor are a number of equally inept and ill trained lesser supervisors.

These supervisors try in vain to organise a workforce of dregs, illiterates, drunks and perverts.

Factories do not attract the cream of the crop.

Factories are there to gather up the dross that drifts to the bottom of the employment barrel, people who are unskilled, uneducated, unemployable in anything else other than factory work.

It is the supervisors' thankless task to try and squeeze an honest day's work out of this rabble.

No easy task.

The people in a factory have a job, not career.

They have no intention of moving on to something better, they are not moving up.

To them, the factory is as good as it gets.

You stay put, you work, you get paid.

You do not leave the factory.

Because people do not leave the factory, they become institutionalized.

They become strange.

Sometimes very strange.

The Bog Wanker

There's a guy at work who keeps wanking off in the toilets while I'm trying to take a crap.It's really getting on my nerves. He can't even be discreet about it, for fuck's sake...You can hear him panting, and there's that unmistakable 'cock being wanked' noise.

The wanking's bad, but I sort of wonder what gets him so randy at work that he feels he really has to crack one off right at that second, even with a bloke tutting loudly in disgust about three feet away from him - but then I wonder if the bloke tutting loudly about three feet away is the reason he is so randy...

Have I become bog wank material?

Why don't you say something, I hear you ask?

That's where it gets farcical...

The first time it happens, I leave the toilet with a shocked and disgusted expression on my face.

A mate of mine, Jock, walks over.

"What's wrong, Lucifer?"

"There's some dirty bastard wanking like a demented chimp in there!"

"No!"

"Yes."

"No!"

"Yes."

"Who was it?"

"I don't know, Jock, but I took a sneaky peek under the toilet door and got a good look at his shoes."

"His shoes, Lucifer? Why were you looking at his shoes?"

"Future reference. I see those shoes walking around, I know who the wanker is."

"I can't wait that long. I'm going to keep an eye on those toilets to see who comes out."

"I've got to get back to work. Keep me posted, Jock."

"Will do, Lucifer."

Jock sweeps up, looks busy, watches the door.

And sees the man who walks out.

Two days later, over the tannoy:

"Will Lucifer please go to meeting room one, will Lucifer please go to meeting room one."

Puzzled, I go to meeting room one.

I arrive to find GroovyManager with a very upset staff member, ModelWorker.

ModelWorker never throws a sicky, works through lunch, all that crap.

Dead boring.

GroovyManager is wearing a Tasmanian Devil tie and a nervous smile.

'Ah, Lucifer! Good of you to come. I'll get straight to the point. People have been accusing Mr ModelWorker of committing an obscene act on himself in the toilets, and they say the person who witnessed it is YOU!"

Shit.

"Me, GroovyManager? I've never said anything about ModelWorker in my life! Somebody was wanking off in the toilets yesterday..."

"Wanking off? Are you sure?"

"Of course I'm sure."

"How are you sure?"

"Well, it was obvious really..."

"How was it obvious?"

"Oh, for Christ's sake, the dirty fucker was panting and moaning and I could hear the smack smack smack as he..."

"Alright! Alright! That's quite enough, Lucifer! If that was the case, how do you know it was ModelWorker who was wan...committing this obscene act?"

"Jock was watching the door to see who came out. All I can think is that he saw ModelWorker come out of the toilets. Word gets round fast in a Factory..."

It was at this point that ModelWorker cracks.

He throws a screaming hissy fit, tears and everything.

He says he's never been so humiliated, he feels stressed, depressed, the lot.

I take this opportunity to take a quick look at ModelWorker's shoes.

They were not the Wanker's shoes.

"Calm down, ModelWorker! I know you're not the Bog Wanker!"

I felt quite smug, ready to present the evidence like a cut price Poirot.

'How do you know?' asks manager.

'I looked under the toilet door, and saw the Bog Wanker's shoes. ModelWorker has different shoes.'

I was triumphant.

GroovyManager and ModelWorker looked alarmed and disgusted.

'What on earth were you doing looking under toilet doors, lucifer?'

Oh.

ModelWorker had nipped in for a piss when Jock and I had been talking. Neither me nor Jock had seen ModelWorker go in.

But Jock had seen ModelWorker leaving.

Bog wanker made good his escape afterwards, undetected.

I had to endure sniggers for being masturbatory obsessive bog peeper for quite a few weeks.

That sort of thing doesn't do much for a bloke's career prospects, I can tell you.

I now realise that if I accuse the real bog wanker, or even approach him on the subject, he can just say I'm lying, and declare me a pervert.

You see, now I've got 'previous' - I've already wrongly accused one person of bog wanking. If I go accusing somebody else it will look like I've got some disorder that makes me look under bog doors hoping to catch somebody wanking.

The Bog Wanker still wanks off in the toilets on a regular basis.

I can't do a thing about it.

Except to tut loudly in the hope he shoots his load quickly, and leaves me to have a shit in peace.

"I'm gonna fuck some sense into you…"

I'd fucked up.

It happens.

A job had gone wrong and it was my fault.

"If you'd been here yesterday evening, Lucifer, I'd have sacked you."

"I was at the pub yesterday evening, Soulless Boss."

"Were you now, Lucifer? Well Zulu and Sytex were here sorting your shit out."

"Zulu likes overtime."

"Sytex doesn't. Now fuck off out of my sight."

I fucked off.

We all make mistakes.

This one was quite big. The whole job had been printed with my fuck up all over it.

It was due out that morning.

My name was mud.

Fuck it.

We all make mistakes.

What bothered me was Sytex.

He was seething.

He wanted to be in the pub last night, but he wasn't.

I was.

He was at work wiping an apprentices arse.

I kept my head down.

"Lucifer, you cunt. Change the chemistry on the processor, and be quick about it."

"Ok Sytex."

I changed the chemistry.

I was on all fours, pulling the barrel out from beneath the machine when a shadow loomed over me.

It was Sytex.

He had his cock out.

I could smell the fucking thing.

"You thick cunt, Lucifer! I'm gonna fuck some sense into you!"

He grabbed me by the head.

And shoved his cock into my ear.

He began to fuck the life out of my ear with his stinking cock.

I've had nicer experiences.

"Take that, you stupid bastard! This'll learn you to make such stupid mistakes!"

It learnt me all right.

It learnt me to keep my cock clean.

In case I ever needed to ear-rape a seventeen year old boy.

I didn't want to leave his ear smelling like mine did.

There really isn't enough soap in the world for an experience like that.

Torquay or Bust.

Weasel never left the UK. He went on holiday either to Torquay or the Isle of White.
Nowhere else.
He didn't drive, never saw the need, and went everywhere by coach.
When he travelled he always wore a smart shirt and his blazer bearing the crest of his beloved York City.
The man was devoted.

On the way down to Torquay one year the coach suffered a blow out on the motorway and was forced to pull onto the hard shoulder.
"I'm afraid we've got to wait for a replacement coach," says the driver, "but nobody is allowed to stay on the coach. Health and safety, and all that."
Off they all get and stand on behind the crash barrier on the grass verge.
Weasel relaxes with a cig, but then a little old lady comes up to him. She squints at his blazer and badge. "Excuse me driver, but can I get onto the coach for a moment? I need to go to the toilet."
He lets her think he's the driver for some weird reason.
"Sorry love, nobody allowed on the coach when we're on the hard shoulder. Health and safety."
The old dear looks frantic.
"I really need to go! What can I do? If I don't go soon I'll have an accident!"
"Why don't you go down there?"
Weasel points don the embankment to some scrubland.
"I can't get down there! I'm seventy six!"
"Don't worry madam," says Weasel chivalrously. "Take my arm. I'll lead you down."
Ever so carefully, Weasel guides the old dear down the embankment to the bottom.
"Just nip behind those bushes," he advises in his strange self adopted official capacity. "I'll wait here for you."
She looks understandably nervous.

"I can't go when I know your here. It's a little embarrassing!"
"Don't worry madam!" says Weasel, "I'll stand up at the top of the embankment. You give me a shout when you're all done."
And with that, Weasel climbs up and respectfully turns his back to the field below.
He starts another cigarette, but then the replacement coach arrives.
"All aboard!"
Weasel stubs out his fag, climbs aboard with the other passengers and off they go...

Ten miles and several frantic head counts later, Weasel suddenly remembers.
The coach swerves off at the next exit, about turn, a further thirteen miles back to the next exit...
They found her where he had left her, absolutely distraught.
Weasel couldn't see how he was in any way to blame.

Does that turn you on?

"You know something, Lucifer? You're one weedy fucker."
I was nineteen. I was thin.
"Thanks for that, Genuflect. Did you know that you are a flabby twat?"
He was twenty six. He'd let himself go.
"Hmmm. I suppose I am. What are we gonna do about it?"
We went to the gym.
Gyms back then weren't like gyms are now.
They were sweaty.
The floors were concrete.
The walls were brick.
The blokes wore moustaches.
It was a place for real men.
I knew I was male, but I wasn't sure how 'man' I was.
I was going to find out.

The guys were working out.
Fuck knows what I was doing.
I lifted shit.
Badly.
I pulled at stuff.
Feebly.
I had a long way to go.
The guy who owned the gym was friendly enough.
Titus wasn't tall, but he was as tall as he was wide.
About five seven wide.
He did pretty good at Mr Universe in the seventies.
He was still formidable.
He kind of strolled around, spotting for some of the guys, shooting the shit and enjoying some man time.
That's gyms for you.
Too much testosterone.
Not really my scene.

Titus saw me struggling.
He strolled over, his monstrous arms at 45 degrees.
He was wearing mirror shades.
In a cellar.
Then I smelled the booze.
Titus liked the juice.
"Now then Lucy. You struggling?"
Funny. Ha ha.
"I'm just warming up, Titus. Finding my depth."
"You'll get nowhere with them weights, sunshine. We only keep them for lasses!"
Titus brought me some 'man' weights.
Oh shit.
He made me do curls.
They hurt.
He started shooting the shit, telling stories.
I gritted my teeth, and sweated.
He quickly brought the subject round to sex.
Too quickly for my liking.
"I used to know some names, Lucy. Tough men. Gangsters, you might say. They were good lads, but they didn't fuck about. Know what I mean?"
I couldn't speak.
He ha told me to do ten reps.
I was on fifteen.
He'd lost count.
"I said, do you know what I mean, Lucy?"
"Yes. I know what you mean, I think…"
"Good. Ten curls, other arm. Go."
Titus swayed slightly, then continued.
"Anyway, as I was saying, these men worked hard, played hard.
"Playing meant orgies."
What?
"The boss was called Steel. He was loaded. I did a bit of enforcing for him now and then. I was part of the inner circle."
I was at nine reps.
I couldn't make ten.
I was shaking like I had Parkinsons.

The weight wasn't going any higher.
"He organised this orgy. We were all sitting in his entertaining room at his mansion, eight of Steel's men, when these prozzies came in, carrying black hold alls.
"Put the weight down, Lucy. I'm embarrassed for you, lad."
He made me do bench presses.
"Anyhow, they all stripped down to stockings and sussies, opened those holdalls and brought out the vibrators. They did a fantastic lezzie floor show, Lucy. Filling every hole, they were."
For fuck's sake…
Titus leant close to my ear on the bench, my puny arms wobbling around above me holding a bar bell.
"Does that turn you on?" he whispers.
I nearly killed myself with the weight.
"I don't know Titus. I might take a break."
Titus didn't let me take a break.
He made me work harder.
"Well, they finished with each other, then crawled across to us lads. They had us cocks out and in their gobs before we knew what was going on!
"Does that turn you on?"
"Gnnnn… how… many… more…reps?"
"One were sucking me balls, the other were working me John Thomas like a fucking lollypop!
"Does that turn you on?"
"I suppose so… they look at bit heavy, Ow! Fucking Hell!"
"Lift them. GO! One, two…
"As I were saying, next thing I knew I were on my back, this bird sat on my face, and I had two other birds parked on my fingers! Had 'em both in a bowling ball grip! You know what a bowling ball grip is?"
"Nnnnnnno…."
"Does that turn you on?"
I was close to puking with the pain.
I wasn't turned on.
"I back scuttled this black lass, and she were sucking off Steel…
"Does that turn you on?
"It went straight up her jacksie liked greased lightning!

16

"Does that turn you on?
"These two lads had one up each hole, and she had one in the gob…
"Does that turn you on?"
I felt something snap in my wrist.
"AAARGH! You're turning me on! Your fucking turning me on!! Are you happy?? I cannot take any more, Titus, You're turning me on so fucking much!! You're killing me!!!"
The gym had gone very, very quiet.
Genuflect was looking at me in open-mouthed horror.
The moustached muscle heads looked hostile.
Titus walked away, shaking his head.
"Fucking poofter…"

I had to take a week off work.
My arms were fucked.
I didn't go to the gym again.

Safe Cracker

"We used to get paid cash y'know, Lucifer. Everyone did."
"I knew that, Scorcher."
"You know what being paid with cash meant, though?"
"No. I don't."
"It meant that factories needed a safe to keep all t'brass in."
"Well, I sort of knew that too…"
"Ah, but did you know that they had to keep getting new safes though? Them safe crackers are clever bastards, tha knows. Always keeping up with the latest designs. Working out how to crack 'em."
"I imagine they would have to."
"Right. Any road, the last place I worked at had just got the latest safe delivered. Top o'the range it were. Brushed steel, big metal wheel on it, four combination locks. It weighed two tonne. They had to take out a window and winch it in with a fucking crane! It came with it's own crew to fit the thing.
"They were just finishing off when I thought I'd take a wander up and have a nosey. This crew of lads were up there own arses, boasting about this safe and how bloody good it were. I took a look at it. 'I reckon I could crack that,' I says.
" 'Fuck off,' they say. 'You never can!'
"They reckoned that safe crackers had been paid to have a go at it, the military had had a go at it, the coppers had had a go at it. None of 'em had managed to crack that safe."
"What did you say, Scorcher?"
"Well I says to 'em, 'you lads lock it up then, and fuck off for a coffee.' That's what they did. They came back ten minutes later, and Guess what?"
"I can't possibly guess, Scorcher."
"I had both doors off the safe, and were smoking a fag without having broken a sweat. All hell broke lose. I just walked off, leaving 'em to guess."
"Go on then, Scorcher. How did you do it?"
"The daft fuckers had put the hinges on the outside. A couple of smart taps with a lump hammer on the hinge pins and the door came

off easier than our lasses knickers."
"You're in the wrong trade, Scorcher."
"Reckon I should have been a safe cracker, Lucifer?"
"Something like that…"

Snow White

If you've ever worked in a factory, you'll know what I mean.
The women aren't much cop.
There are some exceptions.
But not many.
Snow White was an exception.
Blokes would try their luck with the usual gang of dogs on the shop floor.
They didn't approach Snow White.
Different league.
It wasn't just that she had a nice face.
Or great tits.
She seemed... clean.
Too good for ink stained paws.
She deserved a pedestal.
The lads didn't have one.
They left her alone, sneering that she was a snooty bitch.
They still wanted to fuck her.
Badly.

Monday.
9.15am.
Early shift.
Bacon sarnies, pots of rosie, newspapers, lies about how great the weekend had been.
Usual shit.
Door opens.
It's Charger.
He's a suit.
We've been at work three hours.
The suits have been here fifteen minutes.
When they yawn, we shake our heads.
They've got no idea.
Charger's a suit, but he's ok.
He rushes over, a look on his face like he's just found out what his

dick's for.
"Lucifer! You can you process film in here, can't you?"
"Depends."
"What the fuck do you mean, 'depends'? Can you or can't you?"
"Depends."
"Ok. Depends on what?"
"Depends on what you need processing."
"For fuck's sake! I need FILM processing!"
"What sort of film?"
"FILM film!! How many types are there?"
"Lots."
"It's just camera film! From a normal camera. Kodak, I think. Can you do it?"
"Depends."
He was dying now.
I'd had my fun.
"Ok, ok, Charger. Keep your fucking wig on. What's on the film that's so special? Why not just take it to Boots?"
Charger squirmed.
This was going to be juicy.
"I...I can't say."
"Then I can't do it."
I turned back to my paper.
"Why can't you do it, Lucifer?"
"Because you won't tell me what's on it. That's why."
Charger squirmed some more.
But his eyes were shining.
He was going to tell.
Of course he was.
As it happens, I can't process camera film.
I wasn't going to tell Charger that.
Not till he'd spilled his guts.
"Ok, I'll tell. But you've got to keep this secret. Swear to God!"
"I swear to God. Now tell me what's on the fucking film?"
"Me and BadBoy were out on Saturday night. We were on a bit of an office do. Everybody was there!"
I wasn't.
None of the factory lads were.

As 'Everybody' was there, that makes us 'nobody'.
Fine.
"Anyway, Snow White was talking to us, and towards the end of the night she said she was going, and she knew I lived near her. She asked if I wanted to share a taxi! I told her BadBoy was staying at mine, and asked if he could share too. No problem, she said."
My pot of tea was getting cold.
"We got to hers, and she asked if we wanted to come in. Said she had champagne! We didn't need asking twice. We went in, and we fired into this big bottle of champers. She nips off to the loo, and guess what?
She only comes back in all this sexy underwear! Couldn't believe it!"
Neither could I.
"What did she want, Charger? Did she ask you to take a few cheesecake shots of her?"
He looked triumphant.
"Better than that, you sarky twat! Me and BadBoy only went and fucked her! She's red hot, Lucifer! She's loves it up her!"
I was still sceptical.
"Maybe, maybe not, Charger. I'm not convinced. You've still not explained what's on the film."
"It was BadBoy's idea. He whipped the camera out of his jacket pocket, and started pretending to be a camera man on a porno shoot! She went mental at first, but he showed her that there was no film in the camera. Well, she loved it. Posing all over the place. Getting really filthy. Then, at some point, BadBoy only loaded a roll of film, didn't he! What a star!"
He pulled a roll of film from his pocket.
"Can you do it or not?"
"'fraid not, Charger. We can't process bullshit."
Charger was none too happy.
Neither was I. My brew had gone cold.

Friday.
9.10am.
Early shift.
Here's Charger again.

He's looking smug to the power of ten.
"Toilets. Now."
I seem to spend too much of my day in the toilets.
I go in one cubicle.
He goes in the other.
He passes a sheet of photo paper over the top of the door.
He's got the film processed somewhere.
I can't believe what I'm seeing.
Snow White is very, very dirty.
"Shit, Charger! A champagne bottle?"
"I know. Amazing, huh?"
"Yeah. If I had a cock like that, Charger, I'd get it out more often."
"Fuck off, Lucifer!"
"What's BadBoy doing... Oh! Bloody Hell! Mucky Cow."

I was in a bar, with some mates.
"Hi Lucifer. Can I get you a drink?"
It was Snow White.
We went to the bar.
"What are you drinking?"
I was drinking shitty lager.
"I'll have a double Jack Daniels."
We waited for the drinks.
"You know Lucifer, some people say a lot of things about me at work."
"I wouldn't know about that."
"Some people say that you do know."
"Some people are full of shit."
"Well a lot of things get said, but let me tell you, some people are lying. Anything you might have heard, it's all lies."
"Like I said, Snow White. Some people are full of shit."
You included.

My Best Friend's Girl

We played together as kids.
We knew each other at school.
In our teens, we were inseparable.
He got girlfriends.
I didn't.
Even so, he always insisted on me going wherever they went.
He took me on dates, for fuck's sake.
He wasn't a mate.
He was a friend.
My best friend.
Even when he met her, he still insisted we go everywhere together.
The three of us really gelled.
For two years we had great times, good laughs.
He didn't need to take me with him.
He did though.
And I'm glad he did.
Then the inevitable happened.
They split up.
He ended it.
He wanted to be single.
She was hurting.
He still cared for her, but it wasn't his job anymore.
"She's really cut up, buddy."
"I bet she is."
"Look out for her, will you? Make sure she's ok?"
"Sure. How are you doing?"
"I don't know. I had to do it though. I did the right thing, didn't I?"
"I suppose so. I'll keep an eye on her. Make sure she's ok."
"Thanks, buddy."

I kept an eye on her.
I'd always had an eye on her.
You can't spend that much time with a girl and feel nothing.
I didn't spend time with many girls.
I had lots of feelings for her.

We had tickets to a festival.
We all still went.
""Mate, will you share a tent with her? I'm gonna kip in the tent with the lads, but I don't want her to be alone."
"Ok. I'll share with her."
"Thanks. You're a pal."
Yeah.
A real pal.

"Thanks for sharing with me."
"No problem."
"The guys sound to be having a laugh in the other tent."
"Yeah. I'm not bothered. I'm pretty tired."
"Me too."
"I'll get the light."
"Thanks. Night."
"Night."

I felt her breath.
Her kiss.
We didn't say a thing.
We fucked.
I'm a real pal.

She was only the second person I'd ever had sex with.
The first was pretty disappointing.
The second wasn't.

When we came back from the festival, things had changed.
He didn't know that.
"You'll keep an eye out for her, won't you?"
"Sure I will. No problem."

"Are you out tonight?"
"No. I'm around at hers tonight. She's still pretty cut up."
"That's really good of you. You're a real pal."
Yeah.
A real pal.

The penny dropped.
"He's confronted me, you know. About us."
"Shit. What did he say?"
"He said, 'Are you fucking him?'"
"What did you say?"
"I said yes."
"Oh."

I had to make a decision.
Keep seeing her, or stick with my best friend.
It was easy.
I dropped him like a stone.
A real pal.
That's me.

She gave me the confidence I needed.
I grew older, stronger.
I got cocky.
Months turned into years.
I started to screw around.

He went to college, studied music, played in bands.
That's the last I heard.
I was still working in Repro.
I hated it, but it paid for the beers.
I didn't see him again for fourteen years.

"It's getting close to Christmas. Is there anything you really want?"
She looked at me in a strange way.
It made me uneasy.
"I'd like a ring."
"Oh."
I had some big decisions to make.

I dumped her.
She took it really, really badly.
Like I said, I'm a real pal.

Fourteen years isn't a long time.
Not until you look back.
Then you get vertigo.

I read it in the paper first.
Then his brother phoned.
The bands hadn't worked out.
He wasn't going to be a rock star.
He took a little holiday with his parents.
Just to get his head straight, decide what he wanted to do.
He went night fishing off the rocks, under a bright moon.
And there, by the lapping waves, he lost his footing.
He hit his head, and quietly slipped into the cold water.

His parents searched for him next morning.
They found him on the beach.
No parent should have to see that.

Fourteen years does a lot to a man.
You learn a lot of lessons.
Nearly all the hard way.
I finally met my best friend again.
Only he was in a coffin.

After the funeral we went to the cemetery.
I've never cried so hard in my life.
She heard about the funeral, but didn't come.
She should have been there, but she wasn't.

Two years later, I was at a baptism.
She was there.
Our kids started playing together.
My wife was talking to friends
He husband was at the buffet.

"Good to see you."
"You too."
"I like how you've done your hair. It suits you."
"Thanks."

She didn't mention mine.
Hardly surprising.
The years haven't been kind.
"You've got a cute kid."
"Yours are cute too."
"What are you doing now?"
"Erm… I'm still in the same job. Repro."
She was stunned.
"Never! You hated it back then!"
"I know. It's complicated."
It wasn't.
I'm lazy. I know it.
We looked at each other, but didn't say anything.
There was nothing to say.
Time doesn't heal, it just lays a strange sediment over the pain.
It's best not to dig sometimes.
You don't know what's down there.

Neither of us mentioned him.
We didn't talk about the funeral.
All the same, I just wanted to say, "You should have been there."
She should have been there.
I should have been there all those years ago.
I was there at the end.
Too fucking late.

"We're going now. Been nice to see you."
"You too. Take care, won't you?"
"I will. Bye."
She left with her cute kid and her decent husband.
I went back to my family.

It's strange how things turn out.

Ring of Fire.

Sytex didn't do hygiene.
That stuff was for lasses.
And puffs.
He used to come to work day after day with the same bits of selotape stuck to his arms.
He would come in with the same docked tab behind his ear.
He'd slept on it.
He smelled gamey.
He looked gamey.

One time, he looked to be in pain.
"Here, Genuflect. What's wrong with Sytex?"
"It's his piles, Lucifer. You can always tell when it's his farmer's playing up."
"How?"
"He's going for his drawer. Watch what he gets out."
Sytex rummaged around, and pulled out a big, grubby pot of Vaseline.
Then he ambled across the studio like John Wayne, heading for the toilets.
"Pretty grim, huh, Lucifer?"
"Pretty grim, Genuflect."

Later on, I needed the toilet.
Not really.
I just wanted to get out of the studio for a bit.
I'd forgotten about Sytex.
Not for long.

I've never seen anything like it.
There was Vaseline everywhere.
It was all over the door, the toilet, the bog seat, the flush handle.
On the wall was a big, bloody hand print.
Oh God.

"Genuflect! Genuflect! You won't believe what the bogs look like…"
"I know. Blood everywhere? Vaseline everywhere? I've seen it before."
"How did you know?"
He nodded towards Sytex.
I looked.
He was bent over the light table, working.
He looked like someone had shot him in the arse.
Dark blood seeped through the back of his jeans.
"What the fuck…?"
"His piles have burst, Lucifer. It must really hurt."
"Why doesn't he go home? Or go to hospital?"
"I've no idea, Lucifer. I've really no idea…"
He stayed at work all day.
He left blood wherever he sat.
Arse blood.

Years later, Sytex had a heart attack.
They fitted a pacemaker.
He had to stop working.
They sent him for loads of test, but couldn't work out what was wrong with him.
After a while, they worked it out.
He had been bleeding from his dirty arse for so long, his blood pressure had dropped dangerously low, giving him heart arrhythmia.
The doctors sorted his arse out.
He was cured.
I didn't envy the doctors who got that job.

Biscuits

Everybody loves biscuits.
Some people like them more than others.
Kray is a tough fucker, covered in tattoos, shaved head, a few criminal convictions. That sort of thing.
He likes ginger nut biscuits.

"Oi, Lucifer! Go ask Kray if you can have a look at his biscuit!"
I had a lot of work on. The account execs were expecting some proofs, pronto.
Fuck it.
"Hello Kray."
"Alright, Lucifer."
"Can I have a look at your biscuit?"
"Yes you can, Lucifer."
Kray drops his pants, and there, rammed between his broad, hairy buttocks, was a ginger nut biscuit.
"Thank you, Kray."
"Any time, Lucifer."
I really didn't want to know why he had a ginger nut biscuit pushed up his arse.
"Kray?"
"Yes, Lucifer?"
"Why have you got a ginger nut biscuit pushed up your arse?"

It's like this.
Kray liked ginger nut biscuits.
But so did, Rickets.
Rickets works on nights.
Ever seen someone who works permanent nights, and has done for 25 years?
Of course you have.
On zombie films.
Anyway, Rickets favourite type of ginger nut biscuits were Krays ginger nut biscuits.
They were free.

He had found Krays private stash, and was helping himself to them through the night.

The only thing was, Kray knew that Rickets had found them.

Rickets didn't know that Kray knew.

Each evening, Kray 'prepared' a few biscuits for Rickets, and the things he did to them was pretty grim.

Pubes, dick cheese, toe jam, spunk, arse hair, spit, squeezed spots, piss, shit - you name it, it had ended up on a ginger nut biscuit, lovingly prepared for Rickets.

I'd actually witnessed Rickets eating one.

I had to walk away, with a little sick in my mouth.

The jolly japes lasted about a year.

Kray got bored of buying biscuits for Rickets to eat, so he stopped.

Rickets missed his biscuits.

He sent a machine minder out to the shop one night to get him some - they had to be the same brand as he was used to.

The minder came back with the biscuits, and Rickets dived in.

He spat the biscuit out

"What's up, Rickets?"

"I'm not eating them. They taste like shit."

Duck

"Hey, Bear. Don't want to worry you, but Flint and Hugs have been at it again in the garage. It's ducks this time. Right fucking mess."
"BOLLOCKS!!!"
Bear was stressed.
The phone had been going all morning, three machines were broken down, nothing was getting printed, and it was his job to get shit running again.
Now this.
Flint and Hugs were poachers, hunters and badger baiters.
I liked them.
Badgers didn't.

I could never get the badger thing out of my head.
"Why do you do it, Flint? What the fuck have badgers ever done to you?"
"I do it coz it's a right laugh, Lucifer. Ever gone twatting badgers?"
"No."
"Right, well don't knock it till you've tried it."
Try badger baiting?
I think not.
"As for all this 'what have badgers ever done to you?' shit, well them nasty stripy bastards made a right mess of my best dog, Gary."
"Was Gary doing anything to annoy the badgers?"
"Course he was. He was trying to rip their bastard throats out."
"Can't really blame the badgers then…"
"Yes I fucking well can! Stripy bastards…"
I wasn't going to win.

They'd go hunting really early in the morning.
They'd bring their kill in to work, and gut it in the garages.
Sometimes rabbit, sometimes pheasant, even a deer one time.
Gutting and skinning is messy work.
I'd seen the aftermath one time.
It was grim.
And the smell is just as bad.

Bear had been standing amongst the blood and entrails, purple in the face, swearing continuously.
He didn't like them doing it.
It didn't stop them.

This time it was duck.

Ring ring.
"Hello, this is Bear. Yes, yes I've heard about the garage! As soon as I get a second I'm going to go over there and gut those two fuckers with my bare hands, AFTER I've made them clean up their crime scene!"
"Hi, Bear. Have you seen the garage? There's ducks all over the place. Never seen anything like it! There must be thirty of 'em and..."
"I. FUCKING. KNOW!!!! I'm going there now.."
Ring ring.
"Hello? I know, sir. The presses should be in working order in an hour. That's right, an hour. Goodbye."
"Fuck..."
Ring ring.
"Hello, this is Bear. No, the part hasn't arrived yet, Scorcher. When I get it, you'll get it. Alright? Good. Now fuck off!"
Ring ring.
"Hello, this is Bear. No, I haven't seen the fucking garage yet!! I know there's fucking ducks everywhere, I know it's a right fucking mess, but I haven't had the bastard time to get down there and kill everybody responsible yet! It's at the top of my to-fucking-do list!!"
Ring ring.
Bear snapped.
He's a big bloke, but when he has a mind he can move pretty quick. He lumbered across the factory, his face purple, shoving machines and staff out of the way with shovel hands.
He was over the edge.
There would be murder.
"Hey, Bear, if you get a minute, check the garage. Ducks..."
"FUCK OFF!!!"
The door to the back yard shivered on its hinges.

Bear stomped across the yard to the garage.
He broke the door, he pulled it open so hard.
There were Flint and Hugs, caught in the act.
They sat on either side of a kids paddling pool filled with water.
They each held a fishing rod with a hook on the end.
In the paddling pool, three dozen yellow plastic ducks bobbed merrily around as Flint and Hugs tried to catch them.
All the colour drained from Bear's face.
He sagged against the wall.
"It's for the kids Christmas Party at the weekend," said Flint.
"It's Hook a Duck," said Hugs, helpfully.
"Quack quack," said Flint.
Bear left without a word.
He ambled back to his office, and closed the door.
Ring ring
"Hello, this is Bear. No more calls today."
Click.

Torquay 1 York City 0

"Morning Weasel. How was the holiday?"
"Not good, Lucifer. Not good."
"That's a shame. What spoilt it?"
"Well, me and our lass, Olive, went to Torquay because York were playing Portsmouth on the Wednesday. On match day she went to the pool, while I went to the game."
"Was it a good match?"
"I don't know. I didn't get to see it."
"How come, Weasel?"
"It's like this. I was going to get a taxi on the seafront, but I had to be careful. I didn't want to be seen."
"You didn't want to be seen? By who?"
"By anyone, of course!"
"Erm... why?"
"Why? Because I was wearing my York City strip, that's why!"
"I see loads of people in footie shirts, Weasel. No need to be embarassed."
"I wasn't just wearing the shirt. I had a full strip on."
Weasel was painfully thin.
Mid fifties.
Big moustache.
Quite a picture.
"Oh. Long socks?"
"Yeah. Long socks."
"Little shorts?"
"Yeah. Little shorts."
"Football boots?"
"Don't be fucking stupid."
"Sorry."
"And stop fucking laughing. It's not funny. Anyway, I had to run through town, using any cover I could. Trees, bus stops, parked cars, you know the kind of thing. After a bit I got to the taxi rank. I jumps in. 'Take us to Portsmouth mate!' I says. He says 'No. Not worth my while.' I couldn't believe it. I says, 'I'll give you twenty quid,' but he

says, 'I can make that in half an hour. It's high season.' I say 'I'll give you thirty.' and he says 'No' so I said 'Fuck you then!' and got out. None of the cabs in the rank would take it. I ran off behind a bush. They were all laughing at me. I felt like a right tit."

"You never."

"I did. I ran back to the hotel, hiding all the way. I were really embarassed. I got back, but then I realised I'd left the key with Olive, and she were by the pool!"

"What did you do, Weasel?"

"There were some bushes by the pool, so I crept into them, and got down, crawling along on my hands and knees. I could see the pool, but out lass, the stupid cow, she's only gone and set up camp on the wrong side of the pool. I started trying to call to her, but she couldn't hear me. Other people could though. They were starting to get suspicious. So anyway, I saw this kid. I thought I'd get him to take a message to our lass, so I called him over, trying to get him to come into the bushes."

"Fucking hell, Weasel..."

"I didn't bloody know, did I? Anyway, his dad saw me. He pulled me out, and there was a right do by the poolside. I thought I were gonna be lynched! Luckily Olive saw what was happening and stepped in."

"That's awful, Weasel."

"Yeah, I can tell you sympathise by that fucking smirk on your face. Go on. Fuck off."

"Bye then."

What was in the wardrobe, Coffin Nail?

I couldn't figure out how he was still alive.
Coffin-Nail liked his fags.
They didn't like him.
Maybe it was because he kept setting fire to them.
He was a skeleton covered in parchment, his tattoos looking like signs on an ancient treasure map.
If I looked like him, I'd be careful with the fag ash.
He was so desiccated he looked flammable.
The coughing would begin, a rattling clatter like a bingo machine starting up in his chest.
'And the next number is...'
Snort. Spit.
'...a lump of brown jelly with bits of black in it!'
Bingo.

He lit another fag.
"I didn't always work here, Lucifer. I used to clear houses for the council years ago. Do odd jobs for 'em. Fixing stuff that those scum-arsed tenants used to break. They had no respect, those tenants."
"I wouldn't know about that, Coffin-Nail"
"Well take it from me. No respect. You'd be surprised what people leave behind when they do a midnight flit without paying the rent. Photo albums, old books, ornaments and clothing. We used to chuck the lot. Smash it, and chuck it."
"Wasn't any of it worth keeping?"
"We were paid per house, Lucifer. If we fucked about taking every fucking vase and table we found to Hugh Fucking Scully then we'd get paid about a shilling a day! No, smash it and chuck it, that's what we did."
Coffin-Nail's lips pulled back, showing his stained teeth. He looked like a cancerous Mr Ed.
I realised he was smiling.
I hadn't seen that before.
I wished he'd stop.

"Here, Lucifer. Now you mention it, I did find summat worth keeping once."
"Did you, Coffin-Nail? Well, tea break is over, so maybe…"
"I were clearing this house on my own one time. We usually worked in teams, but this day I was on my own. The tenant hadn't left owt behind, except this big wardrobe. The wardrobe were worth fuck all, I'd smash that and chuck it, but it was what I found inside that were worth keeping…"
Oh God.
I was already late. I didn't have time for this shit and his grinning was freaking me out. I decided to do one.
I couldn't help it.
"What was in the wardrobe, Coffin-Nail?"
"It were a box, Lucifer. A big box. You'll never guess what were inside."
"No. I can't possibly imagine."
"I opened this box, and inside were this suit. It were a woman suit."
"A woman's suit?"
"No! A woman suit. Flesh coloured, with tits and a big hairy mott!"
Sweet Jesus.
"Fuck knows what anyone would want one of them for. There's some perverted fuckers out there you know, Lucifer."
"No shit, Coffin-Nail."
"Anyhow, inside the box were these two wigs. A blonde one and a dark one. No joke shop shit, these wigs were top quality. Real human hair. They'll have cost a packet, they will.
"Underneath them were these dildos. Three of 'em! Great big fuckers, n'all!"
"What could you possibly want with that lot, Coffin-Nail?"
"Well, I stuck then dildos in Dettol overnight, in the garage so the wife wouldn't see 'em. Then I took the lot round to this birds house who I was knocking off. We had a right time with 'em, I can tell you."
"I can imagine."
I didn't want to.
"What did you want the wigs for, Coffin-Nail?"
"Well, this bird I were knocking off were bald, so she gave the wigs a wash and she wore 'em, you see."

"Of course. Why didn't I guess. See you around, Coffin-Nail."
"Yeah, see you, Lucifer."

Treacle's Teeth

"You wouldn't believe what happened at the weekend, Lucifer."

"You're right there, Scorcher. Go on. Let's have it."

"I were out on the ale on Saturday night with my mate, Treacle. Well, come Sunday morning, the phone goes. It's Treacle.

'Here, Scorcher. I've had a bit of an accident.' he says.

'What sort of accident, Treacle?' I say.

'I must have had a bad pint or summat, last night,' he says. 'I threw my guts up when I got home last night, and you know what?'

'What?' I says.

'I only went and puked my false teeth down the lavvy, didn't I?' he says.

"Any road, quick as a flash I say to him, 'What time did you puke, Treacle?'

'It were twelve thirty five, Scorcher.' he says.

" 'Right,' I says, 'Get your coat, Treacle. I'll be there in ten.'

"I got round to Treacle's house double quick, he jumped in the motor, and we were off.

"'Where are we going, Scorcher?' he says.

'Sewage works, Treacle,' I says. 'I know a bloke who works there. I reckon we'll be there just in time.'

"We got there just in time.

"We jumps out, and ran full tilt right across to where my mate, Coprolite was working.

" 'Here! Coprolite! My mate lost his choppers down the bog last night!' I says.

" 'What time, Scorcher?' he says.

" 'Twelve thirty five,' I says.

" 'What street?' he says.

"I told him, and he grabs a big net. 'Quick, we've only got a few seconds!' he says. We all ran to this big outlet pipe, Coprolite shoves his net under the pipe, just in time to catch my mates false gnashers as they fall out."

"Really."

"Yeah, really Lucifer. But you know what? Treacle were so chuffed, he just grabbed his teeth out of the net and shoved them straight back in his gob!"

Scorcher shook his head.

"Can't believe some people, can you?"

"No scorcher. You can't."

Bacon. Boxes.

"Bacon."

"Boxes."

"Boxes."

For fuck's sake...

"Bac..."

"Why are you saying 'Bacon' and 'Boxes', Saskwatch?"

He just shrugged. "Funny, Innit."

It wasn't funny.

You've got to be mentally subnormal to think two words repeated loudly over several years, yes *years*, is funny.

I ignored him.

Or tried to ignore him.

He wasn't going away.

He just leant against the desk, his glum horse face gawping at what was on my monitor, size fifteen feet crossed a couple of meters away. He's a big bloke, is Saskwatch.

"Boxes."

"haven't you got work to do, Saskwatch?"

"Yeah, Lucifer, but I can't be bothered."

"What a shame."

"Thing is, I'm feeling a bit low."

"You don't look low. You're six foot seven."

"Not that kind of low. I'm a bit down. You know, depressed."

"Believe me Saskwatch, I know."

You only had to be in Saskwatchs company for five minutes before you wanted stick your head in a gas oven.

"You see, I was out with a girl last night. I took her for a meal."

I wasn't going to get any work done.

"Alright. Where did you go?"

"Went to that new Italian place up the road. It was really nice. I was getting on really well with her, having a laugh, a couple of glasses of wine and that. You know, classy."

"You ooze class, Saskwatch. If it was going so well, why are you feeling down?"

"Well, I needed to go to the toilet, so I stood up, said 'Bacon,' right into her face, and went to the lavvy. When I came back, she'd gone."

"Saskwatch, why the fuck did you say 'Bacon' to her?"

"Don't know. Funny, innit?"

"Well she didn't think so, obviously. Have you phoned her? Found out what happened?"

"Can't call her till tonight, Lucifer. She's on duty all day."

"Duty? What is she, a nurse?"

"Nah. She's a copper."

Christ's sake.

"Saskwatch, you're telling me you said 'Bacon' right into a policewoman's face?"

"Yeah. No sense of humour, some people. Anyway, I'd best be off. See you later."

Not if I see you frst...

"Yeah. Later."

"Boxes."

Good grief.

"Bacon."

View from the Closet.

George is gay.

Problem is, he's not very good at it.

Whereas other gay people are running round having a good time doing gay things, poor George is clinging to the closet door, desperately in denial.

He came out of the closet for a bit, a few years ago.

but then he got back in.

The door wouldn't shut properly, so he sort of peeps out sheepishly at blokes he fancies.

George fancied Romeo.

If you were going to fancy another bloke, Romeo is a pretty good starting point.

Thick, wavy hair, Italian features, a real charmer.

George was in love.

He would stand around the machine, watching Romeo out of the corner of his eye, sighing a bit as Romeo scooped ink into the ducts, or scrubbed rollers with a cloth.

Jock saw him watching.

"You've got your eye on young Romeo, haven't you George?"

"Yeah...sigh... I mean no! What you on about, Jock?"

"Fuck off, George! Everyone knows you fancy Romeo! Don't worry about it. Listen. I'll bet you'd love to touch his cock."

"Jock! What are you on about? You can't go round touching lads cocks!"

"Can you?"

"Course you can, George! Romeo doesn't give a shit! Watch this."

Everybody knew Jock.

He was always fucking about.

You didn't bat an eyelid no matter what he did.

He walked up to Romeo.

And grabbed his cock.

"Fuck off Jock," muttered Romeo as he ladelled more ink onto the rollers.

Jock walked back to George.

"There you go! He's not fussed! Now you try."

George's face was flushed with excitement. "Alright! I will!"

He shuffled up to Romeo.

Reached out.

And squeezed his cock through his jeans.

"I said fuck off, Jock," grumbled Romeo.

Then he looked up.

And saw the sweaty pink face of George smiling back at him.

"Fucking hell!" he roared, throwing down the ink spatula.

George took his cue.

He ran.

Romeo charged after him, howling abuse.

George ducked into the toilets, Romeo in hot pursuit.

"Got you, you filthy pervert!" he cried, and proceeded to punch poor old George about the body.

George was doubled over, squealing.

Romeo towered over him.

"Let's see how you like it!" he snarled, and grabbed a handful of the front of Georges trousers.

Romeo went pale, let go and ran from the toilets.

He carried on working, a shocked look on his face.

"What's up, Romeo?" asked Jock.

"It's George. He had an absolutely fucking massive hard on."

"Oh. So are you going out now, or what?"

"Fuck off, Jock."

Sticky back? Drastic…

Toots was a new rep.

Bickerdike was an account handler.

They were two women on a mission.

They had a chance to land a big contract.

Neither one had been given a chance like this before.

They could not fuck up.

Train to London. 10.30am. Meeting with FatClient.com scheduled: 1.00pm.

"I'm going to honest here, Toots. I'm terrified!"

"Me too, Bickerdike. I can't stop farting!"

Nervous giggles.

"If we're like this now, what will we be like in the meeting?"

Toots shook her head.

"Fuck knows, Bickerdike. I'm not sure I'm cut out for this. Don't know about you, but I'm dying for a fag."

"Yeah, I am as well. Shame you can't smoke on trains."

"Yeah, Shame."

Welcome to the 9.50 train from Leeds to London. A trolley servive offering drinks and light refreshments will be with you shortly. Thank you!

Toots looked at Bickerdike.

Bickerdike looked at Toots.

The trolley arrived.

"Two white wines, please."

They arrived in London.

Both feeling slightly more relaxed.

"Do we have time?"

"Ooh, ages yet!"

"Shall we?"

"Be rude not to!"

"Bartender? Two large white wines, please!"

Drinking before a big meeting is a gamble.

In this case, it paid off.

In the meeting they came across as cool, relaxed professionals, with surprisingly minty breath.

They walked out of the meeting with the deal in the bag.

Contracts would be in the post first thing in the morning.

All that they had to do now was wine and dine the clients on the company credit card.

A bottle of wine in the hotel room as they got ready.

Cocktails in the bar.

Toots and Bickerdike were on fire.

They got the contract!

Woohoo!

Champagne and Lobster.

Large brandies.

The clients loved it.

They loved Toots and Bickerdike.

For a while.

As the booze flowed, the veneer of cosmopolitan respectability wore thin on the girls, revealing a very different side.

Castleford and Doncaster.

Mining towns, terraced houses, Labour clubs and chip shops.

They'd hit the big time.

They were two women on a mission.

They were going to party.

The clients were getting nervous.

Restaurant faded to bar, bar became night club.

Toots was refused alcohol at the bar.

Bickerdike fell over on the dance floor.

The clients quietly left.

Toots got thrown out of the club

She decided to call it a night.

At two.

She collapsed on to the bed in the hotel room, half undressed, snoring loudly.

An hour later, Bickerdike stumbled in.

She wasn't alone.

"Shhh! You don't wanna wake my friend! shis sleepin'! Y' know, people have got you gypsys all wrong! Y' lovely, you are! Reet lovely..."

Bickerdike slumped onto the bed next to Toots, and she also began to snore...

Morning was painful.

Toots woke first.

"Ooh, my poor fucking head! What happened last night, Bickerdike? Bickerdike! Wake up, love."

"Snore.. Wha? Bloody hell... I feel shocking, Toots. What happened? Urgh! What's that on my back?"

Toots and Bickerdike had only managed to take off their blouses before they passed out.

The young chancer who had walked Bickerdike home felt a bit cheated when she flaked out.

He decided to make the best of the situation.

And wanked off over the sleeping girls backs.

"Oh my God, I'm gonna be sick..."

As Bickerdike moaned into the toilet bowl, Toots noticed the door to the mini bar was open.

It had been emptied.

"Fucking hell..."

All the next week they waited for the contracts to arrive in the post.

They never came.

What did arrive was the company credit card statement.

It was back to the job center for Toots and Bickerdike.

The Fuddle

It was Christmas.

Last day of work.

That meant having a fuddle.

A fuddle is getting pissed at work.

On the sly.

Everybody knew a fuddle was going on, but blind eyes were turned.

Six in the morning.

Everybody had a mug in their hand, but the kettles were cold.

A fuddle was going down.

Brandy was popular, for some reason.

Some had whisky, others had potcheen.

Fierce stuff.

I was seventeen.

I had lager.

Tasted like shit at that time in the morning, but a fuddle was on.

By ten, we were pretty fucked.

Word came round.

"Fucking Hell! God is showing customers round! Abandon fuddle!"

God was the boss. Outright owner of the company.

A tough business man.

Didn't take any shit.

He didn't fuddle.

We knew he would head straight for the studio.

Start at the start.

God loved the studio.

Most printworks sent their reprography out to trade houses.

Not us.

We kept it all under one roof.

From the artwork stage, to printing, to delivering, to landing on your doorstep, to being hurled into the bin with frustrated disgust, it was all done by us.

We couldn't blame anyone else for the shit we turned out.

God loved the studio because of the fancy equipment.

Big cameras.

Colourful film.

Tables that lit up.

The mystery of the darkroom with its red light.

Loved it.

Unfortunately the darkroom was littered with tins and bottles from the fuddle.

We had to clean up, and quickly.

Bin bags, hasty scrabblings across the floor, a quick mop of spilt ale, air freshener.

Sytex was pissed on potcheen. We tucked him in the store room to sleep it off.

We pretended to work.

Just in time.

"This way gentlemen, this way. here is our in-house studio, carefully regulated to keep corporate colour correct and turn around times down.

"Film proccessors, blah blah,

"Printing down frame, blah blah,

"And here we have the darkroom!"

Ooh.

Aah.

Isn't it dark, etc.

In they all filed, into the pitch blackness.

God shut the door.

They couldn't see their hands in front of their faces.

God triumphantly flicks the light switch, bathing the customers in eery red light.

In the corner was a pot sink.

Sytex stood there, trousers round his ankles, pissing into the sink like a racehorse.

Nobody said a thing.

God turned off the light, opened the door, and everybody filed out.

They walked back through the studio in silence, and as he left God muttered;

"I need a bloody drink..."

What he really needed was a fuddle.

The Show

You want to see some naked girls?

You know where to go.

A lapdancing bar.

Back then, lapdancing bars were only in America.

We had something different.

We had doffers.

Doffers did the rounds at pubs near to factories.

Fridays, around fivish, blokes would shuffle into their works local and watch two tired looking single mums take off their clothes and wriggle around in a half hearted fashion on a tiny stage set up by the bay window, where the curtains were closed to make the dingy pub appear even dingier.

The hat went round.

If there was enough money in it, they'd do a bit of a lesbian show.

The dizzy heights of Yorkshire erotica.

But there was something else.

There was The Show.

"Lucifer! Bring a fiver in tomorrow."

"Erm, why, Sytex?"

"Because you're coming with us to The Show, that's why!"

"Right. The Show. Do I get to find out what that is?"

"You, Lucifer, are a fucking puff. The Show is what will change you from a fucking puff into a MAN, that's what The Show is."

"Don't think I'll bother..."

"A Fiver. Tomorrow."

I went to The Show.

It was a working mens club.

We arrived in a mini bus, bellowing and singing.

The lads were drinking freezing cold tins of bitter that made your hand ache just holding them.

Freezing tins on a freezing night.

I was eighteen.

Everyone else was in their thirties and forties.

I wondered what the fuck I'd let myself in for.

We went in.

Lots of tables.

Lots of blokes.

Somebody shoved a pint into my hand.

It was nectar compared to that crap in the mini bus.

I gulped it down.

Lights dimmed.

Music started.

Blokes roared.

A blonde woman in a fancy costume shimmied onto the stage, danced a bit, started stripping.

I drank more beer.

Girls slithered amongst the tables taking beer orders, and returned with groaning trays of pints.

The girl on the stage started putting stuff up her fanny.

The blokes roared louder.

She dragged a bloke out of the crowd, and his mates howled with laughter.

She whipped his pants down, got his cock out and started sucking him off.

The crowd went mad.

Sytex jabbed me in the ribs.

"Bet you've never seen owt like this, Lucifer!"

He was right.

I hadn't.

The girl bent over, and the bloke on stage tried to fuck her.

It was like trying to get a marshmellow into a money box.

The bloke on stage gave up, and stumbled back to his seat, humiliated.

"That was rubbish!" shouted the girl to the crowd.

"Who's gonna come up here and give me one?"

All Hell let loose.

Young chancers flocked to the stage, ragging their flies open.

Beer spilled everywhere.

One of the girls serving beer bent over to clean up the mess.

Kray grabbed her, pulled her skirt up, yanked her knickers to one side and shoved his tongue up her arse.

She started screaming.

The girl on stage had disappeared behind pale wall of thrusting spotty arse cheeks, as a horde of pissed blokes tried to get their turn with her.

Some lads were on stage, wanking.

I turned to Sytex, and saw that he was wanking.

Everbody was laughing and drinking and wanking.

The beer girl had broken free of Kray's grip and fled.

The only girl in the room was hidden by those spotty arses.

And still the blokes wanked.

I got my coat.

"Where the fuck are you going, Lucifer?" slurred Sytex.

"Home, Sytex. I'm going home."

"You fucking puff!"
I left him to his wanking.
i walked out of The Show, out into wet night.
I got the last bus home.

Sid's Snake

Sid was depressed.
His dick had had a little stroke.
No, he hadn't been yanked off by Ronnie Corbett.
His cock had suffered a spaz attack.
It had forgotten how to piss.
It had forgotten how to get hard.
It had forgotten how to cum.
Sid is a randy kind of bloke, and he didn't take the news very well.
Despite being in his fifties, he still had a very a active sex life, so he was in a bit of a quandary.
He also had to piss through a pipe.
I saw him in the canteen, looking rather glum.
'How's the cock, Sid?'
Not good, Lucifer, not good."
"Still not managed it yet?"
"No, and God knows I've tried. I've been to the doctor's again."
"What did he say?"
"He reckoned that everything was still the same. No better, no worse. I told him that I'd seen something on the internet that might help. I'm thinking that if I can cum just once, then it might kick it all into action, if you see what I mean?"
I didn't really want to ask, because he looks at some odd stuff on the net, does Sid.
"What did you see on the internet, Sid?"
It had to be done.
"Prostate massage, Lucifer. Know anything about it?"
"No. No, I don't."
"Well, apparently blokes have this doughnut shaped thing up their arses..."
Oh no.
"and if you kind of poke it the right way, it can make you cum."
"That's great Sid. I've actually popped in for a sandwich so.."
Well I mentioned this to the doc, and he seemed a bit uncomfortable, but said it was true. Well, I asked him if it would work for me, and he said he wasn't sure, so I asked if it was worth a try, and he said he

supposed so."
"And?"
"And I asked him to do it to me, to see if it worked."
"You asked a doctor to arse-poke you with his finger until you shot your load."
"Well, yes."
"And he's a bloke?'
"Yes."
"And you didn't see a problem with that?"
"Not really. He's a professional, isn't he?"
"He's a professional doctor, Sid. Not a professional arse poker."
"Hmmm..."
"He said no, didn't he?"
"Yes, he did."
"I'm off. Good luck with your cock, Sid."
"Not having a sandwich, Lucifer?"
"No, I'm not."

The Whistle

That same, familiar whistle.
I hear it every working day.
Five, sometimes six days a week.
For twenty years.
The sort of whistle used to attract your attention.
The sort of whistle that, when heard, makes you look up, see who's calling you.
The sort of whistle a friend uses from across the road when they see you.
And that's the idea.
You hear The Whistle.
You look up.
Nobody's there.
You walk on.
You hear The Whistle again.
You look up.
Nobody's there.
And so on.
For twenty years.
Don't get me wrong.
I don't fall for The Whistle any more.
Not for nineteen years.
I hear the whistle and just keep walking.
And it's not just me who gets The Whistle.
Everybody gets The Whistle at some time or another.
Everybody.
I've been next to Whistlers in action.
"Hi Bilbo. How's it going?"
"Great, Lucifer! Great! Hey, look! There's Scorcher! Get hiddy!."
(Hiddy means hidden.)
"Why?"
"Never mind why! Just get hiddy!"
I get hiddy.
I squat like a moron behind a reel of paper, and wait for The Whistle with a kind of fatalistic dread.
Whistle

"Ha! Did you see that, Lucifer? Did you see the look on Scorcher's face! Ha!"
Whistle
"Ha ha! He looked again! The big fool! He never learns, old Scorcher! Never learns! Did you see his face?"
"No, Bilbo. I was sitting here like a tit behind this reel."
"Aww! Why didn't you look, Lucifer?"
Because I knew what I would see.
Somebody glancing around, a vague expression of bewilderment on their face.
Or mild embarrassment at falling for The Whistle.
Or somebody pointedly ignoring The Whistle, their shoulders hunched protectively against it, because they, too, had become sick to the stomach of this tiresome, feeble, pathetic joke.
Bilbo loves The Whistle.
He must do it twenty, thirty times a day.
Never tires of it.
Always makes his fat belly jiggle with mirth.
I could walk out of the door right now, and cross the factory floor, and I will guarantee you he will whistle.
If you looked hard, you would see his round, red face peeping from between stacks of paper, grinning.
Sometimes I want to smash it in.
You might think I have no sense of humour.
It is, after all, just a bit of fun.
But the fun has worn very, very thin.
To the point that it now grates, and irritates, and makes my teeth ache where they grind together.
It's the repetitive nature of The Whistle that is the problem.
The Whistle makes Groundhog Day seem like a soothing routine.
The Whistle is for people content with mind numbing repetition, the dull and mundane.
Bacon sandwich, pot of tea, hiddy, *Whistle*, giggle, workety work work, hiddy, *Whistle*, giggle, more workety work, a biscuit, hiddy, *Whistle*, giggle, off to the bog, dump, hiddy, *Whistle*, giggle, repetitive tasks followed by more repetitive tasks, hiddy, *Whistle*, giggle, sit in a dark corner and worry that the factory might one day close, hiddy, *Whistle*, giggle, secretly lust after

unattainable page 3 girl, hiddy, *Whistle*, giggle....
And so on.
And on.
And on.
Until death.
Blissful, merciful death.
But there are many Whistlers.
One dies, another steps up to the plate.
Dull eyed, dull witted, middle aged men with chocolate around their mouths and their flies gaping open, men who don't buy their own clothes but leave it to the missus, men who only look at the pictures, men who vote BNP because somebody with an opinion once told them to, men who think steak is the only thing on the menu and football is the only thing on television, men who used to have fights twenty years ago and still like to talk about it, men who actually like working in a grim, colourless, depressing environment like a northern factory, who can't see any problem with it, and who wouldn't want anything else even if you handed it to them on a silver platter.
They work in a factory because they are suited to it.
Genetically engineered to deal with the grind, the toil, the lack of stimulus.
Perfectly suited to get hiddy.
Perfectly suited to Whistle.
Perfectly suited to giggle.
I fully realise that it's me who is in the wrong here.
That gives me zero comfort.
I am trapped in this bizarre twilight world of clattering machines and grinning Whistlers, whey faced office staff and fevered lavatory masturbators, the whirring silence of servers, monitors, back up devices, towers, screens and hubs, a view of every bright dawn through bars and crumpled blinds, in a job I desperately need but desperately hate.
I want a cup of tea.
And when I stand at the water font, mug in hand, I know that when I turn my back, from amongst the machinery and paper and pallets and bins, drifting, taunting, maddening, it will come.
The Whistle.

A Big Fat One

"Didn't think much to the airline, Lucifer..."
"What are you on about, Scorcher? What airline?"
"I've been away. On holiday. Didn't you miss me?"
"No. Not really. Where did you go?"
"Nashville, Tennessee. It were great. Didn't think much to the airline out there, though."
"Why?"
"Well, they came round with the trolley, and they asked me what drink I wanted. I asked for Tetley's bitter. Guess what?"
"What."
"They didn't have none. Can you believe it?"
"I can, actually. They're only going to stock certain drinks, Scorcher. They can't possibly cater to everyone. How many people would actually ask for Tetley's bitter on a flight to Nashville?"
"I did."
"You're probably the only person in about ten years."
"Hmm. Anyway, Nashville were great. I went to the Grand Ole Opry. Fantastic place. Always wanted to go there."
"Nice. Who did you go see?"
"Fats Domino was playing. He were brilliant. A proper legend. He's getting on a bit, so he takes a break between sets. Suited me, cos I were gasping for a pint. I went to the bar, and guess what? They only had Tetley's on, didn't they?"
"They served pints of Tetley's at the Grand Ole Opry?"
"Aye! Not a bad pint either. Well I gulped it down, smacking my lips and sighing. it really hit the spot, you know. A feller next to me asked me what I were drinking that tasted so good, so I told him. Tetley's. He says he'd never heard of it, so I bought him a pint, just so he could try the best drink in the world. I hadn't looked up from my pint, I were enjoying it so much, but I saw this big handful of fat black fingers reach for the glass the bar man put down. It were only Fats Domino himself, weren't it!"
"Really."
"Yes! Really! Couldn't believe it! We got chatting, and you know

he's a really nice bloke. Right down to earth. I told him I was a bit of a musician myself, what with my guitar playing and that."
"You play guitar?"
"Yeah! Didn't you know?"
"No, Scorcher. I didn't."
"Well I do. We were talking about music, and Fats were loving his ale. We really hit it off. Anyway, Fats stands up and says, 'Scorcher, you'd better not be drinking too many of those there Teley's, man!' and I says, 'Why not, Fats?' and he says, 'Because you are playin' the final set with me, up on stage!' Next thing you know, I were up there, center stage, playing guitar for Fats Domino at the Grand Ole Opry. It really made my holiday, that did."
"I imagine it did, Scorcher."
"Yeah, Lucifer. It really did. The flight home were better too."
"Why's that?"
"Well, we were cruising at ten thousand feet, and the stewardess comes round with drinks. She recognizes me. 'Mr Scorcher?' She says. I say, 'Aye, love?' She reaches under the trolley, and you know what she's got?"
"I can guess, but go on."
"Four tins of Tetley's. Those yanks know how to treat you. They really do."

Pot Poo Ree

The compressor room is very loud.
The compressor room is very hot.
The compressor room is so packed with machinery that it's difficult to move in there.
The compressor room is not a place you want to be working.
Troll and Vulcan were working in the compressor room.
Old school engineers, they didn't moan.
Just got on with it.
"Think I've found that leak, Vulcan."
"Good work, Troll. Can you nip the seal up, or are we fitting a new one?"
"New one. Can you smell that? Strange smell, not burning."
"No, not burning, that smell. Not gas."
"No, not gas. Don't know what it is. Makes me feel a bit odd though."
"Yeah, odd. Bit sleepy."
"Hmmm... Sleepy. Hungry too. You still got that packet of Hob Nobs in your cupboard, Troll?"
"Yeah! I could murder a Hob Nob, me. I'm feeling everso peckish, Vulcan. And sleepy. Shall we go get those Hob Nobs, then?"
"Ok. Let me just shut this valve off... shit."
"What?"
"Dropped m'spanner."
"You've got hands like cows tits, you have, Vulcan. Where did it go?"
"Under that compressor. Careful. Bit warm under there."
"I'm always careful... Ow!"
"You alright, Troll?"
"Yeah. It's a bit warm under there."
"Don't worry. I'll get it... Hang about. What's this?"
"What's what?"
"This. This dirty great bag of summat. That's what's causing the stink!"
"What is it? Looks like a sack of grass clippings."

"Smells like that shite the wife likes to leave round the house in bowls."
"Pott Poo Ree."
"What?"
"That's what they call it. Pott Poo Ree."
"Do they?"
"Yeah. Pott Poo Ree."
"Fucking stupid name, that. Do you think this stuff is Pott Poo Ree, Troll?"
"If it is, what the hell is it doing under a compressor?"
"Good point. You'd better go tell Bear. He'll know what to do. I'll wait here with the Pott Poo Ree. Oh, and Troll?"
"Yeah, Vulcan?"
"Bring them Hob Nobs. I'm everso peckish."
Troll returns with Bear.
And the Hob Nobs.
"Now then Vulcan. Troll tells me you've found something... what's that fucking smell?"
"It's this, Bear. In this bag. Pott Poo Ree. Don't sniff it too hard though, it makes you're head feel all funny. Have you got those Hob Nobs, Troll? Smashing."
"That's not Pott fucking Poo Ree. It's drugs. It's pot without the fucking Poo Ree!"
"To be honest Bear, I've always hated owt to do with drugs, but I can actually see the attraction right this minute. I'm off my fucking head."
"Keep it together, Vulcan, and say nothing. Troll, put those fucking biscuits down, stop giggling and go fetch Cardboard Supervisor. This is a police matter."
Troll returns with Cardboard Supervisor.
"Police!" he squeaks. "No police! We'll deal with this ourselves. Internally. We don't want trouble!"
"Oh, come on, Cardboard! This is a lot of drugs here! We can't just chuck it in the bin! Somebody is using our factory to prepare drugs!"
"I know we can't bin it, Bear. We'll burn it. Vulcan, Troll, take this to the back yard and burn it in a metal bin. And don't tell anybody about this. Understand?"
"Giggle. Yeah."

"Giggle. Yes Mr Cardboard."
An hour later.
Ring ring
"Hello, Bear speaking."
"Hi Bear, this is Erebus, in the warehouse. Can you do something about Vulcan and Troll please?"
"Why? What have they done?"
"I've just found them cuddled up in my office. They stink of Pott Poo Ree. I can't wake them up. The fuckers have eaten all my biscuits too. You owe me three packets of custard creams, Bear."

Minty Throne

Whenever I see Minty I hide.
Or walk the other way.
Or pretend I'm in a real hurry.
I never am, by the way.
Minty is a nice bloke, but I don't like him.
Can't stand him, in fact.
Minty is a devout Christian.
He's kind in thought and deed.
Will help anybody.
Give you his last quid.
People know this, they can smell it on him.
And they fuck him royally for every last penny.
He gets pushed around by his family, the window cleaner, plumbers, workmates, neighbours, waitresses, electricians, the lot.
But he's one of these people who turn the other cheek.
The problem is, people aren't slapping him.
They are butt fucking him.
And Minty pulls his arse cheeks ever wider to accommodate these people who are butt fucking him, happily letting them slip another inch into him.
That's what is sickening.
He seems to enjoy getting screwed.
If he's such a good Christian, why does God let all this crap happen to him?
Personally, I don't think God likes him either.
I think he records Minty's prayers on an answering machine, but just deletes them, without playing them back.
I realise I'm sounding very nasty and Minty sounds like a nice guy, but think of it like this.
You've heard of the milk of human kindness.
Well, Minty goes beyond this.
He has the condensed cream of human kindness.
Very tasty, you might think, but just like condensed cream, you have too much and it just makes you want to puke.

Minty likes to keep me informed of his latest butt fuckings.
Each time he tells me, I want to scream in his face for him to stand up for himself, fight back, tell everyone to fuck off, not to let himself get fucked.
But I don't.
He engages conversations with an innocuous question, but cuts in with a sucker punch of his most recent screwing.
I was minding my own business.
Getting on with my work.
I didn't see him coming.
"Hello there, Lucifer."
"Shit! Where the fuck did you come from?"
Minty frowned. He didn't like bad language. Rich coming from a man who likes being bum raped.
"I just thought I'd see how you were doing, Lucifer. Got anything planned for the weekend?"
"Not really, Minty. Just going to the..."
"I'm getting some work done on the house at the moment. I wish I'd never taken this plumber on. Do you know any plumbers, Lucifer?"
He'd got me. The sucker punch. There was no escape.
"No, Minty. I don't know any plumbers."
"Shame. The fellow I've got in to re-arrange my bathroom is a bit of a cowboy, I'm afraid. The prices he charges! You wouldn't believe them. And he's eating me out of house and home..."
"What?! He's eating your fucking food? Why are you letting him do that?"
"He's in the house all day, Lucifer. He's not taking a break for lunch, he's working through. So he helps himself to something from the fridge. Unfortunately, he quite often eats what was going to be my tea."
"Jesus wept..."
"He did, Lucifer, and you don't need to remind me in those terms, thank you very much. Well, I find this plumber's work to be rather shoddy. I hate to say this, but my lavatory had accumulated a fair deposit of limescale in the bowl, due to being in a hard water area, you understand."
"I understand..."
"Well, he assured my that this would not be a problem. He took the

lavatory out, and brought it into the garden. He said it would be a simple matter of pressure washing the bowl. The problem was, when he turned on the jet of water, my toilet exploded!"
"Bloody hell."
"I wasn't best pleased, I can tell you. I was already late for work, and there was pieces of Armitage Shanks scattered all over the herbaceous border, so I instructed him to clean up the mess and replace the lavatory before my wife arrived home. He did that, but my wife was far from happy."
"Why?"
"I arrived home from work, and she showed me. It was quite apparent that it was not a new toilet. It was dirty! It didn't even match with the rest of the bathroom suite! The next day I was forced to have words with the plumber. I asked about the toilet. He argued that the toilet that had exploded had not been a new toilet. 'Where did you get this toilet?' I demanded. 'Out of my house!' he replied! 'And what are you using for a toilet if your toilet is in my house?' I inquired. 'The brand new one I bought at B&Q yesterday afternoon,' he said. Ooh, I was ever so cross!"
"Come on then, Minty. What bog have you got in your house now?"
"I went straight up to B&Q and bought a new lavatory, one that would fit well with the decor of my bathroom! I brought it home, and insisted that he fit it."
"Did you charge him?"
"Urm... I didn't like to..."
"Did he charge you?"
"Well, yes..."
"And he got a brand new bog out of it, didn't he?"
"That's one way of looking at it..."
"And he's eating all you food?"
"Erm..."
"You know what he thinks you are, Minty?"
"No, I don't.."
"The golden tit. He can't believe his bloody luck. He's going to keep sucking on you till the money runs out, you know that, don't you?"
"Well..."
"You need to sack him."
"I suppose I do."

"Are you going to?"
"Probably not."
"Jesus."
"Language, Lucifer!"
"Jesus fucking Christ, Minty."

Cum Dancing

On the last day before we broke up for Christmas, we'd all have sneaky drink in the morning, a fuddle.
Then at half past one it was off to the pub.
It was the only time in the year that the office staff and the factory workers mixed.
Something usually happened.
In repro, you're neither office staff nor factory worker.
More like some crap hybrid.
Scruffy clothes and shiny hands.
Everybody would still talk to you, but in terms of 'us' and 'them', we were 'them' to both camps.
A bit like U.N. observers.
We stood at the bar of the pub, observing.
Cleopatra was a suit.
She was no stunner, but she thought she was.
Blokes gave her attention at work because she was one of the only half decent women there.
In other words, she was under fifteen stone and she wasn't a lesbian.
For a factory, that's a stunner.
She had curly hair that she like to flick about, a pretty good figure, and big green eyes.
She obviously thought her eyes were her best feature, because she caked her eyelashes in mascara, and batted them at anyone who might be interested.
They ended up looking like two spiders that had been dipped in Hammerite and were having an epileptic fit.
On this particular Christmas she thought it would be fun to flirt with some of the shop floor lads.
They bought her drinks.
She liked that.
The spiders spasmed.
They bought her more drinks.
God help anyone with arachnophobia.
Flint was chatting her up.

He was fifty, a rogue.
He had a glint in his eye and a 'tash on his lip.
He must have had a dozen kids to various different women.
Cleopatra was twenty five, and thought she knew it all.
She didn't.
Not by a long shot.
"Bloody Hell, Lucifer," murmured Genuflect. "Have you seen Flint? He's well in with Cleopatra!"
"No wonder. Have you seen how many vodkas she's had? It's my round, Genuflect. Another pint of Moosehead?"
"Please. She wants to be careful, you know. All the gaffers can see her. They don't like that sort of thing."
I got the beers.
I tried to give Genuflect his pint, but he didn't notice.
He was looking at Cleopatra.
Everyone in the pub was looking at Cleopatra.
Flint had his back to the wall.
Cleopatra had her arse pressed against his groin.
She had her face turned to Flint, and they were kissing, really going for it.
There was more tongue than Morrison's meat counter.
Flint had his hand up her blouse, and you could see him tweaking her nipples.
His other hand was down her skirt.
"Bloody Hell," repeated Genuflect, his jaw slack.
I looked around the pub.
There must have been fifty people watching, all with there mouths open.
Flint started strumming away down Cleopatra's skirt, and she began to moan.
His hand was going like George Formby's, only instead of a ukulele, he was playing a tart.
Faster and faster went his hand, then Cleopatra started to shudder.
"I don't fucking believe it..." murmured Genuflect.
She came.
Buttons popped off her blouse, her legs trembled and danced like a washing machine on a spin cycle and the spiders on her face were having a gran mal seizure. She howled like Scooby Doo with his tail

74

caught in the door of the Mystery Machine, and Flint had to stifle her cries with his tongue.
When she had finished, the pub exploded into applause and cheering.
She straightened her skirt, finished her drink, and with a small smile on her face, staggered to the ladies.
On the last day before we broke up for Christmas, we'd all have sneaky drink in the morning then go to the pub.
It was the only time in the year that the office staff and the factory workers mixed.
Something always happened.

Chariots of Liar

"What about us getting them Olympic games then, Lucifer? You reckon you'll go down and watch?"
"Maybe, Scorcher. Wouldn't mind watching the cycling."
"I watched the cycling when I was at the Olympics at Seoul, in '88."
"You were at the '88 Olympics? Competing, were you?"
"Don't be fucking daft, Lucifer! I'm no bloody athlete."
"I suppose you're not..."
"No. I were there helping my mate. He's the only bloke to ever compete in the Olympics and the Paralympics in the same year."
"Wait a minute! Olympics AND Paralympics? How the fuck did he do that? If he's fit enough to do the sport in the Olympics, how can he qualify for the Paralympics?"
"Simple. Two different sports."
"Right. What two different sports?"
"Olympic triple jump and Paralympic wheelchair basketball."
"Jesus H Christ..."
"You see, my mate suffered from schizophrenia - he were born with it."
"Born with it?? How the fuck can you tell if a baby has schizophrenia?"
"Dunno. Anyway, my mate, Leapy, he had it. When he was Leapy he was fine, but when he was Wheelz, he were paralyzed from the waist down. It were so bad, he had two different passports, one for each personality."
"Never."
"Yeah. One for when he were Leapy, and the other one for when he was Wheelz."
"You can't have two passports, Scorcher, you just can't!"
"Yeah you can. when he were Leapy, he were convinced that he was Canadian. He had dual nationality. It were official and everything."
"Where was Wheelz from then?"
"England, of course."
"Yes. Silly me."
"Only when he was Wheelz he thought he was black. That might be

what made him good at basketball."
"That would certainly explain it, Scorcher."
"He did alright at the triple jump, but didn't manage the finals. The Eastern Europeans had that all sewn up. He were a bit gutted about that."
"I'll bet he was."
Well, the Olympics finished, but we had to kind of hang about for a couple of weeks until the Paralympics started. Didn't seem much point in going home. But we had a problem."
"What on Earth could that have been?"
"Old Leapy was staying as Leapy. There was no sign of Wheelz. He couldn't compete unless he was Wheelz."
"How could anyone tell the difference? Why didn't he just pretend?"
"That'd be cheating! Anyhow, people would have noticed his Canadian accent. He'd have been rumbled in a second."
"Of course. Why didn't I think of that."
"The Paralympics got underway, and still no Wheelz. He had to skip the opening ceremony and everything. It got to the night before the match, and he were frantic. Then I had an idea."
"Which was?"
"I took him out on the piss. I got him absolutely arseholed on this stuff called soju. Leapy's a good athlete, so he really couldn't handle his booze. I were alright. I were drinking pints of the stuff. Well, dawn breaks, and I'm watching Leapy as he slumps on his bed. His eyes close, but suddenly pop open again. He sits bolt upright, and says, 'Where am I?' in an English accent! It were only Wheelz", weren't it!"
"And he was sober?"
"Course he was! It was Leapy who'd been drinking, and he were sleepin' it off! I got Wheelz dressed and in his chair as quick as I could, and made it to the Jamsil stadium just in time.
He played brilliant, but his team could only manage fourth, just off the medals."
"Incredible. So where's you're mate now?"
"Dunno. He developed another personality not long after and fucked off to Brazil for a sex change. Haven't see him since."
"I'll bet Wheelz and Leapy got a surprise if they came round first after the op."

"Yeah. They wouldn't have been happy."
"I'd watch the Brazilian womens disabled basketball team very carefully in 2012 if I were you, Scorcher."
"Bloody 'ell! Never thought of that! Thanks for the tip, Lucifer!"
"Don't mention it."

Lemon Squeezy

Shifty meetings in corridors.
Muttered conversations and sideways glances.
Secret emails.
The contract for MassiveBank had become available.
The sales team were pulling out all the stops to land it.
The most important thing to remember:
Don't tell the boss.
Their boss was called Gameshow.
He was Head of Sales.
He was a fucking liability.
He must have been extremely impressed by Michael Douglas in *Wall Street*.
Gameshow had the slick hair, braces, filofax.
He used cringeworthy corporate-speak at ever opportunity.
He had a smile that switched on and off unnaturally.
If he got wind of the looming MassiveBank contract, he would be guaranteed to balls it up.
Everything was done in secret.
Meetings were held in toilets.
The most important room in any factory.
Norse was in cubicle one.
Ferris was in cubicle two.
"All set?"
"All set, Norse. Leeds station at nine. Train down to London, meeting with MassiveBank at one. They're making favourable noises already."
"Good work, Ferris. What about Gameshow?"
"Doesn't know a thing about it. First thing he'll find out is when the contract lands on his desk."
"Excellent. Let's keep it that way. Remember to flush."
"Will do, Norse. See you tomorrow."

Next morning 9.00am.
The team meet in Leeds station.
Some nerves, but quiet confidence prevails.

Coffees, clock watching, murmured conversation, and...
"Hey there, team! Surprise!"
Gameshow.
Spilled coffees, pale faces, murmured curses.
Norse rallies.
"Oh, erm, hi Gameshow. We were worried you wouldn't show. Did you get the email?"
"I certainly did, Norse! Had to hop on your machine to retrieve it. Hope you don't mind!"
"Oh. No, I suppose not..."
"Capital, capital! Right then, troops. What's the campaign strategy? Give me the angle!"
Ferris shuffles nearer to Norse.
"We're fucked, aren't we?"
"I don't know. Maybe not."
"Come on team! The train's here. We'll drill-down over lattes!"
On the train, they brief Gameshow.
Ferris and Norse are to clinch the deal. Secretaries to take notes, account executives to set schedules, Gameshow was there to 'add weight' to the proceedings.
As long as he didn't open his mouth, they would be ok.

One O'clock. MassiveBank HQ.
Ferris starts with a powerpoint presentation of the company capabilities.
Norse follows samples of previous work, mock ups of how MassiveBank's material would look on various brochures and mailers.
Penpusher gives a briefing on costs and schedules.
Everything goes smoothly.
The team are professional.
MassiveBank are impressed.
Big Head, marketing director for MassiveBank, leans forward.
"I'm impressed, Mr Norse. It seems like you have covered all the bases. My only concern is might not have the capabilities to deliver this product to schedule."
"Lemon squeezy."
Everybody looked at Gameshow. He's rocking back in his chair, his

fingers laced behind his slick hair.
"I beg your pardon?"
"Easy peasey, lemon squeezy! I've looked under the bonnet of all Norse's proposals, and it's infinitely do-able."
"I'm sorry?"
"I've not been handling your traffic personally, Mr Big Head, because I've not really had enough bandwidth, but Norse here has looked at everything to the finest level of granularity, he's our product evangelist, so to speak. We're going to tic-tac together next week over the small stuff, but I'm certain, with a little forward planning, that we can probably beat the targets we've shown you here by maybe a week!"
Penpusher jumps in his seat.
"Erm, Mr Gameshow, what about the GoldCash account? We've got them on the schedule..."
"Goldcash? Park it."
"Erm... what?"
Gameshow leaned across the desk, ready to deliver his killer blow. Norse and Ferris look away.
Let's cut to the chase, Mr Big Head. I've got what you want, and I can give it to you, hard and fast."
Tiny groans emerge from the team. Gameshow doesn't hear.
"Me and my crew have taken enough idea showers together to know what's what, Mr Big Head. We're experts in 360° thinking. I'm certain that Massive bank and our company, working together, can create a beautiful synergy. It's a partnership you will not regret!"
The smile switched on. Gameshow actually winked at Mr Big Head.
"You know it and I know it, Mr Big Head. Our products are marketing Viagra! Just leave my team here to do all the clicks and mortar. They pride themselves on taking a holistic, cradle-to-grave approach to your product. They will give you a mailshot that will make you're target demographic hard! Meanwhile, I'm gonna take you to lunch!"
Gameshow stuck out his hand. "What do you say?"
It seems that My Big Head wasn't hungry.
The team trudged along the station platform.
Ferris consoled Penpusher.
His dreams of a Christmas bonus had turned to dust.

Gameshow was unperturbed.
He slapped Norse on the shoulder.
"Chin up, my old China! Mr Big Head is probably ringing the office right now, begging for our services!"
Norse said nothing.
"Yes, he won't let the grass grow too long under that deal. He's just playing hard to get. I like that in a man."
Norse looked at Gameshow.
"You like men to play hard to get?"
"Don't say you like it easy, Norse! You're like me! It's all to easy to nibble on the low hanging fruit. Men like us want to stretch for the client! And when we've wined them and dined them, we like to put the fucker to bed!"
"Do we?"
"Of course! Now get on that train, and get the team a round of lattes! I'll get the next train. I'm going for a blow job!"
"A blow job? What does that mean? Is it a meeting with clients? Are you making a phone call?"
"No! Big meetings like that always get my juices flowing. I'm going to get a prostitute! Here's fifty quid. By coffees for the gang. Ciao!"
"erm... ciao..."

Devil in Disguise

I've got a younger brother, Devil. He looks just like me, only younger, less harassed.
He's one of my favourite people in the world.
Some might call him a laid back character, some might call him an out and out stoner.
I call him Devil.
He's had a lot of jobs, has Devil.
Warehouses, industrial units, restaurants.
In one job he had to stand by the roadside in a fucking massive Pink Panther costume, waving at passers by and attempting to shepherd customers into a carpet shop.
Pink Panther and carpets?
I don't see the link.
He got fired because he was smoking joints inside the costume's head, and people were freaking out at the sight of Pink Panther waving at them with smoke billowing from his eyes.
Devil didn't give a shit.

He got a job in the same factory as me.
He became notorious within days.

The guy who owns the factory, God, is very particular about how it looks. He's a multi millionaire, drives a DB7, a sharp dresser.
He likes the factory to look sharp too - nice grounds, ornamental roundabout, tasteful shrubbery.
Put a pig in a dress, it's still a pig.

He had a big office extension built, and the carpeting cost more than my salary for two years.
It still smelt new when a trail of black inky footprints appeared, walking across it's entire length, leading out onto the factory floor.
Horrified office staff followed the footprints in a white shirted conga across the factory.
They finished at the feet of a blissfully smiling Devil.

He didn't turn in for a week one time.
Why?
He'd had a big fall out with his neighbour the rabbit on the computer game 'Animal Crossing', and he needed to spend some time rebuilding the relationship.
It's true.

One morning, after he finished his night shift, he floored his knackered fiesta, desperate to get away from work.
He'd smoked so much shit on his shift that it left his judgment somewhat impaired.
He plowed into God's fancy ornamental roundabout at thirty miles an hour.
Totalled it.

He worked when he wanted, stayed at home when he wanted, drove the bosses mental.
Then he told them to fuck themselves, sold everything he had and travelled the world.
Pure class.
He left me here, at the factory.
I miss him a lot.

I've worked here a lot longer than he did. A lot longer.

Anyway, word came round the factory like wildfire.
We were losing our biggest customer.
There could be redundancies.
You could smell fear.
Turns out that reprography was part to blame.
We'd been getting the corporate colour wrong for years, our Old Soulless Boss had been ignoring complaints, riding it until retirement.
Enough was enough.
They were coming in for talks that afternoon, then they were binning us.
New Soulless Boss put me on the case.
We worked fast.
Densitometers were put into action, readings taken, proofs spat out.

We really worked our bollocks off.
Updates from the board room didn't sound good, but we gave it our all.
I felt something flickering, a flame that I thought had been pissed out long ago.
Company loyalty.
I wasn't going to let this happen. I was going to get it right!
The door opened, and in walked God, looking nervous, followed by the customers big knobs.
Just as I peeled off the last laminate on a proof, exposing their bright, glossy corporate colour in all it's rosy glory.
They cooed. The aahed.
They were delighted.
We kept the contract.
As they were leaving, God turned to me.
"At last, you managed to get something right, Devil."

After all these years of service, he didn't know who the fuck I was. He just thought I was the guy who tried to evil Knievel his fancy roundabout.

The Shadow

He lurked in the shadows, watching.
Any hour, day or night.
You never knew he was there.
He could see you, but you could never see him.
The Shadow was on the board of Directors.
He was convinced his staff were shirkers and layabouts.
He was also incredibly paranoid.
If they were shirking, they were doing it to get at him.
If production was down, he saw it as a personal affront.
He was notorious for his screaming fits of apoplectic rage, spitting and howling at staff who displeased him.
Everybody displeased him, even the fawning sycophants he recruited from the workforce to spy for him, paying them in high paying overtime.
He had a window fitted in a high room overlooking the factory floor, and he would slink into the unlit room and peer down on his minions from between slitted blinds.
If a worker went to the toilet without permission, he would see.
Sneaky fag breaks were witnessed and noted.
A hastily slurped cup of tea did not avoid his unblinking gaze.
Hated supervisors would then cruise amongst the staff, handing out warnings and bollockings to staff who didn't quite come up to scratch, ladling out bitter vitriol that had been dripped down to them from The Shadow.
The night shift could breath a sigh of relief.
Only a mad man would come in to work at three in the morning to catch malingerers.
Out in the still street, a dark vehicle drifted silently into an empty car park.
The Shadow drifted across the damp tarmac to the door leading into the offices, and entered unnoticed.
Through the unlit corridors he swept, until he reached his lair.
There he crouched, in the dark.
Watching.

The next shift, and the warnings were meted out.
The workers were puzzled, but all eyes slowly turned to the blank eye of the dark window that looked over them.
The workers sent scouts out on a night to spot his car, but The Shadow was too cunning.
He parked a distance away, and slipped through deserted alleyways to his secret entrance.
There he perched, his eyes glittering, watching, watching.
The workers loathed him for it.
He didn't care.

-

2.35am. Wednesday.
The Shadow left his car and slithered through the alleys towards the factory.
He was dressed in black, almost impossible to detect.
He glanced to left and right, before racing across the road to the door, where he crouched, rummaging for his key.
"Excuse me Sir. What do you think you are doing?"
The Shadow nearly had a heart attack.
"What? What? Oh. Good evening, constable. I'm, erm, I'm going in to my office. I work here."
"Do you really, Sir. At 2.36 in the morning? I somehow doubt that!"
"But I do! I really do! I'm on the board of Directors!"
"Well, we'd better pop inside and find out. It seems like there are lights on in the main building. Perhaps we can find somebody who can vouch for you..."
The policeman leads The Shadow into the factory, where everybody looks up, smirks, and looks away.
The policeman calls to Dogsbody, who was operating the nearest enclosing machine.
"Excuse me, Sir. But do you recognize this man? He claims to work here in some capacity."
Dogsbody looked at The Shadow.
The Shadow gave Dogsbody a pleading glance.
"Never seen this cunt in my life, mate."
"But.. but!!"
The policeman asked around.
Nobody seemed to have a clue who The Shadow was.

"Well, well, well, sir. I think somebody has been telling porkies."
"Yes! Those unwashed fuckers in that factory, that's who!!"
"So you say, sir, so you say. We'd better have a little chat about it down the station."
As The Shadow drove away in the back of the patrol car, he looked back at the factory.
In the light streaming out of the open factory door, he could see a dozen silhouettes watching him go.
And they were all smoking.

A Moth and a Rat

The main door to the factory is grim.
It's next to the toilets.
It stinks of piss.
It's full of cobwebs and dead flies.
You wouldn't loiter there, given a choice.
A couple of lads were looking at something on the wall by the main door.
I wandered over.
The lads were in discussion.
"What is it, Rusty?"
"I dunno, Snowy. A moth, I reckon."
"Or a butterfly. Look at the bloody size of it! It's as big as my palm!"
I took a look.
It was beautiful.
It's body was covered in soft beige fur, and huge golden antennae curled from it's head.
The huge pale wings shivered gently, as though it sensed us but trusted it's camouflage to keep it safe.
"It's a hawk moth, but I don't know what kind."
I later looked it up. It was a Poplar Hawk Moth.
Snowy and Rusty looked round.
"I might have guessed you'd know that, Lucifer."
"Why, because I'm renowned for my formidable breadth of knowledge?"
"No. Because you're such a geeky cunt."
"Oh."
The lads walked away.
I should have walked away too, I had jobs to do.
Fuck it.
I'd seen plenty of direct mail jobs.
I'd never seen a moth like this.
Work could wait for a bit.

The lads had a point.
I am a geeky cunt.

So what?
I really loved looking at that moth.
It was so weird, almost alien, and I couldn't believe something so amazing had chosen to take a rest in that shit hole.
After a bit, I got back to work.
Even though, I kept thinking about that moth while I worked.
I couldn't resist it.
I went for another look.
It was gone.
I went outside, hoping it had just moved.
I couldn't see it.
As I turned to go back inside, I saw something moving on the floor.
There, in a pile of gravel and tab ends, was the moth.
Someone had tried to kill it, but had failed.
That soft fur was covered in fag ash, and it's wings were shattered and hanging off.
The sweeping antennae were broken, as were most of it's legs.
It was trying to crawl out of the shit that had been crushed down on top of it, but couldn't get out.
I was mortified.
I picked it up, carried it to a patch of grass, and quietly killed it.
I asked around.
"Here, Rusty. Did you see anyone else looking at that moth?"
I knew Rusty wouldn't kill it. He was odd, but not cruel.
"Yeah, I did. Norms was showing an interest."
Norms.
He would definitely do it.
I found him washing up a print press.
"There's some right cunts about, Norms."
"Yeah, too right, Lucifer."
"Did you see that moth by the main entrance? Some fucker only went and killed it."
Norms looked up. He had guilt written all over his face.
"They never."
"Don't come that. Why did you do it?"
"It were gonna die anyway! That's why it were by the bogs. It were sick."
"You're the one that's fucking sick."

"Fuck off! I just put it out of it's misery."
"There was nothing wrong with it! There was no need, Norms. There was no need!"
"Oh, fuck off."

There was no need.
Maybe it's just me, but I can't understand why someone would do that.
My only guess was that he did it because the moth didn't fit, it was an anomaly.
norms couldn't comprehend it, so he destroyed it.
Either that, or he's just a sadistic bastard.

A couple of weeks later, Norms looked as sick as a dog.
there was a gut wrenching smell on his machine, a smell that was impossible to describe.
I saw Rusty working a safe distance away.
"Here, Rusty! What the fuck is that rotten smell over by Norms?"
"That's the rat, Lucifer."
"The rat?"
"The rat. A rat got into the factory, and Norms went after it. Got it cornered. He didn't kill it though. He was pouring chemicals on it, stabbing it with stuff, being a proper cunt. Anyhow, Goliath caught him doing it."
"Fucking hell! What happened?"
"First thing he did was stamp on the rat. Killed it outright. Then he picks up Norms and just shakes him. He shakes him and shakes him till Norms puked. Then he picks up the rat, takes it to Norms' tea mug, and crams it in. Puts cellophane over the top. He tells Norms to leave it right there, on the work bench. He tells him he's gonna check it every day, and if it's gone, he's gonna fuck Norms up really, really bad. That were four days ago."
I had to look.
I held my nose and went to the machine.
"Hi Norms. Looking good."
"Fuck off, Lucifer."
"In a tick..."
There it was, just where Goliath had left it.

Print factories are pretty warm places.
That rat was half way to being soup.
I couldn't stay any longer.
"See you later Norms."
He didn't answer.
He was puking into a bin.

Statue of Fucking Liberty

"My mate Treacle got him self in a right fix the other night, Lucifer."
"Did he now, Scorcher."
"Yeah. We'd been for a few pints of Tetley's down The Mythical Beast, and he went home early. He were supposed to meet us next day, but he never showed."
"Did you try phoning him?"
"Yeah. No answer. I went back to the pub at lunchtime, but there were still no sign of him."
"What did you do then, Scorcher?"
"I took a walk round to his house. On the way, I saw some cones up around some repairs on the pavement. They'd been pouring concrete, but it were a right mess. There was a big imprint of a bloke's body, right in the middle of this 'ere concrete, and a trail of footprints going off in the direction of my mates house."
"No..."
"Well I broke into a run, Lucifer. There were no time to lose! These footprints were rock hard!"
sigh
"I got to his house, ran round the back, and guess what?"
"I've guessed, but go on."
"There were me mate. Rock solid, covered in concrete, frozen with his house key an inch from the lock. He were just like a statue."
"Come on then. What did you do?"
"I went into his shed, got out his lump hammer and swung it at him as hard as I could! The concrete shatters into a million pieces, Lucifer. It all came off clean. There weren't a bit left on him. And you know what Treacle did?"
"No. No, I don't."
"His hand just kept going toward the lock as if nowt had happened! He popped in his key, lets himself in and shuts the door."
"Really."
"Yeah! Well, I couldn't believe it!"
"Neither can I."

Tellingbone

I can't get my head around porn on mobile phones.
It just seems wrong to me.
Not that mobile phones are in any way sacred.
Quite the opposite.
They're intrusive and annoying, doubly so now that every one of them has a camera.
Not only do they barge into a conversation with their irritating chirruping, demanding attention like a canary with ADHD, but they can also take high definition images of your resulting outrage at being so rudely interrupted.
The thing with porn on phones is it flies in the face of the old adage 'There's a time and a place for everything.'
Do we really need a handy database of fisting and felching with us at all times?
I've got a mobile phone, but there's no porn on it.
-
RamJet was devouring a sandwich and scrolling through his phone.
"Hi Ramjet. how's it going?"
"I'm doing good, Lucifer. Here, want to see something?"
"Well, that depends on.. Whoah! What the Hell's that?? Why would anyone do that to themselves?! Jesus, RamJet..."
"What about this then?"
"Look, it's not really my.. Bloody Hell! Bloody, Hell! That's just wrong. Really, really wrong. Is that illegal? It must be."
"Dunno. Look at this then."
"No. I've got my eyes shut."
"Puff."
"No, RamJet. Not puff. It's not just puffs that don't like to watch Chinese girls shitting in each others mouths. Why have you got that on your phone?"
"Dunno. Just filth, innit?"
"Yes, it is. But why do you need it with you at all times? You're eating a beef sandwich.."
"Ham."

"You're eating a ham sandwich and looking at.. give me that phone... looking at a lady fisting another lady's arse. You can't tell me ham sandwiches and arse fisting are a perfect combination."
"Why not?"
"Fucking Hell, RamJet! Can't you see a problem with that?"
"Now that you mention it..."
"Yes. When you stop and think about it, it's fucking weird. If you want to look at stuff like that, why not do it at home? Why are you looking at it now?"
"Cause I love it. I fucking love porn, Lucifer. Don't you?"
"Everybody likes a bit of porn, if they're honest about it, RamJet. But there's a time and a place! Lunchtime is not the time, and work really isn't the place. Doesn't it get you all frustrated looking at porn all the time?"
"Yeah, it does. I spend half the day with a right hard on."
"Well why do it to yourself? Give your cock a break, for Christ's sake!"
"I can't help myself, Lucifer. I reckon I'm one of those porn addicts. I watch it all the time. It's on my phone, on my computer, it's never off my telly."
"You need help, RamJet. Seriously."
"I don't want help, though. I love it. It relaxes me. That's why I like to look at it while I'm eating."
"Why not try and take a break from it, at least?"
"No point. I've only got an appetite when porn's on. I wouldn't eat if porn weren't on."
"You wouldn't eat? Porn makes you hungry. Now that is really weird."
"You reckon? It wasn't so bad at first. You only used to be able to get hold of magazines, years back. Then porn tapes got easy to find, then DVD's, and then the internet started. It all got a bit mad, after that."
RamJet's expression became all dreamy, and a little smile came onto his face.
"Nowadays, I really can't enjoy my dinner unless I'm watching two birds pissing on each other. It's ace, is porn."
"Remind me never to go to a restaurant with you, RamJet. I'll see you later."

He didn't answer. He was munching away on his sandwich, and his eyes were glued to his phone.
What I want to know is, where will it end?

Own Goal

Huge floodlights loom over the rear yard.
They're for loading and unloading wagons at night.
The thing is, that's pretty boring.
Why not use them to illuminate football matches instead?
The night shift get bored easily.
At midnight they stop work and charge out into the yard.
The lights go on.
Barrels of chemical for goal posts.
Somebody hoofs a ball across the concrete.
Game on.
Things always get heated.
Shouted comments from the sidelines.
Disputes over possession.
Fat, unfit machine minders puking quietly behind the skips.
Games can last for hours.
Not much work gets done.
For people living nearby, not much sleeping gets done either...
-
*Ring*Ring*
Snore.
*Ring*Ring*
"Hmm? Hello?"
"Cardboard Supervisor? This is God."
"Fucking Hell!"
"What a coincidence. That's exactly what I said when the police phoned me at two o'clock in the fucking morning."
"The police? What did they want, sir?"
"They wanted to know why the loading area of the factory was lit up like Heathrow airport all fucking night, and why it sounded like those chimpanzees I have the misfortune of paying sounded like they were murdering each other! Nobody at the factory is answering the phone, so they had no choice but to locate the poor unfortunate who owns the sorry excuse for a business, and that happened to be me!"
"Oh."

"Oh indeed, Cardboard Supervisor. Now I trust that you will sort everything out by morning, and that the necessary heads will roll, and that I will hear nothing more from the local constabulary regarding the nocturnal shenanigans of my dull witted workforce!!!"
"Yes sir. I'll get right on it."
"Good!"
Click.
"Who was that, cardboard darling?"
"It was God. The monkeys have got out of the fucking zoo again, and they sound like they are having a shit fight! I've got to phone the factory. Go back to sleep."
*Ring*Ring*
*Ring*Ring*
*Ring*Ring*
*Ring*Ring*
*Ring*Ring*
*Ring*Ring*
*Ring*Ring*
*Ring*Ring*
"H..H..Hello?"
"Who the fucking hell is that??!"
"Go fuck yourself. Who are you?"
"I'm Cardboard Supervisor, that's who, you piece of shit!"
"Oh! Sorry sir. It's Dogsbody here. What's up?"
"What's up? What's up? I've got God calling me up in the middle of the night because of the noise you arseholes are making, that's what's up! The police are wanting to send the riot squad round to break things up! Now, what the fuck is going on?"
"Nothing."
"NOTHING?! Are you taking the piss, Dogsbody?"
"No, sir! We're all just getting on with our work. Can't imagine what all the fuss is about!"
"Fuck off, Dogsbody! You can't fool me! Where's Mule, the shift supervisor? Why hasn't he been answering the phone?"
"Mule's been very busy, sir. He can't get to the phone. He's working ever so hard! We all are! Honest!"
"I don't believe you!"
"It's true! He's very strict, is Mule! He doesn't let us get away with

nothing! That's why he's supervisor - very responsible man, is Mule!"

A sudden, deafening roar comes from the back yard, screams and whoops and cheers.

Cardboard Supervisor holds the handset away from his ear until the sound becomes bearable.

"Dogsbody?"
"Aherm. Yes Sir?"
"Where's Mule?"
"He's in goal."

Meet The Parents.

I'm late for work.
Fuck it.
Nothing ever gets said.
It's Monday, 6.11am.
Managers and supervisors are still snoring and farting.
I make cup of tea.
In the studio, OhSeeDee is sitting with his head in his hands.
Must have been a good one.
"Morning OhSeeDee."
"Morning Lucifer."
"Rough night?"
"Not really."
"What's up? You look like shit."
"Thanks for that. It was my first meeting with the future in-laws this weekend."
"Right! I forgot about that! You were staying over, weren't you? How did it go?"
"Badly."
"Oh."
"They're really nice people, Lucifer. They made me very welcome. It just went a bit...wrong."
"Come on then. What happened."
OhSeeDee sighs.
"They've got a lovely big place by the coast. Really nice. Must have cost a packet. They're minted, Lucifer. The real deal. Me and Pepper got their mid afternoon. Her folks had tea and cake ready."
"Ooh! I like cake. What type was it?"
"They had two types. Fruit cake and a nice sponge."
"Top drawer!"
"Yeah. Anyhow, we got on really, really well. Pepper's mum asked her to help with dinner, and her old man offered me a game of snooker. He's got his own snooker room! It had a bar in it. Not a tacky one - really nice. He got us a couple of beers, it was dead cool!"
"Sounds ace! What beer was it?"
"Bottles of Speckled Hen."

"Very nice! Nothing shit."
"No, not Carling or anything."
"Wouldn't thank you for it."
"Me neither. As I was saying, I did alright at snooker. He beat me, I beat him, pretty evenly matched. I didn't make a dick of myself, which is the main thing. We went through to dinner."
"What did you have?"
"What?"
"Dinner. What was it?"
"Oh! Deep fried mozzarella with rocket salad, followed by beef Wellington."
"Cracking! It's all sounding great! What was pudding?"
"Pavlova."
"Good choice. You want something light after that lot."
"yeah, I suppose. Anyway, there was plenty of wine on the table, they kept filling my glass. I got a bit fresh, but not pissed. We were all a bit fresh. It was a good night! We sat round the table chatting for ages, but I was getting pretty knackered. I'd been at work that morning."
"Were you? I didn't get asked in..."
"Well I was. At about midnight, me and Pepper went to bed. Her folks stayed up for a bit. I went straight to sleep, but I must have a had a weird dream or something. I started sleepwalking."
"No!"
"Yes. You know how I'm paranoid about burglars, well I hear voices downstairs. Apparently her parents were coming up to bed, so lights were going off, and they were talking quietly and moving towards the stairs..."
"No, way..."
"...Pepper had woken up and found me gone. She goes out onto the landing, and sees me at the top of the stairs wearing nothing but my pants. Her parents start coming up the stairs, and they suddenly see me."
"Oh God. What did you do?"
Apparently I shouted, 'Come on then you fucking cunts! Let's have it then! I'll fucking kill you!"
"Jesus Mary and Joseph..."
"They were a bit surprised to say the least. They tried to laugh it off, but this seemed to get me a bit cross. I started hopping around, screaming, "Let's have it you cunts! Do you know who I am? I'm a

mother fucking gangster!"

"A gangster? You're not a gangster. Why would you say you were a gangster? Are you really a gangster?"

"No I'm not a fucking gangster. I've no idea why I would say that."

"I'm glad to hear that. What happened then?"

"After a bit of an awkward standoff, Pepper managed to coax me back to bed. She told me all about it next morning. I was fucking mortified. There was a strained atmosphere over breakfast, I can tell you."

"Really? What was it?"

"Because of the fucking sleepwalking! I'd called them cunts! I'd called myself a motherfucking gangster! Weren't you listening?"

"I meant what was it for breakfast."

"Oh, fuck off Lucifer..."

Mutual Mastication.

I'm watching Pike.
I like to watch people.
It annoys me, but I can't stop doing it.
Perhaps I'm a voyeur.
I'm definitely a voyeur.
Let's face it.
We're all voyeurs.
That's why 'You've been Framed' is still on telly.
That's why porn is popular.
That's why people who live in flats buy telescopes.
We're all peepers.

I'm watching Pike.
What's he eating?
Everything.
He's always eating.
Jaw champing up and down beneath that scrubby little moustache,
his eyes glazed over.
What's he thinking?
Not much.
Staring into middle distance.
Eating.
He crumples up the wrapper, pops it in the bin.
Good boy.
Jaw still working.
His hand slides towards his pocket.
A chocolate bar.
Looks like a Penguin.
Turquoise wrapper.
Yes, it's a Penguin.
Chomp chomp.
"You greedy, fat, bald headed, tashy-faced cunt bag!"
Bit harsh.
It's Glutes.
He's a body builder.

He's always having a go at Pike.
Pike slowly chews, carefully swallows, and clears his throat.
"Fuck off."
"No, you fuck off, you pig faced, dough bodied, chocolate smeared sack of crap!"
Pike can't answer.
His mouth is full.
Glutes laughs as he goes by.
He's carrying a tupperware container the size of a child's coffin.
It's full of potatoes and beans.
He eats more than Pike, truth be told.
It's just that Glutes turns his calorie intake into muscle by lifting huge weights in his garage to make up for his cock size.
Pike must be pretty well hung.
He doesn't seem to mind being fat.
He watches Glutes go into the locker room.
There's a microwave oven in there.
Pike's eyes are still kind of glazed, his jaw goes up and down, his moustache wriggles beneath his nose, but he's watching.
The door to the locker room opens and out comes Glutes.
He isn't carrying the Tupperware.
"Hey, Pike, you lard-arsed, twat-faced window licker! Is that a Snickers in your pocket or are you checking out my guns?"
Glutes flexes a huge bicep, and swaggers off, laughing.
Pike doesn't say anything.
He looks at something in his pocket.
It's a Snickers.
He watches Glutes go.
Then he wanders over to the locker room.
-
It's cold out here.
Everyone is in the car park.
The fire alarm is going off.
Smoke is drifting out of the factory door.
I look over at Pike.
He's eating that Snickers bar, his face impassive.
I can hear sirens in the distance.
Sytex is shivering.

"Fuck this. I'm nipping in for my coat."
He sneaks through the door.
We wait.
He staggers back out, followed by Bear, who is raging.
"Sack that man!" he screams. "Sack that man!"
Bear is carrying something.
He's got hold of an electrical lead at arms length.
On the other end is a microwave oven, billowing out black smoke.
He hurls it into the car park, where it bounces and clatters across the tarmac.
the door comes off.
A big blob of melted plastic flops out, followed by the cindered remains of several potatoes.
Glutes is crestfallen.
"Aww! That was my dinner!"
A little smile peeps out from underneath Pike's moustache.
"What the fuck are you grinning about?" snarls Glutes. "I'm fucking starving now!"
"Never mind," says Pike. "You needed to lose some weight anyway, you fat cunt."

The Fib Four

"The music industry is a piece of piss nowadays, Lucifer. It were much harder, back in my day..."
"Is that why you're working in a factory, Scorcher, rather than playing the stadiums?"
"Something like that. If I were a young man today, I'd be on Top of the Pops!"
"That'd be going some. It's been cancelled for three years."
"Has it? Never noticed. Thing is, I've got an ear for talent. Not like your Simon Cowell. He just knows money, that cunt. Not got a clue about real music."
"I'm forced to agree with you there, Scorcher."
"Dead right. I ever tell you about that band I saw in the early sixties?"
"Just a sec, Scorcher. I think my phone's ringing..."
"I were down The Cardigan Arms in Kirkstall. It must have been winter, at the start of '62."
"Go on then..."
"These lads were banging out some songs in the tap room. There were only a dozen people in, and none of them were listening. Well, I were listening, Lucifer. Like I said, I've got an ear."
"You've got two, actually."
"Shut it. As I were saying, these lads looked right dejected, they did. Proper fed up. They finished the set, packed up their kit and went to the bar for a pint. I heard 'em talking. They were on about giving it up as a bad job."
"Now my phone really is ringing..."
"Well I slams my fist down on't bar between 'em, making their pots of ale jump almost as high as they did. I says 'There's no way you lads are gonna quit! You've got what it takes. Mark my words, this time next year, you lads will be famous!' Well, they say to me that their manager was a big shot, and even he thought they were going nowhere, and that they should quit. So I says 'Brian Epstein only knows how to sell fucking records, but you lads know how to make 'em. Trust me, I know. I've got an ear!' They seemed to perk up a bit

106

after that! I helped them load their stuff into the van, and I heard one of them humming a song. I said, 'That's a catchy tune! What do you call it?' And he says, 'It's called Love Me Do.' So I says, 'That's gold, that is! Get that on a record, and you'll be onto a winner!' They all shook my hand, and drove off into the night. You know who those lads were?"

"The Monkees?"

"Just fuck off, Lucifer."

"The Beach Boys?"

"Just..."

"Simon and Garfunkel?"

"...fuck..."

"The Beatles?"

"...off. Yes! Yes, it were The fucking Beatles! I met the fucking Beatles!"

"Good for you, Scorcher. You changed the face of pop music, single-handedly."

"I suppose I did, now you put it like that. Who was it on the phone, by the way?"

"I don't know. Probably George Martin, ringing to thank you personally."

"How did he know we were talking?"

"Bye Scorcher."

The Wander

It was a boring day.
In the print industry, work can be seasonal.
Sometimes you're running round like Bernie Clifton on MDMA, and other days you make Stephen Hawking look hyperactive.
This was a Stephen Hawking day.
I looked round the room.
Genuflect was reading a sci fi novel.
Soulless Boss was locked in his office.
Sytex was missing, God only knows where.
Zulu was grinning quietly to himself.
He kept going in to the store room.
He'd come out grinning.
I knew what he as doing.
He was torturing spiders in there.
He liked to press them down onto stick tape, and watch them starve to death over days, sometimes weeks.
A grown man.
Torturing spiders.
I had to get out.
"I'm off for a wander."
I went for a wander.
One of the print presses was clattering away, seemingly unattended.
Looking around, I saw that the operator was Superman.
He was fond of betting on the dogs, was Superman.
He was hidden under a desk, his nose in the racing post, picking the pooches.
I took a glance at what he was printing.
It was a travel brochure.
The print press had run out of yellow ink.
It had run out of yellow ink about half an hour ago.
The entire run was fucked, but Superman hadn't noticed.
I didn't tell him.
Fuck it.
I walked on.

I got near the envelope department.
I knew I had to be careful.
There was some weird types round there.
Somebody jumped out.
It was Slugsy. He'd found a massive cardboard disk, five feet high, the type used to protect the sides of print reels.
He'd drawn a woman's body on it, and cut arm holes out, and he was wearing it, dancing like a loon.
"Blibbleibbleibbleibbleibble!"
"Hi Slugsy. That's a good look on you. I'd keep it up."
"Ta very much! Blibbleibbleibbleibble!"
He turned around and danced away. Other than the cardboard disk, he was totally naked.
Nice.
I walked on.
A machine had broken down.
Pollock was fixing it.
He was singing show tunes at the top of his voice.
"What is it today, Pollock? Le Misérables?"
He didn't answer, just kept spannering and singing.
"You'll get no answer out of that odd cunt."
It was Rusty, the machine minder.
"How come, Rusty?"
"His best mate has fucked off abroad. Emigrated. Pollock's in deep mourning. He hasn't spoken to anyone for weeks. He just keeps singing those fucking songs."
"I know he's always been a bit light footed, but I thought he was married, with kids?"
"He is. I'm not sure he's properly gay, but I reckon he just helps them out, when they're a bit short handed. You know, a weekend thing."
"Maybe your right. Not a bad voice though. What is that?"
"Mezzo soprano, I reckon. Want a biscuit?"
"No thanks. See you later, Rusty."
I walked on.
I could hear a grinding, tearing noise.
A folding machine was going haywire, chewing everything up.
Nobody pressed the 'stop' button.
The operator was Winkle.

He had narcolepsy.
He shouldn't have been running a machine, but he was.
He was asleep.
I tapped the button, and walked on.
I climbed the stairs to the canteen. A new shift was about to start, and Haystacks was eating his pack up before he started work.
Cardboard supervisor hustled in, looking all hot and bothered.
"Haystacks! What the fuck do you think you're doing! There's an urgent job waiting on your machine, and you're up here stuffing your face! We don't pay you to sit here eating, you know!"
Haystacks slowly looked up, checked his watch, and cleared his throat.
"You don't pay me fuck all for another seven minutes, Cardboard, now fuck off."
Cardboard supervisor went bright red, and fucked off.
Haystacks bit into another sandwich.
I walked on.
Something hit me on the back of the neck.
I looked around.
Nobody there.
I carried on.
Something hit me again.
I looked around again.
Still nothing.
This had happened before.
I looked really carefully this time, then I saw him.
The bog roll ninja.
He had wrapped an entire roll of paper towels around his head, leaving only an eye slit.
He had a biro converted into a peashooter, which he poked through his disguise.
That fucker was really, really accurate.
I dodged behind a machine, and made my way to his hiding place.
Took a deep breath.
Jumped out.
He was gone.
Something hit me on the back of the neck.
I didn't turn around.

I was defeated.
Never found out who the bog roll ninja was.
I walked on.
Nutsack and Fresh were arguing.
Nutsack was an old hand at the print game, always wore overalls pulled up too high.
That's why he was called Nutsack.
You couldn't fucking miss them, bulging through those filthy overalls.
Fresh was a new kid.
He'd washed Nutsack's mug out.
He was only trying to be helpful.
"Look at the state of my fucking mug, you stupid little cunt!"
"What do you mean, Nutsack? It's clean! I cleaned it! It took fucking ages! I had to use powerful solvents to get all that black shit off!"
"That black shit, as you call it, is what makes my cup of tea taste like a cup of fucking tea, shit for brains! I'd just got that mug how I like it! Now you've ruined it!"
"Just got it like that? You've not washed it in six months!"
"I know! And it'll take another six months to get a mug tasting right again! Give it here!"
Nutsack snatched the mug off Fresh and smashed it on the ground.
Fresh was speechless.
I walked on.
Somebody was coming towards me.
It was Yogi Bear.
Not somebody's nickname.
I mean Yogi Bear.
Hat. Bear suit. Picnic basket.
Yogi Bear.
"Erm. Hello."
Yogi didn't say anything.
He pulled his head off.
Inside was Sytex.
"What the fuck are you looking at, Lucifer?"
"Er..."
He shoved the head back on.
"Go on. Fuck off."

"right. Will do, Sytex."
I walked on.
So did Yogi.
I heard a big commotion coming from near the toilets.
Blokes were laughing and retching at the same time.
Guisley was walking out of the toilets with his sleeves rolled up.
He was carrying a massive shit in his bare hands.
"I told you it were a big un! Come on! Which dirty bastard done it!"
I did a little sick in my mouth.
I decided I'd seen enough.
I went back to the studio.
Silence.
Zulu was still grinning, glancing occasionally at the store room.
Soulless Boss was still shut in his office.
Genuflect looked up from his book.
"Where you been, Lucifer?"
"Been for a wander."
"What's happening out there then? Owt?"
"Nowt, really."
"Slow day."
"Yeah, slow."

Squirrel Ripper

"It were squirrels, Lucifer."
"Squirrels, Weasel?"
"Squirrels."
"Sorry, you've lost me. What about squirrels?"
"I were telling you the other day! Something were in my loft, scurrying about! I said I thought it were rats, but it weren't. It were fucking squirrels!"
"Oh. That's bad. They can do a lot of damage, I heard. Chewing stuff and that."
"Too right. I had a roofer round to fix some tiles, and he found where they were coming in. They'd climb the tree at the side of the house, jump onto the gutter, then the little bastards would scuttle under the eves."
"What did you do?"
"The roofer blocked up the hole where they get in, and then he goes into the loft. He starts bashing the felt under the roof, listening for the squeaks."
"Sounds a bit harsh!"
"He found this great big bulge in the felt, so he cuts it open, and guess what was inside?"
"Well, going on what you're telling me, was it a squirrel?"
"Worse than that, Lucifer! It were only a fucking squirrel nest!"
"A drey."
"What?"
A squirrels nest. It's called a drey."
"I don't fucking care what it's called! That squirrel nest were in my house, and it had no fucking business there!"
"Fair enough. What happened?"
"Well this roofer lifts this nest out, right careful like. You could hear the squirrels running around on the roof, making a right racket, squeaking they're little fucking heads off."
"Can't say I blame them."
"This roofer opens up this nest, and shows me what was inside. Three little baby squirrels, all curled up asleep. They had their little

tales wrapped around themselves, warm as you like. Fluffy little ears. Really cute."
"That's a predicament, Weasel. What did you do with it? Did you put it back?"
"No, it were alright. This roofer had dealt with problems like that before. He knew just what to do."
"that's a relief. I wouldn't have a clue how to look after squirrels."
"Yeah, it were alright. He had a screwdriver with him."
"What! No!"
"Yeah, he sorted them out."
"Baby squirrels? Screwdrivers? This has gone a bit wrong for me..."
"He stabbed them in their necks. It were over quick."
"Necks? For fuck's sake! Who stabs a baby squirrel in the bloody neck? That's horrible! Who's your roofer? Peter Sutcliffe?"
"No. I didn't know Peter Sutcliffe did roofs. Thought he drove vans."
"He was also handy with a screwdriver, if you remember."
"Yeah, suppose he was. Anyway, that squirrel problems sorted. The adult squirrels wouldn't fuck off for ages though. Stayed on my roof for hours, squeaking and squeaking. Stupid fuckers."
"This is too much for me Weasel. See you later."
"Yeah, see you later Lucifer. You look a bit peaky."
"Yeah, funny that..."

Ringleader of the Midnight Zoo

It was 9pm.
I was ready to leave, and Tommy was just arriving.
Tommy's a good lad, one of the few people at work I'd call a mate.
He was on the night shift.
"Hi Tommy. How's it going?"
"Oh, hi Lucifer. It's going... you know..."
"He looked twitchy and tired, like he was just finishing a long shift, rather than just starting.
"What's up, mate? You look like crap."
"Hmm. Thanks for that. It's just that I hate nights, and they're starting to get to me."
"I thought it was a steady gig. Get yourself tucked away, do your work, listen too the radio..."
"Is that what you think? Listen, can you spare five minutes?"
I wanted to get home, but Tommy's a mate.
"Yeah, I've got five."
We went to his office.
Tommy works on the computers, and his office has a long row of large windows looking out onto the factory floor.
He doesn't look out onto print presses.
He looks out onto the enclosers.
Machines that put bits of paper into envelopes.
Not rocket science.
They're not run by rocket scientists.
They're run by a very odd mix of people.
Very odd.
They call that area The Cabbage Patch, because it populated by rows of vegetables.
Very fitting.
Tommy's office is pretty cozy.
Tea, fan heater, Radio 4.
"This is nice, Tommy. You've got a good set up."
"You think so?" He didn't look so convinced,
I noticed that the windows were covered in paper, up to a height of

about seven feet.
"That looks a bit of a mess, mate. What's that about?"
"You'll see."
He made me a tea. I didn't want one, but he seemed to need a bit of company.
I took a sip, and heard a scream.
"What the fuck was that?"
"They've started, Lucifer..."
Screaming, whistling, gibbering, howling.
The noise pierced the glass, drowning out the calming sound of the radio.
Something thudded off the window.
Tommy flinched.
"What the fuck is going on?"
"It's the Cabbage Patch. It's what they do, all night. It'll be like this 'till six in the morning."
He took me to the window and peeled away a sheet of yellowed A4, opening a window to the cabbage patch.
A man in his forties wearing a torn T-shirt and tracksuit bottoms lumbered by, mooing. He was carrying box of envelopes.
A skinny bloke with incredibly rotten teeth was making hyena noises as he fed sachets of shampoo into a hopper.
Elastic bands pinged through the air, fired by a man in his fifties with a slack, vacant expression. They snarled up the machines and got caught among the mailers. If you ever find elastic bands in your junk mail, that gimp probably fired it.
One worker was keeping his head down, trying to get on with his job. He would flinch occasionally as an elastic band stung him on the neck, or when a half witted lummox bellowed in his ear.
"He's new," whispered Tommy. "He won't last a month."
"Who's that bloke, over there?"
I pointed at a sneering man in his early sixties with hunched shoulders and dry, gray hair. I could see him talking to a small crowd of lackeys who would bellow with laughter at everything he said. They were stood near a kid who was filling mail bags and trying to ignore their obvious piss taking.
"That's Hessian. He's top dog out there, and everyone sucks up to him. He's a proper bully. They've been ripping into that lad on the

mail sacks for weeks. He's a bit simple, but works hard. He got that job through an agency, but Hessian doesn't like that. He hates agency staff, and does everything he can to make their lives Hell. He reckons agency staff are taking their jobs, but the truth is that they need to hire them, otherwise nothing gets done at night due to all the fucking about."

A football thumped heavily off the window, right by our faces. Tommy quickly replaced the piece of paper, to howls of laughter from outside.

Tommy shook his head. "That Hessian is such a cunt. I fucking hate him. He properly loves it here, lording it amongst those witless fuckers in the Cabbage Patch. They make my life a misery, chucking stuff at the windows and making animal noises. It sends me insane..."

"Not good, Tommy. You need to get off shitty nights and get back onto days."

"I wish I could, Lucifer. I wish I could..."

Tommy didn't get off nights, but Hessian was transferred to days. They were easing him off shifts, in readiness for his impending retirement.

He put in an application to work past sixty five.

He was refused.

He lodged an appeal.

It was rejected.

I was standing in the canteen queue.

It was early. My mind was miles away, daydreaming as I waited my turn.

A freezing cold tin of coke was pressed against the back of my neck.

"Fucking Hell!"

I jumped a mile.

There was laughter behind me.

The deep Hurr-Hurr-Hurr of idiots laughter.

I spun around.

Their was Hessian, with two goons.

"That woke you up, kid!" he cackled.

The goons hurr-hurred again.

Now, I'm not a fighter.
It's not my thing.
But that doesn't make me a bitch.
I bent down and whispered in Hessian's ear.
"You do that again, you scrawny piece of shit, and I'll ram that can right up your shrivelled arse."
He didn't like it. People didn't talk to him like that.
"There's no need for that, kid. We was just having a laugh!"
"You've had your laugh, now fuck off."
He fucked off.

No matter how much Hessian protested, they still made him retire.
He was gutted.
He walked around the factory on his last day, shaking hands with people and crying.
I didn't shake his hand.

A few months later I saw him at a bus stop.
He was alone.
He looked to have aged about twenty years.
It was raining.
He had one of those shitty tartan shopping trolleys, bulging with groceries.
The rain on his gray face made it look like he was crying.
Maybe he was.
Tough shit.

Winkle Picker

"For fuck's sake, Winkle, wake up!"
Winkle woke up.
His machine was a mess.
A mail pack had got jammed in the main feed, and dozens more were snarled up in the machinery.
Someone had hit the stop button, thankfully.
Winkle yawned, scratched himself, and slowly started to pick chewed up paper from between rollers and cogs.
This happened a lot.
Winkle had narcolepsy.
He would fall asleep at any time, anywhere.
He'd been found in the canteen, in the toilets, draped over pallets in the warehouse, snoring in cupboards.
He'd fallen asleep stood up, in the middle of a conversation.
Winkle was also a compulsive gambler.
He walked to work most days, not because he didn't have a car, or that it might be dangerous to drive with narcolepsy, but because he'd usually blown his petrol money on the horses.
One time, when the Grand National was on, he went round the factory telling everybody he was running a sweep.
None of the regular staff trusted him, but he managed to convince some contractors to buy in.
These contractors were cable pullers from Newcastle.
Cable pullers are tough as a dog's head. It's a brutal job.
Winkle took their money, stuck the lot on an outsider, each way.
He lost.
He had to stay off work until the cable pullers had gone back to Newcastle.
They'd have pulled his arms off, if they'd got hold of him.

This particular week, Winkle was on nights.
He had managed a rare win at the bookies over the weekend, and the petrol gauge was out of the red.
Just.
He finished his shift, clocked out, hopped in the car and drove away

into the darkness of the early morning.
Down the road, turn left, drop down to the traffic lights and...
Then he woke up.
The car behind had pipped his horn, bringing Winkle back to consciousness.
He rubbed his eyes, put the car in gear, and set off.
"Didn't see the lights change, huh?"
Winkle almost crashed with fright, and jerked his head around to look at the man sitting in the passenger seat.
He'd never seen him before in his life.
They drove across the junction in silence, the man looking calm, Winkle looking panicked and sweaty.
He was trying to think of something to say.
"Turn left here."
Winkle jumped at the sound of the mans voice, but did as he was told.
He didn't want to get hurt.
"Where are we going?"
His voice was dry, croaky. He didn't sound brave.
He didn't feel brave.
He was shitting himself.
"Take the next right up here, past the pub."
Winkle did as he was told.
They were now in a rough area, but because it was so early, the streets were deserted.
"Pull up here."
Winkle was shaking with fright.
The man slipped his hand inside his jacket, and Winkle squeezed his eyes shut praying that he would fall asleep before he was stabbed.
He didn't like the sight of blood.
"how much is that?"
Winkle opened his eyes.
"W...what?"
"On the meter. How much do I owe you?"
It suddenly dawned on Winkle what had happened.
He'd been asleep, and this guy had presumed he was a taxi waiting for a fare.
He squinted at the milometer.

"Eight quid, mate."

"Here's a tenner. Keep the change."

The man got out of the car and walked away.

Winkle let out a long, shaky sigh of relief.

He looked down at the ten pound note in his lap, and a small smile spread across his face.

Ten quid.

There was a horse running at the three thirty that afternoon.

It was a dead cert.

He rubbed his hands with glee, started the engine...

And then he woke up.

It was daylight.

Kids were kicking a football against his car.

The engine was dead.

The car door was open.

The tenner was gone.

Winkle sighed.

He got out of the car, locked the door, and started walking home, the mocking laughter of the estate kids ringing in his ears...

Strawberry Fields for Trevor

"I'm nipping out to check on the strawberry fields, love."
"You go careful Henry. Take the dog with you."
"Aye, will do. See you in a bit."
He stepped out into the darkness.
Bess loped ahead, her nose working overtime in the cool air.
He shifted the shotgun into the crook of his arm as he lit a roll up, then set off towards the fields.
He was hoping to bag a deer, part of a herd he was convinced were stripping his pick-your-own strawberries.
If he could get a freezer full of venison, it would be some conciliation for all the fruit he'd lost these last weeks.
At the gate, he heard rustling in the fruit rows.
"Bess! Heel..." he whispered.
The breach of the shotgun snicked shut, and he quietly cocked the hammers.
He stepped slowly into the field.
As his eyes adjusted to the dark, he saw a humped shape moving amongst the strawberry bushes.
He raised the shotgun, and took careful aim.
The shape stood up.
"What the...?"
Another man appeared, then another.
So it wasn't deer.
It was poachers.
Strawberry poachers.
"Bess," he growled. "Sic 'em!"
The dog didn't need asking twice.
She raced into the field and latched onto the trousers of the nearest thief.
"OWWWW!!! FUCKING HELLLL!!!!!"
The field erupted.
Men jumped to there feet and stampeded through the fruit bushes.
the dog was loving it.
He didn't know who to bite next.

The farmer was struggling to decide who to shoot first.
Then he fired.
"MY ARSE! HE SHOT ME IN THE ARSE!"
The farmer clumped after the fleeing thieves, struggling to re-load the shotgun.
"Come back you bastards!"
They weren't coming back.
The men charged out of the field and dived into the back of a waiting van.
Doors slammed, headlights blazed, and the van bounced across the rutted track towards the main road.
The farmer tried to catch his breath as he read the familiar logos of the print company emblazoned across the panels of the van...

Ring ring
Ring ring
Ring ring
"Hmm? Hello"
"Cardboard Supervisor. It's God here. Why do I find myself calling you in the middle of the night with increasing regularity?"
God was the owner of the company, head of the board of directors. Cardboard supervisor knew his job hung in the balance.
"I don't know why you are calling, Sir. I can't imagine..."
"I'm not calling because I want to fuck you, Cardboard. I'm sorry, but you're just not my type. No, I'm ringing because that set of animals you are supposed to control have been rampaging through the countryside on an orgy of fruit thievery. THe only reason the police aren't around there now is because I happen to be in the same Masonic Lodge as the Chief Constable, so he decided to keep things... discreet. Sort it out, Cardboard. Sort it out."
"Yes sir! I had on idea! I...I..."
"Cardboard?"
"Yes sir?"
"Get your coat on, go round there, and kill someone. If you don't, I might change my mind about wanting to fuck you. Hard."
"Right. I'll..."
click
"Darling, I've got to go in to work. I..."

Snore
"I hate my job..."

Cardboard Supervisor walked into the factory.
He was in a hideous temper.
All he wanted was someone to take his wrath out on.
He was disappointed.
The place was deserted.
Machines were ticking over on stand by.
Piles of work lay neglected.
"Set of cunts..." growled Cardboard as he stalked through the building.
He heard music.
Voices.
It was coming from the canteen.
He crept closer.
Looked through the window.
Checkered table cloths covered the formica tables.
Dogsbody had two huge jugs of fresh cream.
The entire shift of night workers, some sixty people, were sitting at the tables, tucking into bowls of fresh strawberries and cream.
Cardboard was in a quandary.
If he was to start firing people, there wouldn't be a night worker left in the factory.
And he didn't have the guts to burst into the room, shouting and bollocking.
He decided to do what he did best.
Cardboard Supervisor decided to do absolutely fuck all.
He turned around, and crept into the night.

The next day he called Trev into his office.
Trev was a Union rep, and a shift supervisor.
He needed his advice.
"What should I do, Trev? God wants me to make heads roll, but If I punish one, I've got to punish all! I can't sack an entire shift!"
Trev stood by the door, looking thoughtful.
"Honest opinion? I'd let it ride, Cardboard. Get God's copper mate in the masons to tell the farmer that everyone involved had pay docked,

but there's not enough evidence to prosecute. I'll put out a general notice that if it happens again the police will be brought in. Problem solved."

"Hmmm... are you sure, Trev?"

"I'm sure. Trust me, Cardboard. I know these lads."

"Ok. We'll do it your way. Thanks for the advice, Trev. I appreciate it."

"No problem, Cardboard. Any time."

He turned to go, and winced.

"Are you alright, Trev? You look a bit pale."

"I'm alright. Just the old piles playing up."

Cardboard Supervisor watched as Trev limped away, and saw tiny spots of blood seeping through the back of his jeans...

Amateur Photographer

Marvin is horrible man, universally loathed.
He's a supervisor, and somehow he's managed to maintain a Noel Edmonds hair-do for the twenty years I've had the displeasure of knowing him.
No beard.
Just the do.
He used to be an amateur D,J., but it didn't work out.
I don't think he ever recovered.
He came into the studio with a smarmy grin, and talked Soulless Boss into getting one of his lackeys (me) to enlarge some pictures for him. He came across to me.
"Hi! Lucifer! How are you doing?"
"Hello Marvin."
"Soulless Boss just said you'd do me a little favour!"
"Did he? That's very nice of him."
"Yes! It was my daughter's prom night last week, and I've got the photos back. Some aren't as good as I'd hoped, so I wonder if you could do a bit of work on them for me."
He handed me a disk.
"You should have seen it, Lucifer! All the girls left for the prom from my house, and I hired one of those pink stretch limos!"
"That's very classy, Marvin."
"Oh the girls loved it! The limo was so big, I couldn't fit it all in one picture! I'm hoping you can stitch two pictures together. Can you do that?"
"Don't know. Have to see."
I loaded the disk.
There were about thirty pictures.
She was dead centre, perfect teeth, hazel eyes, dark flowing hair, slender, elfin figure. Stunning.
In each picture she looked better than the next, and I felt a little guilty perving over a bloke's daughter, even if the bloke was scummy.
I found the two pictures he wanted joining. The girl appeared on

both snaps - she was at the point where the pictures overlapped.
"Marvin, which of these pictures do you want me to cut off? I don't want to cut your daughter in half; she's posing slightly different in each shot. Which do you want to keep?"
He looks over my shoulder.
"Oh, that's not my daughter."
She's the only girl to appear in EVERY shot. She's in the centre of EVERY shot.
"O...K... Which one's your daughter, Marvin?"
"That's her - on the end."
I didn't need to worry about cutting his daughter's face off the picture. He had already done it.
In fact, she appeared on about ten of thirty pictures.
She was never in the middle.
She was rarely in focus.
He'd cut her off in some of the pictures.
The brunette was the star.
"These are nice pictures Marvin. Really nice."
"Aren't they just? It was a fantastic day! They grow up so fast, don't they?"
He was staring right at the brunette when he said this.

I didn't do his pictures.
I let him keep asking until he got the message.
I don't believe in creating porn for people if it might include their own daughter's blurred face.
I'm a man of principal.

Cabbage Patch Kid

The howls, shrieks, chirrups and yips echoed through the night. Some cowered at the sound, keeping their heads down, flinching if a gibbering scream rattled in their ear.
Above it all came a thundering cry.
"Bacon!"
"Boxes!"
This wasn't the jungle.
This was the factory night shift.
This was the cabbage patch.
It's called the cabbage patch because all the machines are in rows, and the operators stand in rows.
Like vegetables.
Sasquatch was on the night shift.
With his huge hands he scooped up a stack of envelopes.
"Bacon!" he boomed.
A grey sack was held open and Sasquatch thrust the envelopes inside.
"Boxes!" he bellowed.
Scream gibber yip bacon peep moo howl oink boxes baa oi.
Why do the cabbage patch make these noises?
To be honest, I haven't got a fucking clue.
I really don't think they know why they do it.
Hessian liked to whistle at people, then look away, leaving them confused.
He was a 'whistler'.
He thought it made them look a right cunt.
His hunched, narrow shoulders would shake with mirth, and his thin, puckered lips would curl back to reveal rotten, dirty teeth.
"See that knob head looking round with a stupid look on his face!" he would snigger.
Hessian usually had an entourage of goons, who would laugh when he laughed.
"Hurr hurr hurr. Yeah, knob head."

Hessian was top dog on nights.
He called the shots.
"Bacon!"
Hessian looked round, his eyes narrowing.
"Boxes!"
Hessian hissed with irritation.
"That big moron Sasquatch is getting right on my tits tonight. If he does that again, I'm gonna..."
"BACON!"
"... sort him out. Listen up lads. Here's what we're gonna do..."

"BAC..!"
"Here, Sasquatch, you're needed in the warehouse."
"Huh? Who needs me?"
"Dunno. You're needed in the warehouse."
"What do they want?"
"Dunno. You're needed in the warehouse."
"Huh. Alright then..."
Sasquatch clumped to the warehouse.
It was empty.
"Hello?"
No answer.
"Somebody needed me here?"
No answer.
"Hmm. Bacon..."
Men leapt from the shadows, screaming and gibbering.
Sasquatch was knocked sprawling across the floor, and strong hands tore at his clothes.
"Strip him, lads!"
Sasquatch howled with fear, but a strip of parcel tape silenced him. He fought back, but a heavy punch to the stomach doubled him over, and soon he lay trussed on the cold concrete floor wearing nothing but his underwear.
"Bag him up, lads..."

3.00pm. Manchester Piccadilly station.
A guard was wandering along the freezing platform, sheltered from the worst of the wind by large steel cages stuffed with grey sacks

containing direct mail destined for London and the South.
He paused.
One of the sacks was moving.
Rats.
It had happened before.
Rats looking for nesting material. They could chew up a bag full of mail in no time.
Bastards.
He slipped his heavy torch from his belt loop and crept towards the cage.
He slowly lifted it high over his head.
Wham!
"Got yer, yer furry bugger!"
"MMMMMMMmmmmmMMMm!"
"What the...? Fuckin' Hell! There's a fella in this bag! George! George! Get over here! There's a fell in one of these bags! Give us an 'and!"

Sasquatch sat shivering by the stove in the small office. He was mounded with grey blankets, but he still couldn't get warm. An ambulance was on it's way, as were the police.
The guard called George came in, carrying a mug of tea for him.
"Here you go, big lad. Get that down yer. Listen, Pete says he's really sorry for giving you that black eye. He really thought you was a rat scuttling about in there!"
Sasquatch was silent. He sipped his tea and shivered, staring straight ahead. It unnerved George.
"Look here. Are you hungry? We've got some sarnies on the go. Would you like one?"
Sasquatch looked up. He realised he was starving.
"Y..yes please. What sarnies have you got?"
"Bacon."
Sasquatch flinched, and burst into tears.
George shuffled out of the room.
Pete was waiting outside.
"How is he?"
"Crying his poor heart out."
"Bloody hell! What did you say to him?"

"I offered him a bacon sarnie, and he starts roaring his head off! Can't figure it!"
"Hmm. Reckon he's Jewish?"
"Dunno..."

The lads who bagged him up were fired.
Hessian got away scott free.
Sasquatch was never the same again.
It took him years to start saying Bacon and Boxes again.
I heard him this morning, though.
6.00am.
"Bacon."
"Boxes."
I wish some fucker would sling him in a sack again.
Just for a bit of peace.

Animal Crackers

6.15am.
I felt so tired I could have puked.
Soulless Boss has left me a stack of work.
Nice of him.
There was a hand written note.
"Need all this for 8.00am! No wandering off, Lucifer!!!"
I yawned.
Fuck it.
I went for a wander.
I saw Jock.
He was staring at a door, sipping his tea.
"Morning Jock. What you staring at?"
"Morning Lucifer. Don't know if you're familiar with it, but that big green flat thing is a door. What you do, is grab it by that shiny thing and..."
I let him go on, and nodded occasionally to show I was taking it in.
There's always an odd thing in a factory, where the manual workers like to make out anyone with shiny hands is as thick as fuck.
Jock could shift many tons of paper around in a day, lifting and turning it so the reverse could be printed.
the heaviest thing I moved around was a mouse.
No calluses on these hands.
Nice and shiny.
Jock had hands like gorilla paws, hooked and leathery.
"... and when it's locked, it keeps you safe inside, and stops the cunts from getting in. Got it?"
"I think so. So what's on the other side of this door?"
"Hugs and Flint are in there. They're up to something. They were giggling. They've got a bag."
"A bag? Oh shit..."
With Hugs and Flint, a bag meant trouble.
These two loved wildlife.
Loved killing it, that is.
Nothing was sacred.

They'd get up at three, go out with guns and dogs and shovels, and find stuff to kill.
If they'd got a bag, it meant they'd got lucky.
It meant that the cast of Bambi had been unlucky.
The door opened.
Hugs and Flint emerged, cooing and whispering to a rabbit that was nestled in Flints arms.
the rabbit looked content, it's nose twitching as it looked around, tame and inquisitive.
"Here we go," muttered Jock.
We followed Hugs and Flint as they headed onto the factory floor.
A gaggle of women were nattering over cups of tea.
They were all in their fifties, nans and grans who put brochures in envelopes by the thousand, by the million.
Pensions are shit.
They didn't have many other options.
Hugs and Flint approached them.
"Here, ladies, you wouldn't have a drop of spare milk would you? We found this bunny, and it's lost it's mam."
The old dears went spare, cooing and stroking the rabbit, who seemed to love the attention.
somebody produced a saucer filled with milk.
They offered it to Peter rabbit.
Peter took a little sniff, then looked up.
"Go on, precious. take a little sip," whispered a granny.
Peter rabbit lowered his head to the saucer, his little mouth opened...
And a big, gore smeared finger slithered from between it's lips and dabbed itself into the milk.
The nans and grans screamed and screamed and screamed.
The finger disappeared, and Peter rabbit looked up, all perky.
Suddenly his eye popped out, and the finger waggled out of the socket.
Nans and grans scattered in all directions, screaming and sobbing.
Hugs and Flint ran away, cackling hysterically.
Jock looked up at me.
"Bit much that, don't you think, Lucifer."
"I should say so, Jock."
We walked back the way we had come, and found Hugs and Flint

crying laughing in the back room. Peter rabbit lay on the floor, its stomach hanging open. Flints arm was streaked with blood up to the elbow, where he'd had it shoved inside the rabbit's body.
Jock shook his head as he looked at them both.
"Bit much that, lads."
"Fuck off Jock, you big soft fanny," laughed Hugs. He squat down on the ground and pulled a huge hare out of the black bag.
"Look at this beauty! We only caught it about an hour ago. It's a beauty, don't you reckon, Lucifer?"
"It's very nice, Hugs. Not really my type, but you know..."
"What's up with you? Never see that Cadbury's Caramel advert? That bunny were as fit as fuck!"
Hugs shoved the hare into my face, and put on a Cornish accent.
"Don'ts you warnt to fucks me, ole Lucifer boy? Oil suck yours cock, but you'll have to watch moi teeth!"
"No thanks, Hugs. I'm already in a long term relationship. It wouldn't be right."
Hugs was stroking the hare, looking all put out.
"you don't know what you're missing, Lucifer. She's still lovely and warm..."
He dropped the hare on the ground, produced a hunting knife from his coat and started gutting it on the floor.
"Yeah, lovely and warm... Fucking hell, Flint! I'm getting a hard on, here!"
He slipped two fingers into the cavity.
Blood ran down his hand.
"Aww yeah! She likes it, Flint!"
Flint's shoulders were shaking, and tears of laughter rolled down his cheeks.
"Give over, man! I'm gonna piss myself!"
Hugs started undoing his trousers.
"No, really Flint! She's gagging for it!"
"No, give over!"
Hugs didn't give over.
He dropped his trouser, gave his cock a couple of shakes to get it off the slack, and thumbed it into the dead hare.
"Oh, yeah, baby! That's right! That's right!"
He had hold of the hare by it's back legs and started fucking it, hard

and fast.
Blood splattered off his thighs and ran down his legs.
Flint was helpless with laughter. He could hardly breath.
"Come on, Jessica! Give to me! You know you want it! You love it up ya!"
The hare's big ears were flopping all over the place as Hugs rammed it home.
Suddenly, the door opened.
In walked Forsythe.
He's a nice chap, an animal lover and a strict vegetarian.
He had a bowl of porridge he wanted to microwave.
He took in the scene around him.
Dead animals on the floor, blood everywhere, and three men watching another man fuck a dead hare.
The sound of the porridge bowl smashing on the floor was deafening in the silence.
He fled.
We all looked at each other.
"It's not what it looks like," I mumbled, a bit too late.
"Fucking pussy," laughed Flint.
As Hugs cleaned himself up Flint picked up the rabbit, skinned it and chopped it into rough chunks. He put them in a bowl and shoved them in the microwave.
"You're not going to eat that are you?"
"Course I am, Lucifer! We eat what we kill, me and Hugs. We're not animals, tha knows!"
"No. Of course not. Silly me. I'll see you lads later..."
I left them to it, the smell of microwaved rabbit making me wretch.
I sat back down at my desk.
The work was still there, untouched.
It was 7.45am.
I decided to make a start.
Didn't want Soulless Boss to think I'd been fucking about.
Can't work without a cup of tea, though.
I wandered off...

This Time it's Personal(ised)

I went out onto the factory floor.
It wasn't a social visit.
I'd been summoned.
A big machine was clattering away.
It's the machine that adds that 'oh so personal' touch to your shit junk mail, the 'dear Mr Debtridden' bit on the letter selling you a credit card at 29% APR.
Webb was at one end, feeding the printed stuff in to be personalised.
Smithy was at the other end, lifting out the finished product and checking it.
Weakspuds was with him.
He's a manager, a pretty big name in the company.
He knows a lot about machines.
He knows fuck all about how to talk to people.
Weakspuds and Smithy were arguing.
"you see, what it is, Smithy, I couldn't really give a shit about what you're saying. It takes ages to lift that guard rail because of those pistons. I know it's heavy, but you're a big lad. Now take the pistons off, lift the guard by hand, and stop fucking about!"
"But health and safety, Mr Weakspuds, they won't..."
"TAKE OFF THOSE FUCKING PISTONS!"
He slapped a screwdriver into Smithy's hand and turned to me.
"Ah, Lucifer. I've decided to take people like you out of their cotton wool boxes every now and again, to give them a taste of what the real people are doing. How does that grab you?"
"It's lovely, Mr Weakspuds."
"Lovely? What do you mean by that?"
"Nothing."
"Hmm... Well, keep a close eye on me, Lucifer. Watch and learn, watch and learn."
I was keeping a close eye on Smithy. Veins were bulging in his forehead, and he was gripping that screwdriver like a dagger.
He was a man on the limit.
Weakspuds walked in front of me.

I followed.
I knew he'd do it.
He doesn't know he does it, but everyone else does.
His hand crept round to his arse, and started digging away, right up his crack.
He was practically fingering himself.
He took his hand out.
Wait for it...
Wait for it...
Bingo.
He sniffs his fingers.
Dirty bastard.
Watch and learn, watch and learn.
We walked to the other end of the machine.
Webb was there.
He looked just as stressed as Smithy.
It had obviously been a long day.
Any day involving Weakspuds was a long one.
"Webb. You're not running the machine fast enough. Double the speed and load at a faster rate."
"If we run it any faster, Mr Weakspuds, it'll cause a paper jam. This is the fastest it'll go without jamming!"
"Rubbish. You're just doing it all wrong..."
Weakspuds grabbed the speed dial and yanked it around.
He ignored Smithy's bellows of protest from the other end of the machine.
"There you go, Webb! Running like a dream."
Webb glowered at Weakspuds.
"I'm gonna have to put the machine on standby, Mr Weakspuds. I'm busting for the toilet."
"Your toilet break isn't for another hour and a half, Webb. You'll have to hold it in."
"I need a shit..."
"I don't care."
"What am I supposed to do! Just let it slide down the back of my legs?!"
"Weren't you listening, Webb? I... don't...care."
They stared at each other, hard.

They were almost nose to nose.
This was good stuff.
Webb started going scarlet.
He made a tight grunting noise.
The smell of fresh shit drifted into the air.
Weakspuds stepped away, his mouth open.
"You didn't?"
"I did."
"But...why?"
"I needed to."
"You dirty... go get cleaned up! You're stinking the place out!"
What do you mean? I thought you were keen on the smell of shit."
"What are you talking about? Get out! Go get cleaned up, you filthy..."
Webb waddled off, a dark stain spreading across the back of his overalls.
Weakspuds took over from him on the machine.
He turned the speed dial up another notch and started loading paper like a demon.
I watched and learned.
There was a snarling, shuddering noise, a grating of gears, and then silence.
"Oh, what now??" screamed Weakspuds.
"Smithy? Smithy! What have you done?"
I could hear Smithy at the other end of the machine, calling him a cunt.
"What did you say? What did you say?"
Weakspuds started walking to the other end of the machine.
He took the opportunity to shove his fingers deep into his anus and sniff the shitty odour on his fingers along the way.
I'll not be shaking his hand.
"Smithy! What have you..."
He didn't finish the sentence, because he tripped and fell over on the two discarded hydraulic pistons that Smithy had removed from the metal guard.
"What are they doing there, you fucking moron! I could have killed myself on those!"
Smithy just shrugged.

"What's happened? Why has the machine stopped running, Smithy?"
"Paper jam. It was running too fast."
"That's bollocks and you know it! Look, all the paper is snarled up in the outfeed! You weren't collecting it fast enough, you lazy sod!"
Smithy went scarlet.
I don't think he was pushing out a turd like Webb had.
"Now look here, Mr Weakspuds..."
"Shut it, Smithy! Lift that guard so I can reach into the outfeed."
Smithy muttered something, but lifted the guard up.
Weakspuds cleared the outfeed and reset the machine.
We all watched as the personalised sheets flowed smoothly out.
Weakspuds was crowing with self satisfaction.
"That's how it's done, Lucifer. Can't trust these chimps to get it done right! Smithy, get to the other end of the machine and start feeding paper in!"
"But I..."
Go! Now!"
Smithy was holding the metal guard up.
Weakspuds was focused on the outfeed.
Both me and Smithy were focused on Weakspuds thumb, which was positioned directly beneath the guard.
We looked at each other.
Smithy winked.
I had to look away.
There was a large clang, a sickening crunch and a high pitched scream.
I looked back.
The printed copies were still feeding smoothly, but they were splattered with blood.
"My thumb! You've broken my thumb!"
Weakspuds slumped to the floor, unconscious.
Webb came back from the toilets, glanced at the man on the ground, and carried on with his work.
Smithy removed the bloody copies from the stack, and carried on with his work.
"I'll fetch a first aider then, I suppose?"
Both men shrugged.

Weakspuds was on his way to hospital.
I headed back to the studio.
"Not sticking around, Lucifer?" asked Smithy. "Thought you were here to learn a thing or two?"
"I've learned plenty. See you later, Smithy, Webb."
"See you later, Lucifer."

Cornish Nasty

Some fights you just can't win.
I've got no chance against Dave Pebbleshoe.
He's popular.
Women say he's 'sweet natured'.
He's about five foot five.
He's got a comedy Cornish accent.
He's got a massive built up orthopaedic shoe that he has to drag around with him.
He's a bog cleaner.
I'm six foot four.
Enough said.
-
It's 6.30pm. Friday evening, late shift.
Most people have gone home.
I don't finish until 9.00pm.
It's been a stressful kind of day.
There's still a pile of work on my desk, but everyone else has gone to the pub.
No way I'm going to bust my balls over that lot when people are sinking pints.
I take my paper to the toilet.
They are situated at the end of a long, long corridor, dimly lit in the evening.
Very atmospheric.
I get settled, do my business, read my paper.
I hear a noise in the corridor.
Clump, clump, clump.
Getting closer.
Clump, clump, clump.
Everyone's gone home.
Clump, clump, clump.
Who's there?
Clump, clump, clump.
It's Dave Pebbleshoe, the bog cleaner.

He's the supervisor, actually. King of the Bog Cleaners.
You can tell he's a big shot.
He's got keys on his belt loop.
Oh yes.
A real power dresser.
People think Dave Pebbleshoe is a lovely bloke.
I'm not so sure.
It takes more than a big limp and a massive shoe to blind me with pity.
He uses that Cornish accent to top effect when charming the office staff, people who might put a decent word in for him.
He's especially nice to the women, practically tugging his fucking forelock and turning that accent up to Mark 10 as he empties bins and tickles that duster around.
It strikes me that he's angling for a pity fuck.
In his dreams.
I've heard him lay into the other cleaners, treating them like shit.
The accent isn't so strong then.
Funny that.
Clump, clump, clump.
He's outside the toilet door.
The door opens.
He turns out the light.
It's pitch black.
There's no windows.
"Hey! Hey, mate! Turn on the light!"
Nothing.
"Here! Turn the light on! I'm still in here!"
Nothing.
Then it struck me.
There was no clump, clump, clump.
He's still out there.
Waiting.
I shout at the top of my voice.
"TURN ON THE LIGHT!!"
Clump, clump, clump.
Fucker.
I wipe my arse in braille and pull my jeans up.

Fumble with the door, shuffle along the sinks, find the door onto the corridor.
Dave Pebbleshoe is about fifty meters away.
He glances back, nervous.
He did it on purpose.
I can tell.
"Oi! You've just turned the light out on me! I was in those toilets!"
He turns around.
"There's not normally nobody here at this time. I didn't know you was there!"
Bollocks.
He's turned the accent up, not as far as he would for the office staff, but more than he would for a fellow bog cleaner.
Doesn't work on me.
"Whatever. All I'm saying is, just check in future, alright?"
"There's not normally nobody here at this time! You shouldn't be using them toilets at this time!"
Unbelievable!
"I'll use those toilets any time I like, mate. I'm here till nine, if I need a shit at five to nine, I'll take a shit at five to nine!"
"You shouldn't be using them..."
"Look, I'm not arguing. Just check the toilets are empty before you turn off the light, alright?"
I don't wait for an answer.
I go back in, pick up my newspaper, wash my hands.
It's on my mind.
Some fucking people...
I come back out.
Dave Pebbleshoe is still there.
He looks angry.
"Here, mate!" he shouts.
"What."
"I'll start checking those toilets when you stop leaving them in such a state!"
The cheeky fucker.
I decide to hit him with a little bit of my rapier wit.
"Fuck you, you stupid little cunt!"
That told him.

I turn to leave.
Clump, clump, clump.
What the...?
Clumpclumpclump.
I turn around.
Dave Pebbleshoe is hobbling towards me at ramming speed.
His face is scarlet.
His arms are flailing to keep balance and avoid speed wobble, but his fists are clenched.
Oh fuck.
Things have got a bit out of control.
Clumpclumpclump.
"Reeeeeeeeeee!!!"
What's that fucking noise he's making?
It's a weird screech through clenched teeth.
It's pretty intense.
I step out of the way.
He stumbles past.
"Reeeeeee!"
He's coming back.
He starts swinging out with that big orthopaedic shoe, standing on his good leg and kicking it out.
It looks dangerous.
"Give over, knob head! You'll hurt yourself!"
"Reeeeeee!"
"Oww! My fucking shin! Right, that's it!"
I'm no good at fighting, but I'm not going to stand there and take that from a bog cleaner.
I give him a good slap round the chops.
"There! Now give over!"
"Reeeeeee!"
"Stop it with that noise, you gimp... Ow! Jesus, that hurt!"
I slap him again, and again.
I've got longer arms that him.
He can't get close enough to whack me with his shoe.
"Reeeeee!"
Dave Pebbleshoe makes a charge, I sidestep him, and he goes sprawling across the floor.

I stand over him, hands raised.
"Stay down, you crazy fucker!"
A door opens.
One of the secretaries steps into the corridor, and gasps.
She sees Pebbleshoe on the floor, his face all red.
She sees me standing over him, snarling.
I look at Pebbleshoe.
He looks at me.
"Help! This big bloke pushed me over for no reason!"
Oh shit.
I've never heard anybody sound that Cornish in my life.
"No! I never... he... what it is...."
The secretary rushes to help him up.
I step away.
Some fights you just can't win.
It's sometimes best to retreat.
I hurry back to the studio and shut the door.
It'll be all over the factory on Monday.
And I'll have to explain to Soulless Boss why our bins aren't getting emptied...

Bummery Justice

"Anyone seen my wallet?"
"Let us know if you find my keys. Can't seem to find them..."
"I put a tenner in that drawer and it's not there now!"
"There's a fucking thief about..."
It's never good when stuff starts disappearing in a factory.
Old grudges get dragged up.
Accusations fly about.
There's plenty of thieves work there, so you can take your pick.
I've seen thieves accusing other thieves of thievery.
What's that all about?
"There's some right cunts about, Lucifer. Imagine taking cash out of a blokes locker like that? Bang out of order."
"Yeah. Shocking. What you got in the bin liner, Bentine?"
"Pringle sweaters, Two ski jackets, shirts by Thomas Pink and various Ted Baker. Nowt in your size. Want me to put an order in for you?"
"No. I'm good, thanks. Keep an eye on that stuff, Bentine. You don't want anyone nicking it."
"Too right, Lucifer! There's some proper cunts about..."
-
Stuff kept going missing.
Something had to be done.
It was up to Cardboard Supervisor to sort this shit out.
Time for action!
Call the police?
Private security?
Install surveillance equipment?
No.
Knock knock
"Come in!"
"You wanted to see us, Cardboard?"
"Ah, Hugs! Flint! Come in. Sit down. You're both a bit quiet at the moment. Not much work to do."
"You laying us off, Cardboard?"

"No! No! Not at all! Ha ha ha. On the contrary, I've got a job for you. It's right up your street."
Cardboard Supervisor was frightened of Hugs and Flint. He was frightened of lots of things, but he knew it wasn't wise to get people like them pissed off.
They liked to do things. Unpleasant things.
"Sweet, Cardboard. We likes to be busy. What's the job?"
"I hear you boys like hunting."
"Yeah."
"We love it, Cardboard."
"You after a bit of game?"
"Rabbit?"
"Pheasant?"
"Venison?"
"No, no lads. Nothing like that. I've got something different for you to hunt..."

-

The offices were quiet on a Friday lunchtime.
Everyone was at the pub.
The thief knew that.
He just walked in off the street, through the factory, down the corridor, into the offices.
He quickly started opening drawers, going through desks.
He heard a giggle.
He looked around.
Nothing.
Back to work.
Under some files in a drawer he found a twenty pound note.
The thief smiled to himself.
He was in luck.
He heard more giggling and the sudden thunder of heavy boots.
He was out of luck.
They hit him like a juggernaut, and kept running.
The thief struggled, but he didn't have a chance.
They had a cupboard ready.

-

He hit the ground hard.
A fluorescent light flickered on.

He was pinned to the ground and had his pockets emptied.
"Thieving bastard!"
"What we gonna do with him, Flint?"
"Shall we get Cardboard?"
"Not yet."
"Call the rozzers?"
"Those fuckers won't do nowt with him. He'll just get a slap on the wrist. I reckon we should teach him a lesson."
"Right! What we gonna do?"
Flint started undoing his jeans.
"I'm gonna fuck him."
"What!" The thief started thrashing around, but Hugs was way too strong.
"Hold that bitch steady, Hugs! I'm gonna fuck his brains out!"
Flint started ripping the thief's trousers down.
"NOOOO! Pleasepleasepleaseplease no no no no NO! I'm sorry I'm sorry I'm really really sorry!"
"You fucking will be..."
"No no no NO OWWWWW!!!!"
-

Two hours later the police led the thief away, in handcuffs and in tears.
Cardboard Supervisor was white as a sheet.
He was shaking.
Hugs and Flint couldn't stop sniggering.
"You two. My office. Now!"
He didn't say anything else until he had the door shut.
Then he let them have it.
"What the fuck is going on, you maniacs!"
"What?"
"Yeah, what's up, Cardboard?"
"What's up? WHAT'S UP? That boy told me that you'd raped him, that's what's up! Are you mental? Why did you do that?"
"Aww, come on, Cardboard! You know that the coppers don't do nothing to light fingered fuckers like him! He needed teaching a lesson!"
"Yes, of course he did. He needed teaching a lesson, but NOT A LESSON IN FORCED SODOMY!"

Flint sniggered.
Hugs giggled.
Cardboard Supervisor went purple.
"What is so fucking funny??"
"We didn't really bum him, Cardboard," laughed Flint.
"No, we only pretended to," added Hugs.
"Pretended to? It seemed to me like that lad was fairly certain that he had just been buggered in a store cupboard!"
"We never did!"
"No, look. I used my thumb."
Flint held up his thumb. There was a dark ring of blood and shit caked around it's base.
Hugs was almost crying with laughter.
Flint's shoulders shook as he tried to control himself.
Cardboard Supervisor looked away.
"Get out," he mumbled. "Just fuck off out of my office."
Flint and Hugs barged out of his office door.
"Wait one fucking minute, you two!"
They turned back.
"There's thirty five quid and mobile phone missing from the offices. That kid didn't have it on him. Where is it?"
"Dunno, Cardboard. He didn't have it on him when we got hold of him."
"Yeah, we searched him."
"Hugs checked his pockets."
"Flint did a cavity search."
More stifled laughter.
"I should have known better... Oh, just fuck off, the pair of you."
He watched them walk towards the canteen, their pockets bulging with loose change.
He looked away when Flint casually wiped his thumb clean on his jeans.

Womb Raider

Rusty doesn't have a girlfriend.
He's forty four, still lives at home, and he's converted the garden shed into a little den where he can watch his horror flicks and play on his console.
He loads paper into one end of a print press all day, and takes it out of the other end, when it's all nice and inky.
Rusty likes to eat biscuits.
He reads Nuts and the Sport.
He used to collect knives, but sold them when people said it was creepy.
He kept his favourites, though.
Rusty had a girlfriend once.
One of the cleaners was a slack-jawed gob-shite called Shaz.
Raucous, bottle blonde, mouth always full of gum or bad words.
She'd kept most of the wrapping on her brain - it was in mint condition, almost totally unused - but one corner that she did use was cunning.
She figured that Rusty was a hard worker, had no outgoings, lived simply, and must therefore have a decent looking bank account.
Knives and computer games are a fairly cheap hobby.
He wasn't likely to wander, because a man who has never had a girlfriend is just going to be grateful.
She started asking Rusty for lifts home from work.
He thought he'd won the lottery.
A romance of kind blossomed, and they agreed to move in together.
Two things happened that should have got his alarm bells ringing.
As soon as he moved in with her and her daughter;
1. She started spending.
2. She went for a hysterectomy.

Rusty was blissfully unaware.
He was in love.

Some of us lads were talking, asking about why Shaz was off sick.

"Our lass has been for a hysterectomy, but there were a few complications" says Rusty.
"What kind of complications?" I asked.
"Well she were just going in for a partial hysterectomy to start with, you know, the one where they just remove the uterine body, but she got a bit of bleeding, so they had to take out the cervix as well. Anyway, they sewed her up and that was that, but she still got a bit of bleeding, so they opened her up again, and it turned out there was something wrong with her fallopian tubes, so they had to remove them n'all, along with her ovaries."

Silence from the lads.

Jock stood there, shaking his head.
"Fuck me, Rusty," he says. "Until six months ago, you'd never even seen a fanny. Now you know how to take one apart and put it back together again."

Davey Donkeydangle and Mister Frisky

"Hey, Lucifer. You've got kids, haven't you?"
"Depends what you mean, Fluff."
"What? You've either got kids or you haven't. Now, you've got kids, haven't you?"
"Well, if you're asking me if I'm a dad, then yes. If you're asking if I have a cellar full of stolen children, then no."
"What?"
"Never mind. What do you want, Fluff?"
"Look, I've got this children's entertainer booked for my little girl's birthday party this weekend. Only thing is, he can't make it. You got any clowns you can recommend?"
"I know plenty of clowns, Fluff, but none that would be any good for a kid's party. Who's let you down?"
"A bloke called Davey Donkeydangle."
"Come again?"
"Davey Donkeydangle."
"Let me get this straight. You've got a bloke called Davey Donkeydangle coming over to entertain your kids for an afternoon?"
"You saying you've never heard of Davey Donkeydangle? He's a fucking legend, man!"
"I'm sure he is a legend, in the world of Swedish erotica. If some fucker calling himself Davey Donkeydangle turned up at my house and offered to make balloon animals, I'd be arming myself with a garden rake."
"You always do this, Lucifer. You've got a sick mind. You find something smutty in the most innocent of subjects."
"Donkeydangle. Come on, Fluff."
"Well, alright. I see what you're getting at. The thing is, Davey Donkeydangle is an all round entertainer. He does kids parties, but he also does stand up on a night, you know, a bit of blue material."
"Why doesn't he have two names then, something a bit tamer for the kids then Donkeyfuckingdangle for the grown-ups?"
"We asked him that. He said it saved on stationary. He said 'Donkeydangle' was a happy medium."

"Hmm. Let's hope he doesn't get his acts mixed up."
"That'll never happen, not with Davey Donkeydangle. He's a professional, The most popular children's entertainer in West Yorkshire. I told you - he's a legend! We've had him booked a year in advance. They're kicking his door in to get to him."
How come he's cancelled?"
"Well, it turns out they really are kicking his door in to get to him. Hi wife has gone and fucked off with another bloke..."
"Can't say I blame her."
"There's no need for that. You don't know him! He's a lovely fella!"
"Yeah, whatever."
"Well, Davey Donkeydangle phoned my wife yesterday afternoon. He were in floods of tears, poor bloke. Told her he wouldn't be able to make it on Saturday. The wife was devastated. She'd got everything booked, the marquee, the cake, everything. She asked him if there was any chance he'd change his mind, but he told her that matters were out of his hands now. Turns out that after his wife walked out he'd been phoning her none stop, pleading for her to come back. He told her he had a gun, and that he'd do something stupid..."
"He's already done something stupid. He called himself Davey Donkeydangle."
"*sigh* Anyway, next thing you know, the police armed response unit had surrounded his house. They had a trained negotiator shouting at him through a megaphone, asking him to throw out the weapon and surrender peacefully."
"Fucking hell!"
"That's what the wife said. Well, here's how professional he is. He only went and phoned all his bookings for that weekend and cancelled them in the middle of a tense stand off with the police! They had to evacuate the cul-de-sac where he lives for seven hours!"
"Very professional."
"It's not all bad, though. The wife managed to book him for our Maisey's eight birthday party next April while she was on the phone. Just before the police kicked his door in."
"Right. And the fact that he's crying down the phone to his wife threatening to blow his own brains out doesn't put you off at all?"
"Not really. I can't see it ending in a custodial sentence, Lucifer,

unless the keep him in for psychiatric evaluation, or something."

"That's a relief. He should be out of the straight jacket in plenty of time for your daughter's birthday treat. What you going to do this Saturday, then?"

"Dunno. If you don't know anybody on short notice, then we'll probably hire a pony."

"A pony. Why?"

"Pony rides round the garden. We did it for our eldest two years back. They sent a pony called Mister Frisky."

"How did that go?"

"Shit. Mister Frisky started eating the herbaceous border, and when the wife screamed he went went berserk. Bethany from down the street got thrown into a conifer, and Mister Frisky disappeared across the back field at a gallop. It took them four days to find him, and now Mister Frisky won't let kids ride on him anymore."

"Sounds like a lot of hassle to me."

"With Davey Donkeydangle out of action we've got precious little choice, Lucifer."

"What's wrong with letting them entertain themselves? We didn't need ponies or Davey donkeydangle when we were kids."

"It's all changed Lucifer. Kids are different now. They want Davey Donkeydangle. You'll see. In a year or two you'll be begging me for his number!"

"I doubt that. See you later, Fluff. Good luck with Mister Frisky."

"They don't use Mister Frisky anymore, after what happened. The pony they've got now is called Jade, after Jade Goody."

"Jesus wept."

Breaking Up is Hard to Do

Smithy and Webb were deep in conversation.
The machine they were running was running itself.
They were drinking tea.
I stuck my nose in.
Webb was talking.
"I'm sick to death of her, Smithy, but I don't know how to dump her!"
"Just dump her. Say to her, 'You're dumped, now fuck off."
"I can't do that! We've lived together for two years!"
"Course you can. It's easy. All you do is open your mouth, say 'You're dumped, now..."
"I know, I know, but it doesn't work like that. Not in the real world."
"Why not? It's how I got rid of my first wife."
"That's what I mean. It doesn't work like that in the real world. You're not in the real world, Smithy."
"You might be right there, Webb. Ok then, I've got another answer."
"Go on then. Let's have it."
"Bum her."
"What?"
"Bum her."
"Bum her? How's bumming her going to help?"
"Don't ask her first. Roll her over when you're next giving her one, shag her from behind for a bit, then without warning, bang it up her trumper. No lube, nothing. Bang it up there, knock fuck out of her, and don't stop till you're done. She'll think you're a right nutter. She'll be gone by morning."
"You reckon? Thing is, I'm not into bumming. I don't like the idea. It seems a bit gay to me."
"Gay? How's bumming a lass gay?"
"Because you call gays bummers, and by bumming our lass I'll be a bummer, and me being a bummer makes me feel like I might be gay. It's one short hop from women's bums to mens bums, you know. You can't be too careful."
"Don't be so fucking stupid. You've snogged plenty of women,

right?"
"Yeah, loads..."
"Well then."
"Well what?"
"Well because you've snogged women's mouths you've not gone on to snog men's mouths, have you?"
"Course not!"
"Exactly! So bumming a bird's bum isn't going to make you want to bum a bloke's bum, is it?"
"You know, I reckon you're right!"
"Course I'm right!"
"I'll bum her then! I'll bum her tonight! I won't like it though."
Why not?"
"I don't like the idea of putting my cock in her arse. It stinks at the best of times..."

--

I saw Webb a couple of days later.
He was watching the paper coming out of the machine.
He didn't look happy.
"Morning Webb. How's it going?"
"Oh, hullo Lucifer. It's not going so good really."
"You still with your girlfriend?"
"Yeah, worst luck."
"How come? I thought you'd worked out how to get shut of her, something about... you know..."
"Bumming her?"
"Yes. Bumming her. Did you then? Bum her, I mean?"
"Yes. I bummed her."
"What happened."
"She loved it."
"Oh."
"I didn't. I still think it's a bit gay."
"Oh."
"I did everything Smithy suggested. I was shaggin' her as normal, like normal blokes do, and I flips her over, with that great big wobbling white arse of hers stuck in the air, and I shagged her that

156

way, and I thought 'it's now or never', and I just went for it, rammed it up her bum in one go, no messing."
"I'm glad to hear that romance isn't dead."
"I grabbed her by the love handles and rattled her like a fruit machine that wouldn't pay out. Really banged it home."
"And what happened?"
"She bloody loved it. She don't want it any other way now. Only up the wrong 'un."
"That didn't turn out as planned then."
"No. It didn't. I couldn't understand it! When she said that she liked it, I asked her what she liked about it. Know what she said?"
"No. Do tell."
"She said she liked the pain. Liked the pain! I'm living with a fucking perv! It made me feel all dirty. I wanted to put my cock in Dettol."
"What you gonna do now, Webb?"
"I dunno. Bum her, I suppose. If I knew it were the pain she liked in the first place, I could have saved us both an awful lot of hassle and just punched her in the gob..."
"That's one option I suppose. See you later Webb."
"Yeah, laters, Lucifer..."

Feeling Remote.

New technology becomes old technology really fast.
Something new arrives, usually pretty expensive, and we covet it.
Then the price comes down, we buy it by the billion, and suddenly we take it for granted.
It's like that new thing has always been there.
Remote control.
Take a look at the one you use for your T.V.
Covered in shit, dust, chocolate, smudges.
But if you lose it?
You're close to tears with frustration and fear.
You won't even change the channel on the set, because the chances are you have no idea how to.
I know I don't.
But then again, I remember a time before remote controls.
I don't take that little black buttony box for granted.
I appreciate it.
-
Jock had got remote control locking for his car.
This was a big deal back then.
Lots of people didn't have a clue you could even get that kind of thing for your motor.
Jock was chuffed to fuck.
He was showing it to Kray.
"All I do is press this little box on my keys..."
Blip Blip
"And the fucker is safe as houses."
"Jesus Christ! That's brilliant, Jock! Bet that cost you a bit!"
"Naw. My lad got a job with a place that fits these things. Every car'll have one of these soon. He fitted mine for next to nowt."
"Magic! Reckon your lad would fit one for me?"
"Aye, but it'll cost, like."
"How come? It didn't cost for you!"
"Aye, but you didn't wipe his arse and put shoes on his feet for sixteen years."

"Fair point."
A wagon rumbled into the car park.
Jock and Kray saw who was driving.
It was Haystacks.
"I hope your car's well insured, Jock," muttered Kray.
"Me too."
They both stepped well back.
Haystacks parked the wagon safely.
For once.
Haystacks was a fucking dreadful driver.
He must have been thirty stone.
He had bow legs and pincer toes.
He had a terrible stutter.
A real catch.
He drove the company wagons all over the country, delivering direct mail.
He'd rolled more wagons than all the other drivers put together.
Cardboard once took a call from him.
"Hello? C..can I s..speak to C..cardb..board S.."
"It's me, Haystacks. You phoned my direct line. Where are you?"
"I'm at the s..services j..just off j..junction t..twenty n..n..nine."
"Why are you there? You should be in Norwich by now!"
"I h..had a little p..p..problem."
"Shit... Where's the wagon?"
"J..junction t..twenty eight."
"Twenty eight? Why aren't you in it, driving to Norwich, Haystacks?"
"Because the f..fucking thing is u..u..upside down."
"Good grief. Not again..."
"It's n..not all b..bad. The c..coffee here is l..lovely!"
click
"C..cardboard? C..cardboard?"
That's why Jock and Kray were nervous.
After Haystacks had parked the wagon, he waddled over.
Jock nudged Kray.
Kray took Jock's keys.
They were going to have a little bit of fucking about.
"Now then Haystacks!"

"A..Aye up, J..Jock! H..how's things? What a..are you t..two doing out h..here?"
I'm showing Kray my new voice activated car alarm, that's what!"
"V..voice activated! B..bloody hell! How's that w..work?"
"When I got it fitted, they made me speak into this machine. That sets the alarm to react only to my voice."
"F..fucking Hell! Give us a d..demo then!"
Jock winks at Kray.
"Ok then. 'OFF!'
Kray pressed the button.
Blip
"B..bloody hell! W..wait a minute. Show us your h..hands!"
Jock took his hands out of his pockets.
"R..right... now lock it u..up."
"ON!"
Blip blip
Haystacks whistled and shook his head. He was impressed.
"Why don't you give it a try, Haystacks? See if it'll react to your voice."
"Aye, I'll try that! Here we go; O..OFF!"
Blip
"Ha! It w..worked! I o..opened it, J..Jock! That th..thing is a pile of sh..shite!"
Jock shook his head, and looked all crestfallen.
"Bollocks. I'll have to get it reprogrammed! Fucking thing. Will you try it again for us, Haystacks?"
"M..my p..pleasure! O..ON!"
Silence.
"It w..worked a s..second ago! Let me t.try again. O..ON!"
"O..O..ON!!"
O..ON!"
Kray stepped in.
"Maybe you're saying it different to last time. Try speaking a bit lower."
"A..alright Kray. **O..ON!**"
"**O..O..O..ON!!**"
"Try a Scottish accent, Haystacks, like Jocks."
"Och O..ON!!!"

Jock seemed to have bit of a coughing fit.
"Try it a bit higher, Haystacks. You're nearly there..."
"O..on! O..on! On! O..o..nnn!"
Jock had recovered, and snapped his fingers.
"Here, Haystacks! The bloke at the show room told me that emotion can effect the tone of voice. Maybe if you tried it with an angry voice it'll work."
"O..ON! O..ON! O..ON!"
"Get closer."
Wh..where's the sensor for this th..thing, J..Jock?"
"Just in the grill, Haystacks. Get really close... that's it! Now try! Really give it some pasty!"
"O..ON O..ON O..ON!!!"
"Try swearing at the fucker, man!."
"O..ON yercunt! O..ON yerb..bastard!"
Kray scratched his head.
"Can't understand it! Try the sensor by the exhaust pipe, Haystacks..."
Jock was in tears, He had to walk off.
Haystacks was red and sweating, but was determined. He was going to switch that fucker on.
He crouched at the back of the car, and started shouting at it.
"O..ON yer f..fucker! O..ON yer t..twat, O..On o..on O..ON yer c..cunting fuck!!"
"What are you doing, Haystacks?"
It was Cardboard Supervisor.
Kray and Jock had disappeared.
He was alone in the car park, swearing at an exhaust pipe.
"It's Jock's c..car..."
"I know that. I wanted to know what the fuck you were doing."
"I w..was trying to t..turn it o..on."
Cardboard Supervisor looked skyward.
He didn't need this shit.
"No wonder you don't have kids, Haystacks. Now stop chatting up the cars and get back to fucking work."
Cardboard Supervisor walked away.
Haystacks lingered, blinking stupidly.
He waited.

Then...
...he whispered...
"*on.*"
Blip blip
He nearly shat himself.
Jock and Kray nearly pissed themselves.
"B..b..bastards..."

Smooth Gloss Criminal

"I were in a card game with these lads, real villains. Couple of them are into armed robbery, one of them kills for money. Serious people..."
This was Scarface.
He fancied himself as a gangster.
He wasn't.
Far from it.
He was an electrician.
A shit electrician, I might add.
He once took a whole day to put a light fitting up in his own bedroom.
This was after two years of nagging from his wife.
Two years.
He finished the fitting, called his wife upstairs. She opened the door...
And smashed the bulb.
He'd put the light fitting at just the right length and position for the opening door to smash it.
Every time.
His answer?
He nicked a box of bulbs from work, and put them behind the door.
Every time a bulb smashed, he put in a new one.
Job well done.
Scarface was in his fifties.
He liked his gold, liked his designer labels, liked his suntan.
He had a big scar on his face.
He told women he got it in a fight.
He really got it because the lengthy sunbed sessions made something evil grow on his face and a doctor had to cut it out.
It turned septic.
Why?
Because of the amount of sunbed hours he was still racking up while his face was trying to heal.
Clever.

"...and this guy comes into our club, selling jewelry. I turned this gold bracelet over and there was dried blood on it. I asked him where it came from. He says, 'Don't ask.' Serious blokes..."
"SCARFACE!!!"
He jumped out of his leathery skin.
Bear was shouting for him.
Bear was Scarface's boss.
He scurried into Bear's office.
"What you want, Bear?"
"I want you to a job, but I don't want you to fuck it up."
"What do you mean? I always do my best..."
Bear rummaged in a drawer.
He pulled out a screwdriver.
It looked like a normal screwdriver, except the business end resembled molten lava.
"Your best is shit, Scarface. I want you to do better than your best. I want you to try really hard, and maybe, just maybe, you'll manage to do a shoddy job of it. You might even get it right."
Bear waggled the melted screwdriver.
"Two days we were down, Scarface. The explosion almost turned you white, as impossible as that might seem. I don't want a repeat performance."
Scarface grunted. He was already sulking.
Bear continued.
"You're re-wiring the board room. You've got two days."
Scarface perked up. Two days, working on his own. He'd be able to create all kinds of complications and excuses. It translated to at least a week of tossing it off. Maybe even Saturday morning, double time.
"Ok, Bear. I'll get my tools..."
"Oh, and one more thing. You'll be working with Flint and Hugs."
"No! For fuck's sake, Bear, anyone but them!"
Flint and Hugs were machine minders, their job being to load paper and ink into the print presses, but they were the sort of blokes who could turn their hand to anything; joinery, decorating, plumbing, violent sexual molestation of petty thieves and the vicious killing of hundreds of defenseless creatures.
They were psychopaths, and Scarface was terrified of them.
Bear wouldn't budge.

He was going to have to work with them.
With a feeling of dread Scarface packed his tools and trudged to the boardroom.
Flint was fabricating a partition wall.
Hugs was glossing some woodwork.
"Alreet, Scarface!" they grinned simultaneously.
They grinned like Doberman Pinschers.
Scarface swallowed hard.
"Reet, lads," he mumbled, and began to set out his tools
As he worked, he had an idea.
To make Flint and Hugs give him some respect, he decided to tell them some stories about how hard his gangster mates were. That way they might not do anything horrible to him.
He started fiddling about with a wall socket.
"Do you lads play cards?"
Flint and Hugs looked at each other, shaking there heads.
"I do. I've got a game going down York Road at the moment. Big stakes. Some real villains involved."
Scarface got onto his knees by the skirting board and drilled into the wall. It was a long room, he was at one end, Flint and Hugs were at the other.
"Yeah, we're playing poker for big money, but I can hold my own with them lads. Known 'em all my life. Lot of folk shit themselves just looking at these guys, but they'd do owt for me. We're really tight."
"Here, Flint," whispered Hugs.
"Yeah?"
"What's this stupid orange cunt on about?"
"Dunno, Hugs. Seems like he's talking shit to me."
"Too right. What we gonna do about it?"
"Hmmm... tricky one that. I know. Why don't you see if you can hit him with that tin of white gloss?"
"Good idea..."

-

Knock knock
"Come in."
Flint and Hugs shuffled into Bear's office.
He was on the phone.

They patiently waited for him to finish the call.
"Yes, yes, I'll book the machine in for routine maintenance on the fifteenth. Don't schedule any jobs for it until the seventeenth. Ok, cheers, bye."
He hung up.
"Hi Bear."
"How you doing Bear?"
"What are you two cunts after? I don't trust you."
"Erm.. that job Scarface was doing..."
"...was it very urgent?"
"Yes. Everything is fucking urgent in this place. Why? Where's Scarface?"
"He's in the boardroom..."
"...on the floor..."
"...we think we might have..."
"...erm..."
"...killed him."
"Oh shit!"

-

Scarface blinked slowly.
Everything was blurred, his mind and his vision.
He was in bed.
In a white room.
In white sheets.
He lifted his hand.
It was pure white.
Oh fuck, he thought.
I've died.
Then he heard giggling.
He slowly turned his head.
Flint and Hugs were sat by his side.
Scarface cringed away from them.
"Wakey wakey sleepy head!" said Flint.
"Rise and shine!" said Hugs.
"Stay away from me!" said Scarface.
They both started giggling again.
"Bear sent us..."
"... to say we're sorry for nearly killing you."

"Sorry."
"Sorry."
Giggle.
Scarface lifted his hand again.
"What the fuck is wrong with my skin?"
Hugs couldn't speak. His shoulders were going and tears ran down his face.
"It's the tin we threw," spluttered Flint.
"...lid came off..."
"...you want to see your face..."
"...you look like..."
"...a fat..."
They shuffled to the door, howling with laughter.
"A fat? A fat what? What do I look like? Flint? Hugs?"
"...Michael Jackson!"
"What???"
"You're gonna need some thinners..."
"...thinners night..."
"You're fighting for your life inside a.."
"GET OUT! GET OUT YOU BASTARDS!!!"

Baccy Warehouse

Envelopes.
Boring, aren't they?
Not something you get excited about.
There's sometimes exciting things inside them, like cheques, a hand written apology, hate mail, blurred Polaroids of hirsute genitalia, perfume scented love letters meant for someone else.
The envelope is soon discarded.
Forgotten.
Well, think about this.
1. Who made them?
2. How were they made?
3. What is the mental state of somebody who makes envelopes every day?
Any guesses?
No?
Well, swap papers and mark the answers:
1. Devil made them. He's my brother. He worked on the envelope machine with Slugsy, Bilbo, The Thing and Piccolo.
2. Imagine Satan commissioning a machine that would add to the ambiance of Hell.
Imagine the noise. Then double it. That is the machine that makes envelopes.
A grey-black machine that thundered and shuddered, voraciously chomping up envelope templates with such vigour that a fine mist of paper dust coated your mouth, your skin, your eyes.
A machine spitting oil and ink, a machine you could hit with hammers, spanners, wrenches and crowbars and it would not flinch, yet it would choke spontaneously on any random half made envelope, crashing out for days on end.
A machine that puked complete envelopes out of the other end, to be packed into boxes with mind numbing regularity.
A machine you could climb into and hide in, if you so wanted.
A horror, a haven, a porn plastered leviathan, an envelope machine.
3. Barking mad. Singing, capering, snatching-at-imagined-stars mad.

I don't know if they were mad to start with, or if the job sent them over the edge.
Anyone get three out of three?
Engineers kept checking to make sure the machine wasn't kicking out poisonous fumes, just because of the behaviour of it's operators.
They didn't find anything.
Only a deafening, filthy machine, and some odd people.
They were funny people though.
Piss funny.
Always fucking about.
It sent Cardboard Supervisor into depression.

I passed the envelope machine.
I noticed something going on. The lads were excited.
I took a look.
The canopies guarding the moving parts had all been lifted off and lads crammed themselves between the clattering rollers and churning cogs.
They were straining to see through metal air vents to what was happening behind the machine.
Curiosity killed the cat...
I squeezed past a whirring flywheel and pressed my eye to one of the grimy vents.
I could see a large yellow-stained perspex box, the size of a big shed.
It was the smokers booth, known as the Baccy Warehouse.
Half a dozen wheezers were tabbing it, perched on bus shelter style benches around the booth.
Nothing much to look at.
I collared Slugsy.
"What's going on?" Had to shout over the noise from the machine.
Giggling, he showed me a length of blue pipe.
It was connected to an airway, a steel pipe that fed powerful compressed air throughout the factory.
The pipe led to a huge bottle of water.
The bottle of water led to more pipe.
The pipe led to the Baccy Warehouse.
The nozzle of the pipe was concealed.
The smokers were blissfully unaware.

I wriggled into my place within the machine, and waited for the fun.
Scorcher ambled into the booth.
We could see him talking to the others, and someone passed him a lighter.
I glanced back at Slugsy.
He was ready to switch the airway on.
Someone new entered the booth.
It was Lincoln, one of the directors!
He sauntered in, nodding condescendingly to the other smokers.
He drew a pipe from his waistcoat pocket.
That's right.
The cock wears a waistcoat to work.
Smugly starts to fire up the briar...
I turned to Slugsy.
"Slugsy! No!"
Slugsy gave me the thumbs up. He couldn't see the booth.
He couldn't see who was in it.
He turned the valve.
Oh shit.
I couldn't miss this.
Eye to the vent...
It took a second or two to reach the booth.
It was worth the wait.
There's a lot of pressure in those compressed air feeds.
It was like a bomb going off.
One second people were relaxing over their favourite tobacco, blowing smoke rings, murmuring idle conversation.
The next second, the Baccy Warehouse had been turned into a fucking car wash.
The pipe came loose, thrashing about the booth like a demented cobra.
Drenched silhouettes could be seen bouncing of the perspex walls.
Something clattered beneath the wall of the booth.
A water filled briar pipe.
The door to the booth burst open.
Scorcher staggered out, looking bemused.
He still had a soaked cigarette drooping from his lips.
He looked skyward, bemused.

Several other smokers made their escape.
The last to leave was Lincoln.
He was clutching something.
A length of blue pipe.
Shit.
Time to scatter.
Lads ran everywhere, but only one couldn't leave his post.
It was Devil.
He had to keep grabbing envelopes as they churned out of the still roaring machine.
If he didn't, they would spray all over the floor.
He gave me a pleading look.
I shrugged, and ran for cover.
Lincoln, dripping water all over the place, followed the pipe to where it was connected to the airway.
He took one look at Devil, and stalked away.
A minute later, Cardboard Supervisor appeared.
"Devil! Devil! What the fuck have you been doing!? There's water all over the place, and Lincoln is soaked! What the fuck is going on?"
He shouldn't have spoke to Devil like that.
He really doesn't like it, especially when he's not to blame.
Dark red crept up his neck, and veins started to throb at his temples
"What are you talking about, Cardboard? I've done fuck all! FUCK ALL!"
He hurled a wad of envelopes to the floor.
Cardboard stepped back.
"Look what you've done, Cardboard, LOOK WHAT YOU'VE DONE!! Look at me!! I hate it when this happens!"
"Now, calm down, Devil..."
"Don't tell me to calm down, you PISSFLAP!!!"
Slugsy and The Thing rushed to restrain Devil, while Cardboard Supervisor fled.
He wouldn't show his face again on the factory floor for a week.
Everything started to calm down, and people crept out of their hiding places, shaking their heads and laughing.
I made sure Devil was OK, then turned to Slugsy.
He was carefully drying the blue air pipe, and taping it back into

place.

"What are you doing, Slugsy?"

"I'm setting it up again! The afternoon shift still don't have a clue. I can't wait to see their faces!"

"What? Well, good luck with that. I'll see you later."

"You mean you're not stopping, Lucifer?"

"Another time, Slugsy. See you."

He didn't hear.

He was still giggling.

Porn Cracker

Smokers get a bad reputation.
True, some of them deserve it.
There are the smokers who light up at every opportunity, dragging away at cheap, shit fags like their lives depend on it.
Then there is the smoker who really enjoys tobacco, calmly drawing on a pipe or hand rolled cigarette, tasting the smoke, gently, almost reluctantly exhaling.
Smokers fall into the same category as drinkers.
Some relish the bouquet of a fine single malt whiskey, while others desperately guzzle white cider from a bottle the size of the Hindenburg.
I like the smokers who have a genuine love of tobacco, a love of smoking.
They have a more refined, relaxed sense of the pace of life, an unhurried, gentler approach to the work ethic.
That's right.
They toss it off.
I'd often join the smokers loafing around the entrance to the factory, each one of them as idle as the banter.
It made me laugh to see Cardboard Supervisor elbowing his way through them on his way out to lunch, supremely pissed off to see so many people blatantly doing fuck all, and being too utterly spineless to do anything about it.
Good times.
He spotted me in the crowd once.
"Lucifer! What the fuck are you doing out here? You don't smoke!"
"No, but I'm just getting a bit of fresh air."
"Your not allowed to leave the factory to get fresh air! You're only allowed out to smoke!"
"Would I be allowed to stand out here if I smoked?"
"Yes! Of course you would!"
"Ok."
"Well? Why aren't you going back in to work?"
"I'm thinking about taking up smoking."

He stared at me. Hard.
Then the inevitable happened.
His bottle went.
"I want you back at your workstation in ten minutes time, Lucifer!"
"Yeah, will do, Cardboard."
He scuttled to his car, hating himself.
His lunch must always taste like ashes in his mouth.

This particular day there was only two people outside.
Abbott and me.
I liked Abbott.
He was a printer, a big, steady sort of bloke.
He was a rarity for a factory in that he like to read, knew good films, had travelled a bit.
Most blokes where I work only read The Sun, watched action films and went to Tenerife.
As he smoked a roll up we talked a bit about this and that, but really we just enjoyed the sun on our faces, and the illicit pleasure of simply slacking.
It has a flavour all of it's own.
Talk came around to his recent holiday.
"It's a great part of the world, the Far East. Ever been there, Lucifer?"
"Can't say I have, Abbott. I've not been many places, though I'd like to travel at some point."
"Don't put it off, my friend. Just do it. It's a big world out there, far larger than the walls of this shit hole."
He kicked the factory door, for extra effect.
"Yes, I could happily live somewhere like Thailand, Vietnam, Cambodia. You don't need much money out there. A simple life, with good food, a warm climate and friendly faces. Friendliest people in the world, the Thais."
"So I've heard. I love Thai food."
Abbott blew long tendrils of smoke from his nose and squinted into the sun, chuckling to himself.
"Oh, the food! Nothing like the food you get in England, Lucifer. In Thailand the food is fresh, and fiery, and fragrant! The smell alone makes your head spin! Seasoning and spices like you've never

experienced! You really must go, as soon as you can!"
"I'll save my pennies, Abbott. You've sold it to me. I know my wife has always fancied going to Thailand."
"If she's anything like my wife she'll fall in love with the place! She really loved that holiday - can't wait to go back! The people, the places, the culture..."
I nodded, imagining the weak English light on my face was the hot sunshine of Thailand.
"... the ladyboys..."
My little daydream crashed.
"Sorry, Abbott. What did you just say?"
"Beautiful people, the Thais, Lucifer. Beautiful people..."
"Yes, they do seem a very attractive race..."
"...especially the ladyboys."
Oh shit. Here we go.
"Right, love to chat, Abbott, but I'd better be getting back.."
"They have a beauty all of their own, an exotic quality that is very alluring, even to women!"
I couldn't get away. He was off on one. His gaze was focused somewhere in Bangkok, God knows where.
"My wife was quite taken by this ladyboy we saw in a show. Nothing seedy, mind. Very tasteful. High class."
"Ok..."
"She hinted to me that she might like to... go with her. She asked if I would mind."
"Controversial. What did you say?"
"to be honest, I found the idea to be very appealing! As long as I could watch, of course."
"Oh, of course."
"After the show I approached this young kathoey..."
"Kathoey?"
"Yes, kathoey. It's what they are referred to in Thailand. You see, in Thailand they are not regarded as men or women, but as phet thi sam, or third sex. A different thing entirely."
"Oh. That makes it alright then."
"Yes. Well, I approached her, and she seemed very keen on the idea. We all went out for a lovely meal at a restaurant she recommended. It was a magical evening!"

"I'm sure it was."
"Afterwards she came back to our hotel room for drinks. We had to pay her of course, but it didn't feel cheap in any way..."
"You mean she was expensive?"
"No! Not like that! I mean it all seemed very tasteful."
"Sorry. That's the term I was thinking of. Tasteful."
Anyway, soon she undressed, and started to kiss my wife. They laid on the bed, and soon they were both completely naked!"
For fuck's sake...
"It was a highly erotic scene, Lucifer! I've never seen anything like it! She was hung like a pony!"
Taxi!
"My wife was crying out in ecstasy, and that lithe young woman was fucking her like an animal."
I've never felt so uncomfortable in my life. I prayed that he'd hurry up and get it over with...
"Well, I couldn't help myself..."
"What? No..."
"I undressed..."
"My boss is going to be looking for me, Abbott. I've really got to be getting back..."
"...and pushed it right up her tight little arse."
"Jesus..."
"It was the best sex I've ever had!"
"With a man. The best sex you've ever had, with a man."
"No! Don't you understand? She is kathoey, of the phet thi sam..."
"More like fireman Sam, Abbott. You can dress it up how you like, mate. The summary is, you went on holiday, you paid a Thai bloke with tits to fuck your missus, then you bummed him."
"You've got it all wrong! I'm not gay! It's not like that, Lucifer!"
"Whatever, Abbott. I'm not knocking you, what goes on tour stays on tour and all that, but don't dress it up as something it isn't. That's the ladyboy's job. If she's got a massive cock, she's a he. That's a fact."
Abbott threw his roll up on the ground and stamped on it.
"I thought better of you, Lucifer! I expected that kind of talk from the lads in there, but not from you!"
He stormed off.

I stood in the sun for a while longer.
Maybe he was right.
Maybe it was some kind of beautiful experience, and it was me that was missing out.
Or maybe Abbott was just a raging pervert.
I don't know.
All I know is, bumming a tranny prostitute who is screwing the missus isn't high on my sexual to-do list.
I took another lungful of clean air, and went back to work.

Roadkiller Heels

Ring ring
"Hello, this is Cardboard Supervisor."
"Cardboard, this is God."
God owns the factory, everything in it, and the grubby souls of all the people who take his shilling.
"God! What a surprise, sir! Hahaha! How are you this morning? In fine fettle, I trust?"
"Shut up, Cardboard. If I wanted a blow job I'd ask for one. I want to know why I've just walked through my own factory, and seen a hideously ugly man staggering around with a broom wearing a grubby pink boob tube that says, 'Too hot to handle' on the front. In glitter."
"Oh. 'Too hot to handle'?"
"Yes. 'Too hot to handle'. And he was wearing a steel toe capped boot."
"Steel toe capped boots?"
"No. A steel toe capped boot. Just one. On the other foot he was wearing a dirty white trainer. And he was ugly. Very, very ugly."
"Very ugly?"
"No. Very, very ugly."
"Oh, very, very ugly! That will be Roadkill. I'll pull him in."
"Do that, Cardboard. Just looking at him in that outfit made me want to vomit. He shouldn't be allowed out like that for health and safety reasons. Can we sack him for being ugly?"
"I'm not sure... probably not. No, I'm fairly certain. You can't. I think we tried it with another employee a few years back and they took us to court."
"That's a pity. Then again, if we started sacking hideous people then I wouldn't have any staff. Hahaha. Oh well. Sort out that horrible goblin or I'll sack you, Cardboard."
"Yes sir! I'm onto it, sir! I'll..."
Click
"Hello? Hello, God?"

Cardboard slammed down the phone and stalked onto the factory floor...

Roadkill needed a fag.
He always needed a fag.
The only thing he needed more than a fag was a drink.
A fag and a drink, then he'd be right as rain.
As it was, he felt like shit.
He did a bit of sweeping up, emptied a couple of bins, ignored the stifled laughter of the lads working the machines.
He looked down at his top.
Too hot to handle.
His beer gut bulged alarmingly from beneath the stretched pink cotton.
For fuck's sake...
"ROADKILL!!!"
He almost had a heart attack. He gripped his chest and clenched his teeth. Soon the pain passed.
"Fuckin' Hell, Cardboard! No need for that..."
"No need for that? No need for that? You're stood in the middle of the factory looking like a disabled prozzy, and you wonder why I'm shouting at you?"
"A disabled prozzy? I wouldn't go that far, Cardboard."
"I fucking well would! Why are you wearing a pink boob tube, you tit?"
"I had a few ales last night, to be truthful. Got up a bit late, and couldn't find my t-shirt. I put on the first thing that came to hand. This is our lass's. I didn't notice what I looked like till I took my coat off."
"A few ales? How many ales do you have to drink to make you dress like that and not notice?"
"A couple.."
"A COUPLE???"
"...of dozen."
"Jesus wept. Ask the maintenance department for a set of overalls, Roadkill. You make my eyes hurt. What about your shoes then?"
"Some rotten fucker has nicked one of my boots and one of my trainers."

What? Why aren't you wearing the shoes you arrived in then?"
"Well, it were dark this morning, and I couldn't find my shoes, so..."
Cardboard buried his face in his hands.
"Don't tell me. You came to work in your wife's shoes?"
"Er... yeah."
"Bloody hell, man, weren't they far too small for you?"
"Not really. I've only got little feet."
"What's the problem then?"
"I'm not used to the heels. I wobble about."
"What??? Never mind. Never mind. Go to the stores and sign for another pair of boots."
"Can't wear them boots, Cardboard. They hurt my feet."
Hurt your feet? You've got one boot on right now! Is that hurting?"
"No."
"Well what's the difference between that boot and a new boot?"
"New boots hurt my feet. I've got very delicate feet."
Cardboard Supervisor started to turn red.
"So boots aren't good enough for you now, eh? I'm not sure that Jimmy fucking Choo does high heels with steel toe caps, but I can check the fucking catalogue!!!"
"No need to shout, Cardboard. I've got a right head as it is."
Cardboard lost it.
"No wonder you've got a right head, you fucking alky!! You downed twenty odd tins of beer last night and came to work dressed like Eddie fucking Izzard!! Now you won't put on proper regulation footwear! I know what you want, you stinking little cunt. You want me to send you home, don't you? You want me to send you home, but you won't go home though. You'll go to the pub. You'll go to the pub all afternoon, and drink another twenty odd ales, then tomorrow you'll come to work in another ridiculous get up!! What will it be?? Dressed as your mum? Dressed as a dog? 'Sorry Cardboard, it were dark, all I could find to wear was this fucking collar...' Well, I'm not having it. You WILL work, you WON'T be going home, and you WILL wear the safety footwear provided!!!"

Twenty minutes later, Roadkill wiggled down the road in his wife's heels.
He'd been sent home.

He lit a fag and inhaled.
And inhaled.
And inhaled.
When the glowing tip started to melt the filter he breathed out.
He let out more smoke than a burning tyre.
That felt good, he thought.
Much better.
But only half better.
He needed something else.
He needed a drink.
He looked at his wrist.
His wife's watch said 11.05am.
His local would be doing two for one until twelve.
If he hurried he could make it in time.
The clicking of his heels increased pace, and with surprising grace and ease, Roadkill started to run.

A Little Romance

Dogsbody stood at the end of the enclosing machine.
Scratching his arse.
Yawning.
Staring at nothing.
Every thirty seconds or so he would shovel up the personalised envelopes that churned out of the machine and cram them into a box.
Then he would scratch his arse.
And yawn.
Nothing much went on in Dogsbody's life.
Nothing much went through his mind.
His life was drudgery.
He knew that.
But at least while he was at work, drudgery paid.
And he didn't have to look at his wife.
In between scratching his arse and yawning, Dogsbody shuddered.
He knew what his wife would be doing at that precise moment.
Laid on the couch in a cup-a-soup stained nightie, smoking fags and drinking a blue WKD in front of the Jeremy Kyle show while the kids set fire to things in their bedroom.
No, work was shit, but it was better than being at home.
With a glazed expression he watched as the cleaners clocked in and limped, waddled and shuffled to their work.
They filed past, and...
Hello.
What's this?
A new cleaner.
Long dark hair.
Brown eyes.
Massive tits.
Very nice!
Admittedly she was less than four feet tall, but you can't have everything.
She was the loveliest dwarf he'd ever seen.
She realised he was staring, and glanced across at him.

Dogsbody quickly looked away, pretending to concentrate on his work.
He couldn't help himself.
He looked back.
She was still looking at him.
Oh God!
She smiled!
Then she was gone, heading to the offices to vacuum, dust and empty bins.
The envelopes began to pile up, but Dogsbody didn't notice.
He was looking at a closing door, and thinking of one hot midget.

As the days went by, he waited in excited anticipation for her arrival each day at four.
The heavy clunk of the punch clock was enough to set his heart racing.
The pitter patter of her tiny feet gave him goose bumps.
One time he saw her bend over to tie her shoe lace, and he caught a glimpse of a black thong.
He was stunned.
He didn't know they made stuff like that in kids sizes.

Two weeks later, and Dogsbody was clocking off for another day.
It was nine o'clock at night.
He hadn't seen her for a couple of days.
It made him feel strange and empty.
As he walked across the car park he wondered if he might be falling in love.
He couldn't stop thinking about her cute little hands, and the smooth skin of her large forehead.
Yes, he was in love.
He sighed, and trudged to his car.
There was a note under the windscreen wiper.
It was only just held in place.
She couldn't reach any higher.
With fumbling hands he opened it.
"I've seen you watching me. I think you're cute!
If you want to go for a drink, give me a ring. X"

There was a phone number.
Dogsbody was ecstatic.
That night he sent her a text.
"it is me. dogsbody. off the mashine. i thinc yoor rilly hott. i wud rite like to go out wi yoo, maybe too pub. if yoo fansi it give us a bell. by th way wot is yor name. from dogsbody. xxx"
He waited.
And waited.
Nothing happened.
The next day at work, his phone buzzed.
It was a text.
From her.
Hi dogsbody. glad you got my message. my name is Tracy..."
Tracy! What a beautiful name!
"...You are my kind of man, dogsbody. I think you are very handsome. I knew you were looking the other day. I saw you looking at my knickers, you dirty man. I fancied you the moment I saw you. I would like to do all sorts of things to you. What would you like to do with me? xxx"
Dogsbody felt faint.
His mouth was dry.
His heart punched painfully against his rib cage.
He tried to hide his hard on behind a pile of envelopes.
The years of bitter dissatisfaction at work and home suddenly seemed about to end, and a new option presented itself to him.
Light at the end of a dark tunnel.
The sun's weak rays banishing the bitter cold of night.
He was going to have red hot, no holds barred sex with a nympho of restricted growth.
His knees went weak, and with sweaty thumbs he clumsily began to write a text, tentatively describing how he wanted to fuck her brains out...

He didn't see her at work any more.
Her shift had been changed.
They kept in touch by text.
Lots of texts.
Dirty, filthy, texts, full of bad spelling and sordid fantasies.

He struggled with the phone, wishing he owned a dictionary so he could spell words such as 'facial' and 'vibrator'.
Did you spell 'fisting' with one or two 't's?
English had never been his strong point.
He didn't have any strong point, for that matter.
But that wasn't important any more.
Tracy wanted to see him.
He'd got the text that morning.
He was going to meet her at The Pheasant, that evening at eight.
Anything could happen.
Anything.
Everything.
He only hoped he didn't make a fool of himself and cum too early.
He was nearly cumming just thinking about it...

It was 7.50.
Dogsbody slipped through the side door of The Pheasant, hiding the large bunch of flowers behind his back.
He felt like a right tit.
He knew he should have left the flowers in the car.
Too late now.
He wished he'd worn something less conspicuous, but he'd wanted to look smart, make a good impression.
He was wearing the only smart outfit in his meagre wardrobe.
His wedding suit.
He'd been married for twenty years.
The lapels were seven inches wide.
The suit was chocolate brown.
His tie was purple paisley.
He'd told his wife he was going to play snooker with the lads.
She caught him trying to sneak out in his suit.
She asked him where he'd be playing - 1978?
They'd had a right row.
She'd threatened him with divorce.
He didn't care.
All he wanted was Tracy.
Lovely little Tracy.
He hoped she was wearing something that showed off her tits.

It would be a piece of piss to look down her top.
His mouth was dry just thinking about it.
He needed a drink.
Dogsbody went to the bar.
As he waited to get served he glanced around the pub.
He didn't think she had arrived.
He couldn't be sure though.
It was quite a high bar.
He'd have a look round when he got a drink.
The barman arrived, but before Dogsbody could order anything, he put a drink down in front of him.
It was a single whiskey.
Dogsbody looked puzzled.
"What's this?"
"It's from a lady in the other room."
Tracy!
Dogsbody's heart leaped.
The barman continued.
"Yeah, she said you'd come here for a short, so here it is."
He picked up the glass, and his phone buzzed.
It was a text message.
'Come and get me! I'm in the other room!'
Dogsbody pushed open the adjoining door, but Tracy wasn't there.
All his work mates were, though.
Laughter and wolf whistles exploded as he walked in.
Everyone was calling him a wanker, a pervert.
He was stunned.
"Where's... Tracy?"
One of the women from the mailroom was tapping on her phone.
Dogsbody's own phone buzzed.
'Tracy left work weeks ago. She was scared off by you grinning at her.
We left that message on your car, you pervert!!'
Somebody threw something at him.
It hit him on the chest and flopped to the floor.
It was a strap on dildo.
Fucking hell.
He remembered all the texts he'd sent.

All the dirty secrets, all his fantasies.
Now everybody knew.
He ran, the screams and laughter of his work mates ringing in his ears.
He dropped the flowers in a filthy puddle, and slumped behind the wheel of his car.
He'd have to go home and face the wife.
He'd have to face his work mates on Monday.
Tracy had been nothing but a dream, a fantasy.
He should have known it was too good to be true.
Why would a sexy dwarf like her go for a loser like him?
She was out of his league.
Mind you, he had thought he'd noticed her mate giving him the eye once or twice.
He felt honoured that she's give him the eye, seeing as she only had one to give.
It was a very nice eye though.
And he'd always like a girl with a fuller figure.
Like an hour glass.
Well, a pint glass, really.
Maybe he'd give it a go with her.
He'd never forget Tracy though.
That had been love.
Dogsbody yawned.
Scratched his arse.
Started the car, and drove home.

Operation Superlesbian

The Shadow was interviewing people for jobs in the mailroom.
He was on the board of directors.
He didn't have a soul.
He was sly, sneaky, underhand, ruthless.
Nothing made him happier than screaming at a member of his staff until they cried.
Job well done.
Knock knock
"Come in."
A short, stocky man with a crew cut stomped into his office and sat down.
He sat down without being asked.
He wouldn't get the job.
Still, thought The Shadow, I've got to go through the motions.
"Name?"
"Ermintrude."
The Shadow had been sketching in a pad, doodling pictures of stick men becoming trapped in printing machinery, when he suddenley stopped and looked up.
"Ermintrude?"
The man glowered at him.
"Ermintrude."
He quickly sifted through the C.V.'s on his desk.
He found the one he was looking for.
Ermintrude was single.
Experienced.
Late twenties.
No kids.
And he was a woman.
Interesting.
"So, err.. Ermintrude. By the looks of your C.V. you seem to be perfect for the job! When can you start?"
Ermintrude looked shocked, and suspicious.
"No disrespect, but you've not even interviewed me. How come I get

the job?"

The shadow laughed quietly, his hands laced behind his head.

"There's two answers to that question, Ermintrude. One is, quite frankly, bullshit. The other is the truth. Which do you want?"

She sat back in her chair, eyeballing him.

"Better start with the bullshit, Mr Shadow."

Ok. Your credentials are perfect, you are the right age, you have good experience in the role and you come across as a positive, upbeat, team player. Happy?"

"Not really. Let's have the truth."

"Ok. You're a bull dyke."

Ermintrude growled and started to get out of her chair.

The Shadow patted the air, indicating for her to calm down.

"Keep your wig on, love. No need to take offense. I meant it as a complement. As a matter of fact, you are just what we are looking for."

Ermintrude cracked her knuckles.

"Why's that?"

"Because I've got a quota of women employees I have to fill, and to put it bluntly, your lot won't fuck off for six months at a time on maternity leave. Got it?"

Ermintrude still glowered.

The Shadow smiled at her.

"Don't look so cross. You've got the job! And here's another little proposition. If any more of your lot want a job here, tell them it's in the bag. I'll even bung a little sweetener your way for every dyke you point my way. Deal?"

Ermintrude shrugged.

"Ok. Deal."

They shook hands, and she left the office.

The Shadow cackled to himself.

This was perfect!

No more maternity pay, no more useless part timers to train up. Just a workforce of superlesbians, steadily working away without fear of them getting knocked up.

He picked up the phone and spoke to his secretary.

"Marjorie? Is their anybody else waiting for an interview?"

"Yes Mr Shadow. There are eleven young men waiting outside."

"Right. Tell them to fuck off."
"Oh!"
The Shadow slammed down the phone.
Yes, this was perfect.
Nothing could go wrong.
-

Things had started to go wrong.
He was six months into Operation Superlesbian, and he was getting steady stream of complaints.
He had hired a dozen or so women that Ermintrude had recommended, but now they were getting out of hand.
They had been aggressive and intimidating to other members of staff.
They kept hitting on the straight women on his staff, even managing to turn a couple of them.
Their husbands were furious.
What's more, they kept fucking each other in the toilets.
God only knows what they got up to in there, but it sounded like a Roman orgy.
On top of all that, explosive arguments had been erupting over who was going with who to the Christmas party.
The Shadow was at the end of his tether.
Unfortunately, there was nothing he could do about it.
He was stuck with the lesbians.
-

It had been a good year at the factory, and God decided to push the boat out for the Christmas Party.
For the first time ever there was a respectable venue, superb food, and free wine on every table.
Some of the older workers had gone so far as to hire tuxedos for the event.
The air was buzzing with excitement.
Not everyone was happy though.
Tensions were running high in the lesbian camp.
Some of the bull dykes didn't get the girl dykes they wanted for the evening, and they were far from happy.
Ermintrude slouched against the bar, staring daggers at Clarabelle and slinging back Jack Daniel's.

She wasn't happy.
Clarabelle had come with Vicky, but Vicky had been seeing Ermintrude on the side and Ermintrude has wanted Vicky to come to the party with her.
Instead she had been forced to come with Roxy, who still was technically her girlfriend, but everyone knew that Roxy was shagging Yvette, and Denise too, if rumours were to be believed. They could all fuck off.
Ermintrude only wanted Vicky.
She slammed back another whiskey...

The party was in full swing when things came to a head.
Dinner had been cleaned away, and everybody was enjoying a dance.
The Shadow sidled close to where God was dancing with Mrs God.
"This really is a super do you've arranged this year, God," he greased. "It will go down as a most memorable event!"
"I only hope it's memorable for the right reasons, Shadow," he growled back. "Mrs God has just been telling me that those short ugly men you've recently hired were having quite a row outside the women's lavatories..."
Shit.
Shit shit shit shit shit!
The Shadow abandoned his wife and made his way across the dance floor.
Too late.
It all kicked off.
"Bitch!"
"Slag!"
"Cunt!"
People screamed as snarling lesbians started punching the living crap out of each other, throwing chairs and smashing glasses.
No hair pulling for these girls.
You can't grab a crew cut.
A couple of printers tried to separate them, but staggered away with blood pouring from broken noses caused by well placed head butts.
Spilled beer sloshed onto the dance floor, turning it into an ice rink, and frightened wives fell like nine pins as they tried to flee the

bloodshed.

"Ladies! Ladies!" screamed The Shadow, desperate to halt the mayhem.

A chair shattered across Ermintrude's broad shoulders, but she shrugged it off and planted firm right hook to Clarabelle's jaw. Clarabelle staggered backwards, spitting teeth and foul language, her hand scrabbling across a bloodstained table cloth in search of a weapon.

She found a wine bottle, gripped it by the neck, and hurled it with all her strength at Ermintrude.

Who ducked.

The Shadow wasn't so quick.

The bottle of Chateau neuf du Pape struck him square between the eyes, sending him reeling to the floor among the blood, glass and beer, the sounds of battle and Boney M fading, fading...

The jolt of the stretcher being loaded into the back of the ambulance brought him briefly back to consciousness, and he squinted his eyes against the painful flashing blue lights of the police vans.

He saw a copper sitting on a tail gate, nursing a bleeding nose.

A regional news van was parked on the grass outside the hotel, and the lurid orange anchorwoman was interviewing a grinning Dogsbody who was still holding a pint.

There was no sign of God, or Mrs God, or Mrs Shadow, for that matter.

He closed his eyes.

That hadn't gone well.

Not well at all.

He wondered what the Hell he was going to do for staff on Monday morning, now that Operation Superlesbian had been scuppered.

He'd have to call the agency, see who was available short notice.

As he drifted back into unconsciousness, he wondered if he could specifically request only really hideous women apply for the jobs.

That way nobody would want to fuck them.

Not even the bull dykes.

Who Dares Whinnies

"Now then, Scorcher. What's that you're reading?"
"How do, Lucifer. Just reading here in the paper about our boys."
"Your boys? I didn't know you had kids, Scorcher."
"I don't."
"Oh. Well, what the fuck are you on about then?"
"Our boys. OUR BOYS! You know, them heroes fighting in Afghanistan! Brave soldiers, our boys."
"I suppose so."
"Suppose so? What's all this 'suppose so' shit, Lucifer? You don't sound very supportive of our boys! They're out there fighting for your freedom, you know!"
"It just seems like another scrap over oil to me, Scorcher."
"How dare you! HOW DARE YOU! These young lads, barely out of school, out there in the dust and sand, getting blown up by these O.M.D.'s..."
"I.E.D.'s."
"What?"
"I.E.D.'s. Your boys keep getting blown up by I.E.D.'s."
"Oh. Right. What does that stand for?"
"Improvised Explosive Device."
"So what does O.M.D. stand for?"
"Orchestral Manoeuvers in the Dark. They were a band in the Eighties, Scorcher."
"Were they? Never heard of 'em."
"I think they became less popular after they started blowing up British troops."
"Sound like a set of bastards to me. Sorry for snapping at you, Lucifer. I forget that civilians like you can't really picture the horrors of war."
"What, and you can?"
"I can, 'cos I've been there, Lucifer."
"Here we go..."
"Yeah, I've witnessed armed conflict at first hand, all over the world."

"Come on then, Scorcher. Tell us where you've fought."
"Everywhere... and nowhere... what you laughing at?"
"Nothing, nothing. What do you mean by 'everywhere and nowhere'?"
"Well, my regiment saw action in all the major conflicts of the last sixty years, the world over, but officially we weren't there. They were clementine operations what we were taking part in..."
"What? Little oranges? You fought battles all over the world, against little oranges?"
"What the fuck are you on about, Lucifer? What have oranges got to do with owt?"
"Clementines are little oranges, Scorcher."
"Shit. I always get mixed up. What's that word for secret stuff, sounds like little oranges?"
"Clandestine?"
"That's it! I took part in clandestine operations with the regiment for fifteen years, I did. It were brutal, Lucifer. Hell!"
"Tell us some war stories then, Scorcher."
"Can't."
"Why not?"
"Can't."
"Why? Have you forgotten?"
"No! I remember it all like it were yesterday! The thing is, They made me sign the Official Secrets Act. I can't say owt for a hundred years!"
"What are you going to do after that? Write a book?"
"Dunno. Maybe."
"Go on, Scorcher. Give us a hint."
"Well, let's put it this way, do you know that film, Apocalypse Now?"
"Fuck off, Scorcher! You were never in Vietnam!"
"Didn't say I was! Some of the scenes for Apocalypse Now were shot outside Tropical World at Roundhay Park in Leeds. Well, we did a lot of our training manouevres around there."
"Really."
"Yeah. And we were in Vietnam too. Can't talk about it though."
"Ok then, Scorcher. What's this regiment you were in? How come it's so secret?"

"Special Forces, Lucifer. Best of the best. I spent fifteen long, bloody years with the S.H.S."
"S.A.S., Scorcher. They're called the S.A.S."
"Fuck off! I'm not talking about them soft puffs! No, I was in the S.H.S."
What's that stand for?"
"Special Horse Service."
"You're going to have to give me a minute here, Scorcher..... ok, ok I'm alright now. Did you just say Special Horse Service?"
"Aye, and If I had Trigger here with me today, God rest his soul, you wouldn't be laughing like that!"
"I'm sure I wouldn't. So how did that work then, Scorcher? Did they parachute you into combat zones on the back of your horse?"
"So you do know about the S.H.S then!"
"Fuck me..."
"Yeah, those were the days. We taught those horses to gallop in mid air, so when we hit terra firma, Whoosh! we were off! You don't need no Land Rover if you've got a horse, Lucifer!"
"Wouldn't a horse be a bit conspicuous in a war zone, Scorcher?"
"Not at all! WE always wore local costume. Think about it - a lot of these places where guerrilla armies are kicking off, the only way of getting about is by horse! We were just beating them at their own game. Deserts were a bit trickier though."
"What, because of the lack of water?"
"No, cause everyone rides camels. Our horses stood out a mile off."
What did you do, Scorcher?'
"We made camel outfits, of course!"
"For you or the horses?"
"For the horses, Lucifer. Best days of my life with the regiment, Lucifer. I've got the regimental tattoo and everything."
"Give us a look."
"There you go..."
"Oh, come on! A proper look! That was barely a fucking glimpse!"
"Use your fucking eyes, Lucifer! Look - a horse's head, symbol of the regiment! Believe me now?"
"No."
"What? Why not?"
"That's not a horse's head, Scorcher. It's Scooby Doo."

"How dare you! That's a genuine regimental tattoo, that is!"
"So what do those words mean?"
"It's latin! It means 'On Hooves of Steel'! It's the regimental motto!"
"Let's get this straight. You're trying to tell me that 'Scooby Dooby Doo' means 'On Hooves of Steel' in Latin?"
"Yes."
"Bollocks."
"I don't care what you think, Lucifer. You watch them reports on News at Ten tonight. If you see some bloke in the background on horseback, it's more than likely one of our lads from the S.H.S.!"
"Like I said, Scorcher, bollocks."

Smell a Rat

Some sights are far from welcome on a Thursday morning at six.
Sights such as Sewer Rat.
Sewer Rat is a print assistant.
He's in his fifties, with a wizened face, bald head, giant ears, and big, sharp buck teeth.
He's got a perma-tan.
Not like George Hamilton III.
No, more like a tramp.
It's the sort of tan you get from park benches, rather than sunbeds.
His look is not a good one, believe me.
Surprisingly, his physical attributes are not the thing I find most offensive about him.
The thing I find most offensive about him is his clothing.
To be more specific, it's his shorts.
So, we've got a bloke who actually resembles a large rat, wearing a plaid cotton shirt, work boots... and tiny little denim shorts.
Tiny.
You can see them cutting into his groin.
He has this strange habit of resting one foot on stacks of pallets, in a bizarre, almost pioneering, pose.
It doesn't matter how high the pallets are stacked, Sewer Rat will get his foot up there, and rest his elbows on his knees.
Not everyone can carry off such a striking pose.
Sewer Rat certainly can't.
Those itty bitty shorts are already at bursting point.
Something has to give.
So whenever he strikes his 'pioneering lumberjack' pose, his ball bag squelches down the leg of his shorts and flaps against his leathery thigh.
Sewer Rat works the night shift.
He waits at the door of the factory, peering out into the darkness, waiting for something.
The lads who are starting their morning shift are greeted by the sight of a distinctly rodenty looking man flashing his scrotum at them.

Muttered curses and protests are directed at Sewer Rat, but he ignores them.
He has bigger game in mind.
He hears his prey first.
Those big ears twitch.
His lips peel back from those long yellow incisors as he starts to grin.
He has heard the sound of a Vespa scooter.
Sewer Rat scurries around to the warehouse door at the far end of the factory, and listens.
The Vespa is pulling into the loading bay.
He knows who it is.
It's Kray.
Kray hates Sewer Rat.
The feeling is mutual.
He waits, waits, until Kray has locked up his scooter, taken of his gloves and helmet, and is walking towards the warehouse door.
Then he slams home the deadbolt, locking Kray out.
Sewer Rat snickers and cackles as Kray tries in vain to get into the factory, before scuttling back to the locker room.
Sewer Rat is one of those people who sweats profusely.
It drips off his long nose and trickles across his bald head.
I was making a cup of tea.
Sewer Rat fishes in his locker for his towel before he swaggers over, a look of triumph on his brown, sweaty face.
He props one foot on a pile of pallets, his bollocks slither out, and he proceeds to wipe his glistening face the towel.
"Hee hee! Did you see that, Lucifer? Did you see that?"
"What? Your nut bag? I can't miss it, Sewer Rat."
"Eh? No, I mean Kray! I got him good this time! It's the third time this week! He'll never get back round to the clock machine in time, and they'll dock his wages for being late!"
Very good. I can see you're pleased about that."
"Pleased? I'm over the fucking moon! I really hate that cunt Kray. Just knowing he's pissed off makes my day!"
"You want to be careful, Sewer Rat. What goes around comes around. If he finds out it's you that's locking him out, he'll have his revenge."

"Pah! I'm not frightened of him! Anyway, he hasn't got a clue who's fucking him over! That's the beauty of it!"
"Whatever. I'll give yo a word of advice though."
"Yeah, Lucifer? What's that then?"
"It's a bit nippy out there. You might want to put some trousers on before you head home."
"I don't need trousers. I've got my shorts on! Look!"
"Oh, Jesus..."
"Nothing wrong with getting a bit of air to the old legs! Good for the circulation!"
"Does that rule apply to your scrote, Sewer Rat?"
"What? Look, I'd better be off. Kray's coming, and he's furious! Hee hee!"
He was right.
Kray was livid.
"Which bastard keeps locking that warehouse door? It's meant to be kept open, every fucker knows that! Have you got any idea, Lucifer?"
I don't like to get anyone into trouble.
I'm not a snitch.
I always think it's best to keep out other people's business.
"Sewer Rat did it, Kray."
"Right! I thought it was that horrible, vermin faced fucker!"
"What are you gonna do Kray?"
"I'm off to see Puglsey!"
"Pugsley? What do you want to see him for? He's got nothing to do with it."
Kray winked at me.
"Ah! I'm off to see Pugsley because he's diabetic!"
I was none the wiser.
I decided to hang about.
Soon, Kray returned.
He had an empty insulin syringe.
"What's that for, Kray?"
"Watch and learn, Lucifer, watch and learn..."
Kray took the syringe to the locker room.
Before I knew what was happening, Kray had whipped his cock out and was pissing into a plastic bottle.

"Ah! First of the day, Lucifer. Always the richest!"
"Fucking hell, mate What have you been drinking? It stinks!"
Kray held up the bottle to the light, swirling it around to show its deep orange colour.
"We were on the whiskeys last night. Always makes my piss nice and ripe!"
He filled the syringe with piss, slipped the needle through the keyhole of Sewer Rat's locker, and squirted it inside.
He did it five times.
"There! It'll have a good fifteen hours to ferment in there on that towel of his. That'll teach him to fuck with me!"
-
Next morning, the smell of Sewer Rat hit me before I clocked in.
It made me gag.
There he was, leg on a pile of pallets, a great wedge of chicken skin poking out of his shorts.
He was reeking to high heaven.
For some reason, he didn't seem to notice the smell.
Sweat trickled down his face, and he wiped himself with that foul, piss soaked towel.
"Morning Lucifer! Any sign of Kray out there? Don't want to miss him at the warehouse! Hee hee!"
"I didn't see him. I'd give it a rest if I were you."
"Why do you say that, Lucifer?"
"Because I reckon he's beginning to smell a rat. We all are, for that matter."
"Pah! There's nothing that fucker can do to me, Lucifer. I'll take the pis out of him for as long as I like!"
"As long as your willing to take the piss, Sewer Rat, I'm sure Kray is willing to give it. See you later."
"Yeah, see you, Lucifer."

Bedhead

I've swapped shifts.
I usually work alongside OhSeeDee.
He's a bit obsessive about things, but he's ok.
Today I'm working opposite Jinnero.
Let's take a look at him.
Ginger hair, for a start.
Really thick, kept short, makes his head look like a dark orange tennis ball.
Some tufts of hair missing.
Stress related, apparently.
I'm not surprised.
Big old eagle beak of a nose.
Flared nostrils.
He's about four meters away, but I can hear his nose whistling every time he breaths.
Very, very annoying.
His ears are really big and red.
Really red.
Remember sneaking up on your mates and flicking their ears from behind?
We used to shout 'tabs!' just as we flicked their lugs.
It really hurts.
Jinnero has the sort of ears that are begging to be flicked.
They stick out like jug handles.
God, I want to flick them so badly.
His leg is juddering.
I mean, really spazzing out.
He's hunched over his keyboard, eyes about ten inches from the screen, and that leg is bouncing up and down at three beats per second.
I wonder if it aches at the end of the day, and he doesn't know why.
How many calories does a juddery leg burn up?
Fuck knows.
A lot, probably.

What I do know is that it's very, very annoying.
He's getting cross at something on the screen.
He's muttering, and jabbing his keyboard hard.
Very hard.
For fuck's sake, calm down.
Wow.
It's the first time I've ever seen anyone headbutt a keyboard.
All the keys are jammed together, and he's trying to free them up using the edge of a ruler.
What a gimp.
I've just realised how fat he's become.
He used to be skinny.
Not any more.
Look at that gut.
He's got more chins than a Chinese phone book.
When did that happen?
When did he get so fat?
"Hey, Jinnero."
He's freed the keys and he's typing again.
He doesn't look round.
"Yeah?"
"When did you get so fat?"
A brief pause in his typing.
Only brief.
"Dunno. Just put weight on, didn't I."
Tap tap tap.
Judder judder judder.
Whistle whistle whistle.
I turn back to my computer.
"I reckon I started putting on weight after that thing with the bed."
My ears prick up.
That thing with the bed?
Sounds good.
"What thing with the bed, Jinnero?"
Jinnero doesn't look around.
The nose whistle speeds up a bit.
As does that spazzy leg.
"We'd been living together for about eighteen months. She was a bit

202

younger than me."

"A bit?"

"She was eighteen."

"Eight years younger than you. Bit of a difference."

"Yeah, but not too much. She was very mature for her age."

"Fair enough. Go on."

"Well, she liked going out with her mates. You know, into town. It's not really my thing, going out, so I used to give her some money for drinks and that."

"What were you doing while she was out?"

"I was building my own PC at the time. Either that or I was on the Playstation. She'd give me a ring when she wanted to come home, and I'd go collect her."

"That sounds a bit boring."

"Huh. That's what she said. Said I was dull. Boring. I'm not boring, you know."

Yes you bloody well are.

"Of course you're not, Jinnero."

"Anyway, we started arguing all the time. I don't like that sort of thing. It upsets me."

He starts scratching at one of the bald patches on his tennis ball head.

I look away.

"I came home from work one time, and she's gone. Packed her stuff and left. I rang her mum's house, but she wasn't there. Turns out she'd moved in with another bloke."

"Oh dear. That's a bit shit, Jinnero."

"That's one way of putting it, Lucifer."

He's still not taken his eyes of the monitor.

His fingers still jab the keys.

His nose whistles.

His leg judders.

Those ears have gone very, very red.

Tabs!

I resist the urge.

"A few days later I get this knock on the door. It was this little Pakistani bloke. He says he's come for the bed."

"Why did he want the bed?"

203

"He was the bloke she'd moved in with. They'd been seeing each other for months. When I went to work, he'd come round and they'd...they'd...you know."
I knew.
"Fucking hell, man! Did he tell you all this!"
"Yeah. He seemed to think this information justified him taking the bed. The thing is, when she moved in with me, it was the only thing she brought with her, that bed. I paid for everything else, all the bills, mortgage, food, everything. She was still at school, you see."
I hide my laughter by pretending to cough.
It doesn't fool Jinnero, but he pretends to ignore it.
"So anyway, she seemed to think that I should give her the bed! No fucking way!"
If that leg goes any faster it's going to fall off.
He's getting very excited.
"The Pakistani bloke's got a van with him. He intends to take it with him, and he wants me to help him carry it downstairs! Can you believe it!"
"What a cheeky cunt. You should have slapped him."
"Oh, well... maybe, I don't know."
"Did he get the bed? Please tell me you didn't give him the bed!"
"I didn't give him the bed."
"Nice one! You showed him..."
"I paid him for it."
I'm looking at Jinnero, open mouthed.
"You did what?"
His ears were glowing like fire now.
"I paid him. She'd bought the bed from Argos, so we looked it up in the catalogue to see what it was worth..."
"Jesus Christ..."
"I didn't give him the full amount! No way! It was three hundred in the catalogue and I only paid him two fifty."
"What? Jinnero, you should have told him to fuck off. You should have slapped the little fucker. You should have dragged that bed out of your house, set fire to it on your front lawn and danced around it, laughing! You should NOT have given him anything! Not a fucking bean!"
"I didn't like to."

"Why the fuck not?"
"Because he might have thought I was racist."
"Racist? Racist? What the fuck has race got to do with anything? That nasty fucker was screwing your bird on your bed in your house! Then he has the cheek to come around to your house, tell you how he poked your bird on your bed in your house, and he enjoyed it so much that he'd like the bed, please! You should have punched him, Jinnero. Right on the sneezer."
"Well, I didn't. I paid him. That's how I reckon I started getting fat."
"How does that work then?"
"When he drove off, I went back inside, and started on a crate of beer that I had in the kitchen. Been drinking like that ever since."
I take a good look at Jinnero.
His face is pale and puffy.
His eyes are red and watery.
His gut oozes over his belt, showing a wedge of pale skin and ginger fluff beneath his stretched t-shirt.
Yep. He's a boozer.
I almost feel sorry for him.
Almost.
"Tabs!"
"Owwww! My ear! You flicked my ear! God, that really hurts! Why did you do that?"
"Because you deserved it."
It felt good.

I Know What You've Been Doing!

It was a really busy day.
The studio was stacked out with work.
Account Executives would burs through the door every five minutes demanding their job get top priority, and the phone didn't stop nagging.
Soulless Boss was running in circles and screaming, handing down all the grief that was raining on him.
I, however, had discovered a nice sunny spot outside, just out of view of the security cameras.
No breeze, very little traffic noise, no agitated dick heads getting all worked up over some shitty credit card mailing.
I had my eyes closed, smiling.
The bricks of the factory were warm on my back.
blackbirds were marking their territory with song.
Good tobacco smoke was in the air.
Nice.
Very nice.
Wait a minute...
Tobacco smoke.
I didn't see any smokers.
I opened my eyes.
"Hello Lucifer. Enjoying the weather?"
"Shit the bed! Hello Abbott. You startled me."
Abbott is a printer. A big, easy going kind of bloke.
I'd felt little uneasy around him after he disclosed a rather unsavoury piece of information a while back, but we were cool again.
He leaned against the wall next to me, a little too close, to be honest, but I knew why.
I checked his position.
Yup, he was just out of view of the security cameras, too.
Respect, Abbott.
"Yes, Lucifer, I like the weather, today. It's kind on us patrons of the weed, and those who respect it."
He winked at me, removing a fleck of tobacco from his tongue.

I smiled lazily.

"Nothing wrong with smoking, Abbott. I used to smoke a little myself, but had to quit. I never became rabidly opposed to it like some folk. Can never understand that. Why suddenly detest something you once loved?"

"It's all about respect, Lucifer. You might not smoke, but you still respect the tobacco, still respect the smoker. Perhaps those who once loved smoking now hate it as they might hate a woman that they can no longer have; with a jealous hate. Perhaps they hate smokers for staying with that woman, for tasting the forbidden fruit, for living in sin..."

He chuckled to himself, exhaling grey tendrils like a mellow old dragon.

Had to hand it to him.

Abbott had a nice turn of phrase.

"Guess you're right. Sometimes I miss smoking. Times like now. I could really enjoy a cigar. Smoking a cigar in the sunshine is one of life's great pleasures."

"I've got a panatella if you're interested?"

"That's kind of you, Abbot, but I'm ok. Like it or not, I'm going to have to get back to work at some point."

I half closed my eyes again, and leant back against the warm bricks. Abbott took a long, measured pull on his roll up, and looked up at the sky, shaking his head.

"Yes, Lucifer, these evil swine work us like dogs. Like dogs! What job have you got on at the moment?"

"That mailing for NastiBasterds™ Credit. They're breathing down my neck for it."

" NastiBasterds™ Credit? When is that due out?"

"Yesterday."

"Oh. Who's the account executive for that particular piece of dross?"

"Cleopatra. She's phoning very two minutes demanding to know where her job is."

Abbotts eyes widened.

"Cleopatra, eh? Small world! I was at a dinner party last Saturday and she happened to be in attendance!"

"Yeah? Which party was that then?"

"It was over at Harrogate. Do you know the Phillipsons? The

husband is a big noise in marketing."

"Nope. Not the sort of social circle that I get invites from."

"You'd fit in a treat, Lucifer! I'll get you an invite for the next soirée. Well, she was there, Cleopatra, with her fiance. Tony, I think his name was. lovely couple. I'd just nipped to the lavatory, and I came back to find my wife with them."

"That's a coincidence. What did Cleopatra have to say?"

"She couldn't talk at the time, as she was eating."

"Canapés?"

"No, my wife's pussy."

"Beg pardon?"

"My wife's pussy. She was eating my wife's pussy."

"Fucking hell. Didn't anybody else in the room have something to say about that?"

"No, no! Of course not. They were too busy screwing each others brains out!"

"Hmm. It was one of THEM parties, wasn't it, Abbott."

"Is there any other kind?"

"There is, actually. There are the kind of parties where female acquaintants don't eat out your wife's fanny in the middle of a room full of strangers fucking on the furniture."

"They sound like dull parties."

"They're not too bad, to be fair, but there's probably not the element of excitement that you're used to. Cleopatra, eh? She doesn't seem like the type. But then again..."

"Oh, she's hot to trot, Lucifer! She was eating that fanny like a dog with a hot chip."

"Nice image. And what was her bloke doing while all this was going on?"

"Wanking, naturally."

"Naturally. I won't ask what you were doing."

"Well, I couldn't ignore that little pink treat winking up at me..."

"I'm gone. Work to do..."

"...I asked her fiance's permission first..."

"You gent, Abbott. Look, I'd better be getting back..."

"It was incredible, tight as a Scotsman's fist..."

"Bye."

-

I got back to work.
Abbott had unsettled me.
Again.
After five minutes, who should walk in but Cleopatra.
"Soulless Boss! Where on Earth is that work for NastiBasterds™ Credit that I've been waiting for? I've got a courier in reception waiting for it!"
"We're working on it, Cleopatra!! It's Lucifer's job but he's... back! Lucifer, where the fuck have you been?"
"Bog."
"Typical. Cleopatra, you'd better talk to Lucifer. I've got a meeting to get to."
She came over, acting very prim.
I couldn't look her in the eye.
"When will this be ready, Lucifer?"
"An hour."
"I haven't got an hour! The courier is here, now!"
I shrugged.
"Can't work any faster. It'll be an hour."
"That's not good enough!"
I glanced up at her, and just a I feared, the graphic image that Abbott had painted flooded my mind.
"What are you smirking at, Lucifer?"
I know what you've been doing!
"Nothing."
Her eyes narrowed.
I know what you've been doing!
She stared at me, hard.
My eyes gave it away.
"I know what you've been doing!"
She gasped.
Shit.
I'd said that one out loud.
I turned back to my work, looking guilty.
"Email me when the job's ready," she muttered, and walked away.
I watched her leave.
I know what you've been doing!
I know what you've been doing!

Ten minutes later Soulless Boss took a call.
He hung up and shouted to me.
"No rush on that job, Lucifer! It's going tomorrow. Cleopatra's had to go home sick."
Oh dear.
I felt a bit guilty.
Who was I to judge her?
If she wanted to get bummed by vague acquaintances while muffing out their wives, then that was her business.
Maybe I was jealous, looking down on somebody for tasting the forbidden fruit, for living in sin...
Fuck it.
At least the job wasn't needed any more.
While Soulless Boss wasn't looking, i snuck away, out into the sunshine.

Beauty and the Yeast

There's a hierarchy within the factory.
Director look down on managers.
Managers look down on office staff and shop floor staff.
Office staff look down on shop floor staff.
Printers look down on machine assistants.
Machine assistants look down on floor sweepers.
The studio department doesn't figure in this equation so much.
If a print works is a prison, then the studio is the nonce wing.
Isolated, locked away, misunderstood.
Bit weird.
I wouldn't ask any of my studio work mates to babysit, that's for sure.

The relationship between printer and machine assistant is the most interesting one.
Similar types of blokes.
Similar knowledge of the machine.
but the printer can kick the machine assistant's arse and make him wash the machine up while he fucks off early to the pub.
Because of this, people think machine assistants are thick.
They're not.
At least, not all of them.
I admit, some of them are the stupidest cunts to ever shamble the Earth, but it's not the rule.
I've known some pretty smart machine assistants.
The difference between a machine assistant and any other worker in the factory is ambition.
For example, you'd win at blackjack if you played a machine assistant.
They'd stick at the first cards they were given.
Even if they were a two of hearts and a four of clubs.
They'd be happy with those cards, the cards would be just right for them, thank you very much.
Perfectly good cards.
Not a winning hand, though.

The thing is, they would be HAPPY wit those cards.
Generally speaking, most machine assistants are happy, contented characters.
No responsibility, no ambition, beers on a Friday, footy on Saturday, roast on a Sunday.
A simple life.
If you have ambition, you end up grumpy, fucked off, disillusioned, greedy, nasty, Machiavellian.
Who has it best?
Sometimes, it's the bloke holding a two of hearts and a four of clubs.
-
At nine, I made a cup of tea.
Third of the day.
Old Stan the machine assistant was leaning against a silent print press, tea in hand, nibbling a biscuit.
I brought my tea over to him.
"How do, Old Stan."
"How do, Lucifer."
"Press not running?"
"Not at the mo. Romeo's supposed to be running it. He had an appointment with the doc this morning."
"What's up with him?"
"Dunno. He wouldn't say."
"Something wrong with his cock, then."
"Aye, lad. It'll either be his cock or his arsehole. The two unmentionables. Ey up. Here he comes now."
Old Stan lobbed the last of his biscuit into his mouth and glugged his tea over it, slurping the mouthful of mush. He was ready to work.
"Now then, lad!"
Romeo didn't speak.
His face was white.
He got into his work gear and fired up the print press.
Old Stan shrugged and set to work.
I slowly drank my tea.
Things looked interesting.
They worked in silence for a bit, then Old Stan spoke.
"So, is your cock alright then?"
"Fuck off, just fuck, off you horrible old cunt! Mind your own

fucking business or I'll stick this...this... teaspoon in your eye!"
"Steady on..."
"And you can fuck off too, Lucifer, you fucking nonce!"
Nonce.
I'd rather not have that label stick, to be honest.
We left Romeo alone for a bit.
Old Stan wasn't fazed.
He'd seen it all before.
He'd minded machines for dozens of printers, if not hundreds.
He knew Romeo would come out with it when he was ready.
So did I.
That's why I hung around.
Sure enough, a spanner clattered to the ground.
Old Stan and I looked up.
"It's Juliette."
Old Stan winked at me.
"Is love a tender thing? It is too rough, too rude, too boisterous; and it pricks like thorn!"
"Itches like fuck, more like, the cheating fucking whore!"
"Oh."
This was shock news.
Romeo and Juliette had been an item for a good while now.
She'd never seemed the cheating type.
Romeo was bitter, to say the least.
"The cunt! The fucking cunt! Wait till I get my hands on her..."
"Steady on now, lad. What's the doctor said then?"
"It were me knob, Stan. It went all red, and started itching, and it stung like fuck when I went for a piss! I was getting really worried so I went to the doctor."
"Very wise, lad, very wise. And what did the quack have to say?"
Romeo looked away. I thought he was going to cry.
"He told me SHE gave me it. Sexually, like. He's given me some cream. SHE'LL need more than cream when I'm through with her!"
Old Stan patted his back.
"Steady now, lad. What is it she's given you then?"
Romeo dropped his head into his hands.
"Thrush. She's given me a dose of fucking thrush! Bitch!"
Old Stan and I looked at each other.

"Thrush? Is that all?"
"Is that all? IS THAT ALL?? It doesn't matter what she's given me, Lucifer, but that fucking cow had to have been doing something to catch it in the first place!"
Old Stan looked uncomfortable.
"Listen, lad. It's not as it seems. Your lass hasn't been cheating on you. You see..."
"Not cheating? Course she has! That night she was late in from town, now I know what she was doing! It's over. Over!"
"No, no. What it is, with some ladies, it's just, sort of, well...."
"...cheating cunt, that's all there is to it. Dirty cheating..."
"...bit of a ladies problem, and their bits get all kind of, well..."
"...gonna find out who's fucked her, and smash his head in..."
"...no! Just a bit of cream, and..."
"...chuck her out on the street, burn her fucking cloths..."
For the first time ever, Old Stan lost it.
"Romeo! For fuck's sake, will you listen to me? She's not been fucking around, she's got thrush cause women get thrush sometimes! They don't get it off another bloke! They get it cause they sometimes get a sweaty fanny, and it get's all yeasty and goes off, and if you fuck them when their fanny is like that then you'll get it too! Now put the cream that the doctor gave you on your fucking cock and stop being a fucking baby!"
Old Stan walked away, and started inking up the print press.
Romeo stood still for a bit, blinking.
"Fucking Hell... so she's not been cheating, Lucifer?"
"Seems not, Romeo."
"And thrush is just one of those things, women's stuff, like?"
"Yep."
"So everything will be ok, as long as I take this cream?"
"Oh true apothecary! Thy drugs are quick. Thus with a kiss I..."
"What the fuck are you talking about, Lucifer?"
"Oh. It's Shakespeare, you see, and..."
"Shut up, you nonce."
"Fair enough. Hope your cock gets better, Romeo."
"Thanks. I hope Juliette starts washing her fanny more, Lucifer."
"How silver-sweet sound lovers' tongues by night..."
"Nonce."

The Love Hammer

"Hindu."
"Ten sixty six."
"erm... wait a minute... Charlotte Brontë?"
"Blue whale."
Hungerford."
"Cadbury's."
"I haven't got a fucking clue."
"It's Coronation Street, you thick cunt, Lucifer!"
-
I like quizzes.
Quizzes are a rather sad way for people without qualifications to prove they're not stupid.
I've known some great quizzers who are unemployed, are fork lift drivers, are mill workers, are on parole.
They might be on a lot less than ten pounds an hour, but they know what the capital of Somalia is called.
Mogadishu, of course.
It's your round, and get some crisps in.

I used to do quizzes at a local pub.
Me and Mrs Lucifer teamed up with a lovely couple in their eighties.
The four of us would sometimes thrash teams of six, eight or even ten (cheating bastards).
One night the quiz-master asked who performed the first non stop transatlantic flight.
The old gent starts pissing himself laughing, and mutters, 'Sammy Davis jr.'
"Sammy Davis Jr? I don't think he was renowned as a great aviator!"
The old guy shakes his head, still laughing.
"No, it's how I remember the answer - Alcock and Brown."
-
"Isle of Wight."
"Rasputin."
"Skip that one, Jock. You know I'm shit at sport."
Jock did the quiz at his local club on a Thursday.

He'd test the questions out on us lads in the week.
"If you lads can't get the answers, then those thick fucks at the club won't have a cat in Hell's!"
The locker room has a good radiator.
Nice and toasty in there, even if it does smell of printer's feet.
Pot of tea, a biscuit and a few questions.
"Golden Gate bridge."
"Cat Stevens."
"What were the last words of Admiral Nelson? Now that's controversial, Jock. It's not what you think. His last words were in fact..."
The door to the locker room was kicked open.
It crashed against the wall, shuddering and shedding flecks of paint.
"TWO DUCK DOWN PILLOWS AND A KING-SIZE EGYPTIAN COTTON QUILT, KID! SORTED!"
Cyclops strode in, huge and lumbering.
"Nice try Cyclops, but that's the wrong answer."
"YEAH, YEAH, SIX PILLOW SLIPS AND FOUR SHEETS, SINGLE BED."
"No, not that either."
Cyclops was on the phone.
'Doing some business', as he put it.
Cyclops was a printer, but he had a lucrative sideline going in selling bedding.
Nothing stood in the way of him and deal.
Not even printing.
I could see the list of questions in Jock's hand being slowly crushed.
He glowered at Cyclops.
"Here, big fella, we were just in the middle of something..."
Cyclops snapped his fingers at Jock and drew his fingers across his lips.
Zip it.
Jock turned scarlet, and started to growl.
Cyclops ignored him.
"CREAM COTTON VALANCE, FOUR KING SIZE FITTED SHEETS..."
We didn't wait to hear the rest of it.
The quiz was over.

"I really hate that big, fat, slobbering, boss-eyed cunt," rumbled Jock as we walked to his machine.

"Yep. He's one ignorant bastard."

"Did you see how he kicked that door, Lucifer? I wouldn't mind, but it's me that has to do all the re-painting when the doors are fucked. Not him - me."

Bang.

The door was kicked open again.

Cyclops lumbered out of the locker room, snapping his phone shut.

"JOCK! YOU'VE GOT TO WASH THE MACHINE UP ON YOUR OWN! I'VE GOT AN ORDER FOR BEDDING SO I'M LEAVING EARLY!"

"Go steady on the fucking doors, Cyclops. I only glossed them last month."

"HA! I'M DOING YOU A FAVOUR THEN! YOU CAN GLOSS THEM AGAIN NEXT MONTH, ON OVERTIME! THINK OF IT AS A BONUS!"

Cyclops grabbed himself by the balls, his lazy eye swimming all over the place.

"TALKING OF BONUSES, I'VE GOT TO GIVE MY CLEANING LADY HER LITTLE TREAT FOR DOING A GOOD JOB. IF I DROP THIS GEAR OFF QUICK, I'LL BE HOME IN TIME TO CATCH HER PUTTING MY NEW HEAVY GRADE COTTON DUVET COVERS ON THE BED. WE CAN TRY 'EM OUT, SEE IF THEY'RE COMFY! THAT GIRL CAN'T GET ENOUGH OF MY LOVE HAMMER!"

He left, kicking the door open as he went.

"Love hammer?"

"It's what he calls his cock, Lucifer. His love hammer."

"He is a fucking love hammer. Look at the state of the machine."

Cyclops had left the print press in a shitty state. Rags, ink tins and paper were strewn everywhere.

Jock looked tired. I didn't like to see a cunt like Cyclops taking the piss out of a decent bloke like Jock.

It wasn't right.

Jock didn't say anything.

He folded the crumpled page of quiz questions into his trouser pocket, and slowly started cleaning up.

It wasn't right.

-

Next day I went looking for Jock.
Couldn't find him.
I was walking back to the studio when I glanced into the maintenance department through a grimy window.
Cyclops was there, sitting on a tatty, oil stained chair.
His face was a mess, covered in blood and bruises.
His neck looked like a dog had savaged him.
A flock of first aiders dabbed at him, and Bear was talking on the phone.
"Oh fuck..."
The door opened and Jock staggered out, tears streaming down his face.
"Oh fuck, Jock! What's happened? What have you done?"
Jock turned round.
He was pissing himself laughing.
I had to help him into the locker room.
Soon he calmed own enough to speak.
"What goes around comes around, Lucifer me old mate!"
"Come on then! What's savaged cyclops?"
"He dropped off all that shit he sells and went home to fuck his cleaner, only she wasn't there. He couldn't understand it. Well, this morning her car turns up, but it wasn't her. It was her husband."
"Fuck."
"Exactly! This husband, he had a baseball bat. Cyclops's love hammer was no match for that! The door was locked, so this bloke smashes every window in the house, and climbs into the front room. He twats Cyclops, and drags him around the room by that big stupid gold chain he wears, tore his neck to shreds! Then he only goes and drives his big stupid head through the partition wall."
"No!"
"Yeah! His big stupid head stuck out of his dining room wall like a big game trophy! This bloke gives Cyclops a few more twats with the bat for good measure, then fucks off, leaving him hanging there!"
"I guess he found out about the bonus system Cyclops was running with his cleaning staff. So is that when Cyclops came here?"

"It gets better! The big slobbering cunt staggers out to his car and drives off, but he's out of petrol. He pulls into the petrol station and starts to fill it up, but the husband suddenly pops up and brays him all over the forecourt!"

"They've got everything at petrol stations these days, Jock. Charcoal, flowers, groceries..."

"....prolonged aggravated assault. This bloke drives off, leaving Cyclops in a pool of blood and petrol. Cyclops realises that he's got to get some back up, so he picks himself up and drives to his local boozer, where all his shady mates hang out. They all rally round him and get him a beer in, and just as he starts telling the tale, someone shouts 'Look out!' Cyclops didn't even manage to get a gobful of beer before the husband wrapped a fucking barstool around the back of his head! He'd seen Cyclops's car in the car park, and thought he'd pop in to say hello. Cyclops's big hard mates didn't lift a fucking finger to help."

"I suppose you get the mates you deserve. What happened then?"

"He legged it here, to work. He knew the security locks would keep the psycho out. Coppers and an ambulance are on there way."

"Fucking hell! He's lucky he wasn't killed. There'll be no printing on that machine today, Jock. What are you going to do?"

"No worries there, Lucifer. Click down the button on the kettle, and you'll find some biscuits in that locker... that's the one. Now then."

He pulled a crumpled piece of paper from his pocket.

"What is the capital city of Somalia?"

"That's easy. It's..."

Blazing Saddles

"Nice bike, Lucifer."
"Thanks, Scorcher."
"I used to have one of those, back in the day."
"Did you now."
"Yeah. Good bikes, Jack Bobson's."
"Bob Jackson's"
"What?"
The bike. It's made by Bob Jackson's."
"I know. That's what I said."
"Right."
"Looks like you've got a puncture there, Lucifer."
"What makes you think that, Scorcher?"
"Well, you've got the tyre off, and your holding an inner tube and..."
"Yes. I've got puncture. You're right. You not busy then? Nothing to do?"
"Naw, dead at the moment. As I were sayin', I used to do a spot of ridin', back in the day."
"Oh."
"Yeah, nothing competitive, like."
That's nice"
"Nothing too competitive."
"I see."
"Maybe a little race, here and there."
"Aha."
"I only rode the Milk Race once."
"Here we go..."
"It were back in the sixties. I was doing alright, not winning, but not losing. There were some big names riding..."
"Like who?"
"Wot?"
"Who was riding? I'm a bit of a fan of cycling history, Scorcher. Who were the big names who were riding?"
"You wouldn't have heard of 'em."
"Try me."

"Well, let me see, there was Eddie Merckx..."
"He never rode the Milk Race."
"Who didn't?"
"Eddie Merckx."
"Who said anything about Eddie Merckx? I said Freddie Merts."
"Oh yes. Of course. Freddie Merts."
"Yeah. Heard of him?"
"No."
"Told you you wouldn't have heard of 'em. Any road, on the stage from Leeds to Blackpool I took off on my own. The crowds went mad, seeing a local lad having a go."
"I'm sure they did, Scorcher."
"Well, the crowds thinned out as we got into the countryside, and soon it was only me and this copper on a motorbike, cos my lead had stretched out so far. I was sure to win."
"What happened then?"
"The copper got a flat. I stopped and offered to help, cos I knew a bit about motor bikes, what with having built my own and that..."
"Wait a minute. You're saying you stopped in the middle of the Milk Race and offered to help fix a copper's flat tyre?"
"Yeah. I had plenty of time. Anyhow, the copper waves me on. 'You get off, son,' he says. 'You'll win it for sure!' So off I went."
"Did you win then?"
"I rode on, as fast as I could, cross the moors, down t'valleys, but still with no sign of another soul on the road. After another hour, though, I saw a sign. I raced up to it, and guess what it said?"
"I dread to think."
"It said 'Welcome to Scotland'."
"Fuck off."
"It did! I thought, shit, what happened there? It turns out that my lead was so big, they hadn't got the road ready for the race to come through, with no signs or diversions. I took a wrong turning."
"What did you do then?"
"I turned round, o' course! I got my clog down and legged it to Blackpool. I felt a right tit tearing down the Golden Mile."
"Why? Because you were all on your own?"
"What you on about, 'on my own'? I caught up with the bunch on the run in to town, but I was so knackered I only came seventh in the

sprint. I should have pissed it."
"Did the other riders take the mick then, Scorcher?"
"You fucking bet they did, Lucifer! Merciless, they was! They didn't believe me that I'd taken a wrong turn and gone to Scotland..."
"Surprise surprise..."
"...but I soon shut 'em up. They went very quiet when they saw what I pulled from my back pocket to mop the sweat from my forehead."
"Give us it then."
"A tea towel that said 'A Gift from Scotland' on it. I nipped into a gift shop on the border there. The shortcake was a bit crushed, but those greedy fuckers didn't turn their noses up at it!"
Scorcher winked at me.
"There's a tale to impress you cycling pals with, Lucifer."
"Oh, I'll tell them all right, Scorcher. See you later."
"Yeah, laters."

The Car Chase

I can drive but I don't.
I ride a bike.
I used to take buses but I don't anymore.
Too unreliable, dirty, full of nutters.
Cars cost a bomb.
Riding a bike is free.
I ride a bike.
I started riding a bike to get away from public transport.
I used commute to work by bus.
Going to work was fine; I'd read a book, stare out the window, stroll up to the factory for clocking in time.
It was the trip home that spelled trouble.
Nine at night, lurking under the street lights, hiding behind bus shelters, wearing dark clothing in the hope of being overlooked.
No chance.
The throaty growl of the engine, the screech of brakes.
Fuck.
He'd seen me.
"Lucifer! LUCIFER! What the fuck are you doing hiding back there, you paedo? Get in, I'll give you a lift!"
"Hi Ballboy. Listen, I think I'll just wait for the bus, I'm..."
"I said get in the fucking car!"
"Seeing as you put it so nicely..."
I got in the car.
Ballboy floored it, fishtailing through honking horns and swerving cars.
"HAHAHAHAH!!! Set of cunts!!"
Ballboy was mad.
He called everybody cunts.
His answer to everything was the screamed instruction to, 'Suck us off".
He picked fights he could never win.
He had a Ford Capri MkIII that he drove like a getaway car.
It scared the living crap out of me.

I glanced at the speedo.
We were doing ninety in a forty zone.
"Take it steady, Ballboy..."
"Suck us off, Lucifer!"
He slammed on the brakes.
I ended up in the footwell.
"Hahahahah! You daft cunt, Lucifer! Why weren't you wearing your seatbelt?"
"I couldn't reach it. The g-forces wouldn't let me lift my fucking arms."
We were sat at traffic lights.
He was revving the Capri.
I was struggling to get my seatbelt on.
"How do you sort this catch out, Ballboy?"
"Ballboy?"
He wasn't listening.
He was staring at a black Rover parked across the road, his eyes narrowed.
"Ballboy?"
A woman fell out of the passenger side of the Rover, tried to run, but a big guy in a Crombie overcoat hurried after her, slapped her around and shoved her back in the car.
"Ballboy?"
I was alone in the car.
Ballboy was out of the car, running towards the Rover.
"Oi! Oi you, cunt! What the fuck do you think you're doing?"
The big guy leapt behind the wheel of the Rover and took off.
Ballboy ran back, jumped in the car and gunned the engine.
"You get that seatbelt on yet, Lucifer?"
"Not really, Ballboy. That catch is a bit..."
"Tough shit."
Ballboy howled through the red light, chasing the Rover.
I wished I was back at the bus stop.
"What the fuck's going on?"
"Didn't you see the cunt slapping that bird, Lucifer?"
"Well, yes, but..."
"Nobody does shit like that in front of me and gets away with it!!"
"Oh."

We could see the Rover up ahead, weaving through traffic.
Ballboy was taking all sorts of risks to keep up with him.
"You wouldn't fancy just dropping us at this corner here..."
"Suck us off, Lucifer! We're gonna show that fucker!"
I didn't like all this 'we' business.
I really didn't know what we were going to 'show' that 'fucker' either.
Personally, I had nothing to show him except a second hand Graham Greene paperback and a packet of French cigarettes.
Not a combination guaranteed to strike fear into the heart of a potential foe.
"Maybe we should just call the police..."
"Fuck that!"
"We don't know what we're dealing with..."
"Ha! I'm not scared. I've got quite a reputation round the pubs of Horsforth, you know!"
Horsforth is a very conservative suburb of Leeds.
It's not in the least bit 'hard'.
I was getting worried.
The Rover swerved onto the Ring Road, with our Capri in hot pursuit.
Hot pursuit.
For fuck's sake.
"Get that seatbelt on, you snivelling shit!"
"Steady on. No need for.... oh fuck..."
I got the seatbelt on sharpish.
The Rover was howling around a large roundabout, smoke billowing from it's wheels.
Ballboy wasn't slowing down.
He wasn't steering either.
"No! Fucking hell, no! Ballboy..."
He wasn't listening.
He hit that roundabout at about sixty.
Bedding plants exploded everywhere.
He churned right over the top of the roundabout and crashed onto the road on the other side, cutting off the Rover.
Ballboy was out of the car like a whippet, tearing towards the black car.
The big guy climbed out of the car.

He looked pretty put out.
He pointed a sawn-off shotgun at Ballboy.
Ballboy stopped running.
Oh shit oh shit oh shit oh shit.
After a long drawn out moment, a moment designed to let seriousness sink in, the big guy slowly got back into the car.
We could see the woman sobbing in the passenger seat.
Ballboy didn't move.
Very wise.
The Rover drove away, and Ballboy came back to the car.
"Fucking hell."
"yeah, Lucifer. Fucking Hell."
"He had a fucking gun."
"No shit. Did he? I didn't fucking notice!"
"No need to be sarcastic."
"Huh. I reckon we should call the cops on that fucker. What was his registration?"
"I don't fucking know! I was to busy watching my life flash before my eyes to see his number plate!"
"He wasn't even pointing the gun at you, you useless cunt!"
"Who says anything about the gun! I'm on about your fucking driving!"
"Oh, just... just suck us off."
Ballboy set off, his exhaust scraping on the ground below us.
We didn't say anything more until we got to my house.
We were thinking about that girl.
We were thinking about that gun.
I got out of the car.
It felt good to have my feet on the tarmac.
I'd have kissed the ground, only someone had walked dog shit right across my front gate.
"Do you want me to pick you up tomorrow?"
"What?"
"I said, do you want me to pick you up tomorrow, Lucifer. I'll give you a lift in to work, if you like."
"Thanks, but I'm ok."
"How you getting to work then?"

"I'm going to get a bike. See you later, Ballboy."
"Yeah, suck us off, Lucifer."

Brief Encounter

"What do you want, Lucifer? Can't you see I'm rushed off my fucking feet?"
"Hi Bear. I'm looking for Spiderman. Is he here?"
"Can you see him? Does it look like he's here?"
"Erm... no."
"Exactly. Now fuck off and let me get some work done."
"Where is he?"
"What?"
"Spiderman. Where is he?"
"He's in the offices! There's an electrical fault with the phone system. He's sorting that shit out for me."
ring ring
"Hello? Don't be so stupid I..."
Bear answers the phone, shouts at someone.
I wait.
The door opens.
Spiderman staggers in, gasping.
He looks shaky.
His hair is all over the place.
His face is red.
"Fucking Hell, Spiderman! Are you alright?"
He staggers to a chair.
"I...I..."
"what is it? Have you had an electric shock?"
"I...need..."
"What? A bandage? Cold compress? A cup of fucking tea? What do you need??"
"I...need...tissues..."
"For fuck's sake, Spiderman. Not again..."
-
Spiderman is a colossal pervert.
A great bloke, but about as pervy as they come.
His nickname is Spiderman because he does a great Spiderman impression.

Not that you ever see it.
his Spiderman impression happens on the way home from the pub.
He sneaks into gardens and steals knickers off washing lines.
then he hides in alleys, one pair of knickers on his head, one pair wrapped around his cock, wanking.
The gusset hides his face. The leg holes look like huge eyes.
Spiderman.
Don't touch his sticky web.
It's nasty.
-

I made him a cup of tea while he sorted himself out in the stockroom.
He flopped down into a battered chair.
There was a suspicious damp patch covering his groin.
I tried not to look at it.
"Your pants have got spunk on them, mate."
"I know, Lucifer. Tell me about it. It went off like a garden sprinkler. I didn't manage to get any on her shoes though."
"Shoes? Jesus..."
"Can't blame a bloke for trying."
"Come on then. Let's hear it."
"Well, Bear sent me to the offices. The phones were all fucked. It was lunchtime, so only half the staff were in there. It meant I could get under the tables and have a look."
"Have a look at what, you dirty bastard?"
"The phone lines! Of course, while I was down there, it would have been rude not to have a little look round..."
Spiderman's eyes rolled in his head, and an odd smile twitched his mouth.
Creepy.
"I didn't find much of interest in the handbags. Just a change of knickers and some nice smelling tissues."
"Did you...?"
Spiderman patted his pocket.
"No. I'm saving them for later."
"Oh."
"What happened was, I routed a fresh phone lead through hole between the desks, and when I looked through to see where the lead

had gone, I saw her."
"Who?"
"I dunno. I could only see her legs."
"Love at first sight."
"You got it. Those pins were red hot, Lucifer. She didn't have a clue I was under there..."
He let out a little moan and his hand started to stray towards the front of his overalls.
"Do us a favour, Spiderman. Don't wank in front of me."
"What? Oh, yeah. Sorry. Anyway, She crossed her legs. She had stockings on! Benders, fancy knickers, the lot. It were too much for me! I had to do something!"
"So you went to the toilets?"
"No way! With that sweet floor show going on? I wasn't gonna miss that for nothing!"
"You didn't."
"I fucking did! I pulled my toolbox closer to give me a bit of cover, whipped out Spiderman junior, and let him have it."
"Good grief! What if somebody had seen you?"
"That were part of the thrill! I could see this lass eating her lunch about six feet away! She was eating a fucking banana! I was in Heaven, Lucifer. Heaven."
You should be in prison, you gimp. That's front page of The Sun activity, you know. People would set fire to your house if they knew about it."
"Don't care. I reckon everyone does it, but I'm the only one who admits it."
"Believe me, Spiderman. That really isn't the case."
"Bollocks. Anyway, watching those lovely legs slithering about and that lass noshing a banana, I wasn't going to last long. There was no way I could get it on her shoes from that angle..."
"Why do you want to spunk on he shoes, for God's sake?"
"Dunno. Always wanted to, for some reason. Don't you?"
"No. Not really my thing."
"Suit yourself. So If I couldn't reach hr shoes, I had to settle for the next best thing."
"Which was?"
"Her handbag."

230

I closed my eyes.
"No."
"Yeah!"
"You jizzed into her handbag?"
"I didn't get it all in there. Some went on my overalls too..."
"Bloody Hell..."
"...and on the floor, some hit the desk, a bit splashed the bin and I nearly got myself in the eye."
"Is that all? Fucking Hell, Spiderman, you need to be hooked up to a milking machine in a sperm bank. Or castrated."
"I know. I wish I could sell it. I'd make a fortune."
"Believe me, you wouldn't. People don't want a fucking knicker sniffer polluting there gene pool."
Spiderman looked hurt.
"That's not very nice, Lucifer. I'm not harming anyone, you know."
"Not until they find spunk on their chapstick, anyway. Listen, I've got to get back to work."
"I'm too knackeredjust yet. My legs are all shaky. I'll just have a rest and finish my tea..."
ring ring
Bear answers the phone, talks for a bit.
"Spiderman!"
"Yeah, Bear?"
"The lightbulb has blown in the women's toilets, can you..."
His face lights up, he grabs his toolbox and sets off at a jog.
"Woohoo! I'm on it!"
He barges past me, and a flash of pale pink cotton winks at me from his grubby overall pocket.
He grabs a sign from a cupboard to hang on the toilet door.
It says, 'Out of Order'.

Work Experience

"Crisps, Lucifer?"
"Yeah, go on then, J-Dogg. Ready salted."
"That's dull. Not beefy, or prawn cocktail?"
"Truth is, I'm a dull person. Ready salted, all the way."
"Fair do's. What you drinking?"
"I'll have a pint of bitter."
"Bitter? It's an old man's drink! Why not a lager, or a cider?"
"Because with cider you go all wonky and when you sneeze you accidentally shit yourself, and lager makes me burp foam like a fire extinguisher. Bitter, please."
"Huh. Anything else?"
"Yeah, do they do scratchings?"
"Ooh, pig bits! Good call! I'll get two bags."
"Nice one."
J-Dogg went to the bar.
He's my favourite bloke to go to the pub with.
We talk lots of shit.
What's your favourite dinosaur.
Which is the hardest brand of crisp.
Which cartoon character would you most like to fuck.
You know the sort of thing.
I love pubs.
No surprise there.
Pubs are where the beer is, but I also like pub goers.
You get characters in pubs, you don't get them in bars.
In bars, people want to be noticed.
In pubs, people want to be left alone.
The bloke next to J-Dogg at the bar was alone.
He wasn't in the pub to find friends.
He was there to drink.
He was steadily sinking the pints and staring at the telly flickering in the corner.
I accidentally caught his eye.
I looked away.

Bit creepy, if I'm honest.
A packet of pork scratchings hit me in the face.
"Ow."
J-Dogg was back with the goods.
"Beer! pig bits! Sundry shit! Tuck in, motherfucker."
"Cheers, J-Dogg. Hey, check out the Vietnam vet at the bar. He's got the scariest thousand yard stare you've ever seen!"
"Huh? Oh, him! That's Tommo. He's harmless, but he's all fucked up."
"Fucked up? In what way?"
J-Dogg giggled and lowered his voice.
"I went to school with Tommo. He wasn't the brightest of kids. When we were fifteen we all got sent to different places on work experience..."
"Where did you go?"
"I got work experience as a sparky. That's why I'm a sparky. Anyway, that's not important. Tommo got work experience at a welding shop. When I came back from working with the sparky, I was dead keen to become a sparky. When Tommo came back from the welders, he was dead quiet."
I looked across at the bloke at the bar.
He'd killed another pint and was ordering more.
Same dead expression.
J-Dogg kept talking.
"Well, one lunchtime he just came up to me, said he had to tell someone and that he wanted to tell me, 'cause we were friends."
"Were you friends?"
"Nah, but I took piss out of Tommo less than the other lads, so I suppose that might have made me a friend in his eyes. Anyway, he gushes out his story. He'd gone to that welding shop on work experience. They all worked on these long benches, welding shit all day. At lunch everyone fucked off to the pub, but Tommo didn't have any money so he ate his packed lunch at the bench. One of the welders had a packed lunch too. Tommo said this welder was a big biker, shaved head, tattoos, beard, but he was friendly enough. He got chatting to Tommo about this and that, and Tommo told him that he was in the scouts. The biker starts going on about how scouts can tie knots, but that there wasn't a knot he couldn't escape from. The

biker gets Tommo to tie his hands, and in a flash he was free! Tommo tied him again, with a really complicated knot this time, but the biker got loose just as fast. Tommo asked him how it was done, so the biker offered to show him. He ties Tommo's hands, and then ties his wrists to his ankles. Tommo realises he can't get free, and in his own words, 'I struggled, but he pulled down my trousers and pants, and before I knew it, he were inside me!"
I choked on my beer.
"Fucking Hell! The biker bummed him?"
"Not so loud! Yeah, he bummed the shit out of him. Right there in the welding shop. When he finished he let Tommo go, but said he'd find him and kill him if he said anything."
"Poor bastard! He told you all this?"
"Yeah. He were snivelling and blubbing as he told me. Said that I was the only person that knew. He said that he had to tell somebody, get it off his chest, like."
"No bloody wonder. What did you do?"
J-Dogg took a long pull on his pint.
"I told every fucker in the school what had happened. I couldn't help it! A story like that is too juicy to keep to yourself!"
"You rotten fucker."
"Fuck off, Lucifer! It's not my fault he went and got bummed! If anyone's to blame he ought to blame himself!"
"How's that work then? He's the victim in all this."
"Bollocks. He shouldn't have been so fucking stupid as to let some hairy arsed Hell's Angel tie him up with his ringpiece pointing to the heavens. You let a bloke do that to you, then you deserve everything you get."
"A good hard arse raping? He deserved it? Look at him! That bloke at the bar is a fucking wreck!"
We looked at Tommo.
He was blank faced, his eyes were blood shot, he was unshaven.
A sudden look of horror flashed across his face.
"Shit," muttered J-Dogg, "Drink up, Lucifer. We're off to the next pub."
"What's happening? What's up with him?"
J-Dogg nodded at the television, where Tommo was staring with growing horror.

234

A show was just starting.
It was the Hairy Bikers Cookbook.
"Christ, let's get out of here before he goes into melt down!"
We left our beers and hurried outside, grateful for the wind and rain. Anything was better than the sound of a bloke alone in a pub, sobbing into his pint.

Puppet on a Thing

It's never easy being the new boy.
Even the most civilised office space can feel daunting to the fresh meat.
Factories are another level again.
They can be seriously scary.
When customers are given the guided tour of the print works, they huddle close to the sales rep, pale and frightened.
It's like they are on a grim urban safari, and the rep is the only one packing heat.
Feral beasts lurk behind greasy machines, ready to pounce.
The deafening chatter of the presses echo from the grimy walls like the mocking cries of mindless apes.
The rotting stink of overflowing bins assails delicate nostrils.
A primal cry floats above the industrial din, a territorial howl from a mad eyed alpha, challenging the suited intruders.
"Here! You cunts! Suck us off!"
The rep hurriedly ushers the shocked suits to the safety of the offices where refreshment is offered. Frayed nerves are soothed with tea and biscuits. Heavy blinds screen the horror.
They've seen enough of the wild.
For some of us though, the wild is our new home.
For those of us without qualifications or a university education, it is where we are sent.
We must face the feral beasts.
We must fearlessly defy the cries of the mindless apes.
We must make cups of tea for the howling, mad eyed alpha.
Like Max in the land of the Wild Things, the screaming, shrieking, gibbering fiends become your friends.
Kind of.
-
It took a while to find my feet in the wild.
There were plenty of journeys home on the bus spent in shocked silence.
Lot's of creeping around, avoiding others, reluctant to be their sport.

Painful balls from inky maulings by the coffee machine.
Disappointment at finding myself in such a shit hole.
You get used to it.
-
I'd thought I'd seen it all until I met Mule.
Mule was fucking enormous.
He must have been six feet seven, easily twenty two stone.
Big black moustache nestled under his nose.
I was bustling on my way somewhere, and he stepped out from behind a machine.
I froze.
He grinned.
"Erm... hello."
Mule kept grinning.
"You're new, aren't you?"
"Yeah."
"It's Lucifer, isn't it?"
"Yeah."
"I'm Mule. Have you met my friend?"
"Don't think so..."
This giant slowly pulls his arm out from behind his back.
He's wearing a glove puppet.
I quietly start to freak out.
"W..what's that?"
He thrusts the puppet at me.
"Hello there, Luci-her! Hy nay is Garnagy!"
"What? What are you saying?"
"Garnagy! Hy nay is Garnagy!"
"What? I.. I don't understand! Garnagy?"
Mule loses his temper.
"Are you stupid or something? His name is Barnaby! He wants to be your friend!"
I wanted to go home.
"Look, I'm a bit busy, I've got to..."
"Shake his hand."
"What?"
Shake Barnaby's hand. Be his friend."
One of Mule's big, fat sausage fingers poke out from the puppets

clothes, and started to waggle at me.
"Shake his hand, Lucifer."
The finger was dirty.
"Shake it."
I didn't want to.
"I said shake Barnaby's hand."
I slowly raised my hand.
I heard a loud rumbling approaching.
We use pallet trucks to move heavy loads around the factory. They basically look like giant orange scooters, and people use them to travel around on. You're not meant to, but that didn't change anything.
Taters came hurtling by on a pallet truck.
Taters was the sort of bloke who didn't have a particular job, but seemed to be doing something new each day.
His main task was to needle Mule.
He was legendary.
"Hey, Lucifer, don't shake that puppet's hand! It smells of kid's arseholes!"
He thundered away.
I quickly dropped my hand.
Mule turned purple.
"You foul mouthed fucker, Taters! It's not true! I've never done that! Never! NEVER!!"
I ran off.
-
Taters lounged at the coffee machine, leaning on his pallet truck like it was a Harley.
"Yeah, you want to avoid that gimp Mule, Lucifer. He does a lot of caravaning, and belief me, he get's thrown off sites all over England for scaring kids with Garnagy. It's just not normal."
"He really freaked me out, Taters. God only knows what a little kid would make of it."
"Mule reckons he used to be in the Navy before he came here. We reckon he was really in jail. We reckon he's a nonce."
"I reckon you could be right. Look out! Here he comes!"
Mule was lumbering towards the coffee machine.
Taters climbed aboard his pallet truck and rolled out.

"Hey, Mule! Where's Garnagy? I heard he's been hanging out in the toilets offering handjobs to the lads!"
"Fuck you, Taters! Wait till I get hold of you! I'll..."
"Wank me off? Keep that puppet away from me, you rapist!"
Mule was foaming at the mouth.
I left, quickly.

-

Scrawled in pen on the toilet door:
"What do you call Garnagy in a gimp suit?"
"Marigold!"
It was scribbled out the next day.

-

The Mule bating went on all week.
On the Monday, Taters didn't show for work.
Neither did Mule.
Or Barnaby.
I heard what happened later in the day.
Taters was cycling home on Friday night.
Mule followed him in his 4x4.
On a bad roundabout, Mule made his move.
He ran Taters over, knocking him to the pavement.
Then Mule got out of his car, walked over to Taters, and beat the living crap out of him, right there at the roadside.
He used Barnaby as a boxing glove.
It was a toss up to decide who was the most battered afterwards.
Taters or Barnaby.
Barnaby ended up in the washing machine.
Taters ended up in traction.

-

I was fetching coffees again when I next saw Taters.
His orange pallet truck wasn't moving so fast, probably because of the whiplash collar round Taters neck.
And the pot on his leg.
"Hey Taters! I heard about what happened. You look like shit."
"Thanks for that, Lucifer. I'm not too fussed, to be honest. Don't get me wrong, it didn't tickle at the time, but I won't be cycling to work anymore."
"How come? Have you got permanent injuries?"

"Nah. I sued Mule for assault, and got ten thousand in compensation. He got a criminal records and a suspended sentence. I've got a nice shiny Ford Escort in the car park. I'm sorted!"
"Fucking Hell. Good work, Taters. Did Mule get the boot?"
"They couldn't do nowt, cause he waited till he was off company property before he twatted me. They've warned him to keep away from me, though."
"I'm not sure that'll stop him, Taters. Here he comes!"
Taters whinced a bit as he got on his truck and rumbled away behind a print press.
Mule collared me before I could get away.
"Hello Lucifer. You never did get to meet Barnaby, did you?"
I gulped.
"No, I never got the pleasure, Mule."
The puppet came out from behind his back.
It was missing any eye, and faint stains covered it's head.
Some things never wash out.
"Shake Barnaby's hand, Lucifer."
"I'd rather not..."
"Go on, shake it."
"The finger poked out."
I reached up...
A shout came from the other side of the print press.
"Don't shake that thing, Lucifer! It's not Garnagy's hand! It's his cock, and it smells of cub scouts!"
The pallet truck rumbled.
Mule bellowed.
I dropped the coffees and ran.
-
Like Max in the land of the Wild Things, the screaming, shrieking, gibbering fiends become your friends.
Whether you like it or not.

A Doffer you can't Refuse...

Tuesday, wrote Mister Kipling, was really fucking boring.
I'd been up since five.
At work for six.
Started doing some work at seven fifty five.
Now it was ten.
I'd had four cups of tea, one bacon sandwich, a walk around the factory, about two hundred yawns and one dump.
In the toilet I read the paper.
It was The Sun.
Not my choice.
It was on the cistern when I went in there.
There was a bloody thumb print on page five. How?
Someone had drawn a moustache on Sam Fox and coloured in her nipples. Why?
I washed my hands very, very thoroughly.
Now it was five past ten.
I wished something interesting would happen, like Soulless Boss having a heart attack or that account executive with the big knockers letting me look down her top again.
No such luck.
Instead, the phone started ringing.
"Lucifer! It's for you."
Me?
I never got calls.
They frowned on personal calls at work.
Soulless Boss was frowning.
I took the call.
"Hello?"
"Aye up, you cunt, Lucifer!!"
Oh no.
It was Denny.
Denny's one of my mates from where I live. Great bloke, bit odd, does some strange things.
"Who was that stuffy cunt who answered the phone?" He guffawed

deafeningly.
Loud enough for Soulless Boss to hear.
He scowled at me.
I ignored him.
"No-one, Denny. Listen, what do you want? I'm a bit busy, and..."
"Hahahaha! You? Busy? Don't make me fucking laugh! The only thing you're busy doing is wanking in the bogs!"
Soulless Boss growled.
"Ha. Ha. Yeah, look, what do you want, Denny?"
"I want you, outside work, Friday lunchtime. I'll pick you up."
"Why? Where are we going?"
"The doffers!"
"Oh God..."

A doffer is like a stripper, only more bored and knackered looking.
Doffers do the pub circuit, dropping their shabby knickers in tatty boozers and using stinking Ladies toilets as changing rooms.
Sometimes they accidentally drag their fleabitten feather boas through puddles of piss from the leaky bogs.
If you feel something splash your face in the middle of her creaky gyrations, you know what it is.
Quite often the doffer is a prostitute as well.
Half an hour after she's shaken her spotty arse on stage she's down a dark alley, sucking off a taxi driver.
It's bad enough going to these places after a skinful of ale, but on a Friday lunchtime they can be downright depressing.
The most notorious was the Belle Vue.
It lurked on the edge of Bradford's red light district.
This is where Denny wanted to go.
-
He phoned again on the Wednesday.
Soulless Boss was starting to lose his rag.
"You're coming with me, aren't you Lucifer? Say you're coming."
"Look, I'll be there, Denny, alright? Just stop phoning me at work."
"Why? Is that stuffy cunt giving you shit again? OI! STUFFY CUNT! STOP GIV.."
I hung up.

Soulless Boss had turned purple.
I scuttled back to my desk.

Denny phoned again on Thursday.
Soulless Boss had an argument with him.
Then hung up.
"Lucifer!"
"Yes, Soulless boss?"
That arsehole has called for you again. Tell him if he rings again, you're getting the sack."
"I can't tell him that."
"Why the fuck not?"
"You've hung up on him."
"Oh, fuck off, Lucifer."

Friday.
D-day.
D for Denny.
If I'm honest, my heart really wasn't in it.
It was a nice sunny day outside.
Not the sort of day you wanted to spend in a stinking pub drinking watered beer, inspecting a doffer's stretch marks.
Twelve o'clock arrived.
So did Denny.
He parked his crappy Saxo outside the studio and leaned on the horn until I rushed out.
"What the fuck are you doing?"
"All aboard the doffer express! You ready, Lucifer?"
"Yeah, suppose so."
"Oh, cheer up, you miserable cunt! We're on our way to paradise!"
He burned rubber out of the car park, Bradford bound...
-
"Make sure you lock your car, Denny."
"Ok, ok. Let's go!"
We walked into the pub.
Sunlight oozed through the cracks in the heavy, dusty curtains, drawn to stop people in the street seeing the girl on the rickety stage.
The music was distorted by the cheap speakers, music that was

meant to be sexy, but sounded more like the soundtrack to a slasher movie.

We squinted in the gloom, in the thick smoke.

Single men perused newspapers, ready to feign surprise when a naked girl tottered onto the stage.

Oh! What's happening? I didn't realise it was THAT kind of pub! Well, as I'm here...

Etc.

I went to the bar.

It was my round.

With Denny, it was never his round first.

What you having Denny?"

A pint and one of those pork pies."

"What? A pork pie?"

"Yeah! They're fucking awesome!"

"No they're not. They're covered in fly shit!"

"Fuck off and get me a pie, Lucifer."

"Your funeral..."

As I was getting served a voice blasted over the speakers.

"And now, gentlemen, please put your hands together and give a warm Belle Vue welcome to..... Tricksie!"

Sporadic applause.

Half-arsed wolf whistles.

Work boots stamped by blokes holding pints.

The rustle of hurriedly folded newspapers.

The toilet door opened and a girl hurried out.

Her feather boa looked soggy.

I tried to indicate for Denny to get a table further from the stage, but he didn't notice.

Oh well.

I carried the drinks to the table.

"Here's your pie, here's your pint."

"Fucking awesome! Come to daddy!"

He took a quick swig of beer and sunk his teeth into the pie.

His eyes closed in ecstasy.

"Mmmm...magic!"

The girl on the stage wasn't too bad, to be honest.

Mid twenties, blonde, big tits.

As I'd paid my fifty pence entrance fee, I decided to get my monies worth.
Within ten seconds of mounting the stage she was naked.
Her clobber seemed to just fly off.
She'd dropped the boa, thank God.
I put down the newspaper I'd pilfered from the next table to deflect any piss that came our way.
Denny had his back to the stage, his gob full of pork pie.
The girl on the stage noticed he had his back to her.
She slithered across to us, leant down, and blew seductively in Denny's ear.
He turned around and saw her.
"Fuck off, love."
He spoke with a mouthful of pie, so greasy crumbs sprayed her face and stuck in her hair.
She fell backwards with a look of horror, before quickly regaining her composure.
She decided to shake her tits at the punters on the other side of the stage.
I was baffled.
"Why did you say that to her, you mad twat? You've been nagging me to come here for three days, and now we're here you're telling the girl to fuck off!"
"What, her? I'm not fussed about seeing them slags. I'm only here for the pies. They're fucking magic. Why don't you try one?"
"What? Why don't you fuck off..."

Good Lost Cause.

Bored.
I'm never bored when I've nothing to do.
I can always think of something.
No, I'm bored when I'm given something boring to do.
Such as work.
Reprographics is boring.
Really, really boring.
When someone asks me what I do for a job, I start yawning before I can even answer.
When I'm at work, I yearn for something interesting to happen.
Like a jet plane crashing into the building, or a disgruntled employee going postal with an assault rifle.
Screams, gunshots, shattering glass.
Anything to break the tedium.
-
Bored.
I'm at work, looking at a direct mail job with eyes that refuse to focus.
It's as though my body refuses to acknowledge the awesome crappiness of the job.
Cup of tea?
Just had one.
If I have another I'll piss myself, and I can't go to the toilet because it's 10.30 and the bog wanker will be in there, yanking himself daft.
I want something to break the tedium.
Nothing.
Nothing.
The door flies open.
Something!
It's Soulless Boss.
He's flustered.
"Incoming!"
"No!"
"Yes!"

"Shit!"
He hides in the store room.
I duck under the desk.
I wanted something to happen, but not this.
I wait.
It's really shitty under my desk.
The gritty linoleum is strewn with grey patch cables and power leads.
These act as dust traps, gathering lint and an alarming abundance of what looks like pubic hair.
Silverfish scuttle about their business.
Massive spiders lurk in the corners.
A millipede is nibbling desiccated orange peel.
How the fuck did it get under my desk?
It really needs a clean, but the cleaner won't do it.
Not after I called him a fucking cunt.
My working environment gradually went downhill after that little conversation, I can tell you.
It smells of old cuppa-soups and despair.
I'm not coming out though.
I remain perfectly still.
I hear the door.
I hold my breath.
High heels click across the floor.
I wish that they would just fuck off.
Eyes squeezed shut.
Go away.
Go away.
Go...
"LUCIFER!"
bang
"Shit the bed! Owwww!"
I open my eyes.
Fat feet spilling out of tight shoes. Fat ankles. Fat legs.
I look up.
Fat face.
"Aw. Did you bang your head, Lucifer?"
"Yes, Dimples. I banged my head."

"Aw. Are you crying?"
No. My eyes are watering, but I'm not crying."
"Why are your eyes watering?"
"Because I banged my fucking head!"
"Language!"
"Huh. What do you want."
I know what she wants.
She wants money.
Dimples always carries a bulging manila envelope and a paper bag with a card in it.
She's always collecting for someone.
I fucking hate putting money into collections.
Births, birthdays, weddings, leaving-do's, retirements.
Dimples waddles from department to department, filling her envelope with the cash of her begrudging victims with an irritating, mindless giggle and a brainwashed, buck-toothed smile.
If ever there was an argument for releasing Peter Sutcliffe early, it's Dimples.
She thrusts the envelope under my nose.
"Collection for Daisy!"
"Daisy? Why should I give money for her?"
"She's having a baby!"
"What? Another? She must have about five kids already! She's only just back off maternity leave, isn't she?"
"Yes, but she's pregnant again!"
"Jesus. She wants to get her tubes tied, she does."
"Nothing wrong with big families, Lucifer! She loves kids!"
"She loves cock, more like. Anyway, what about all the crap we bought for the other kids? She'll have more gear than Mothercare by now!"
Dimples tuts.
It makes her look like a squirrel with a thyroid problem.
"It's an expensive affair raising a family, Lucifer. You should know."
"I do know. And it's even more expensive when I'm supporting Daisy the cow and her bloody herd as well. All she wants is to park her barge arse on the couch in front of Jeremy Kyle all day while the kids run riot. Work's an inconvenience to her. No, I'm not paying this time, Dimples. She's had her lot from me."

She looks shocked.
"You're a nasty man, Lucifer! Having a lickle baby is a wonderful thing, but you make it sound so... so..."
"Cynical? Yes. I've got a tenner in my wallet and it's got to last me the week. I'm not blowing it on some lazy cow who's legs are permanently bowed from all the men going in and the babies coming out. If that's everything, Dimples, I'll get back to work."
She tries to give me a hard stare.
She looks like a Care Bear pushing out a fart.
"Bastard!"
"No, I'm a realist. You office staff are always collecting for this or that! You don't get us shop floor lads sniffing around the offices because one of us has got his wife up the stick! You get paid more than us as well!"
The door bangs shut.
Dimples has gone.
I dust the pubes and insects from my jeans and sit down.
Monitor.
Keyboard.
Key.
Bored.
Sigh.
Soulless Boss slithers out of the store room, checks the coast is clear, and heads out of the door.
Thirty seconds later he shoots back in.
"Incoming!"
He's back in the store room.
Fuck.
I look under the desk.
Don't fancy getting under there again.
I decide to brazen it out.
The door opens.
In walks Buster.
He's a printer, covered in crap and ink.
He's carrying an inky manila envelope and a bag with a grubby card in it.
"Doing a collection, Lucifer. You wanna put in?"
"Depends, Buster. Who's it for? We don't normally collect on the

shop floor."
"It's for Superdad."
"Shit, what's he done now? He can't be expecting another kid, because his wife has fucked off, hasn't she?"
"Yeah, took off with the nipper last year. That's when he got into all that 'Father's for Justice' shit. Dressing like Superman. Drinking on his own."
"Hmm. So why are you collecting for him?"
"He's dead."
"What? Dead? Fucking hell! When did he die?"
"Last weekend, they reckon."
"How did he die?"
"Well, it was his little lad's birthday, so he organises this party for him in the garden, with a big bouncy castle and everything. The blokes had a hell of a job getting it into his back garden, by all accounts. It was wedged in tight when it was fully inflated.
"Well he waits for his lad to turn up but he doesn't show. He rings his ex-wife, but she tells him it's not his weekend to have custody. What with all the drinking, Superdad has got his dates mixed up. He takes the news pretty bad. Puts on his Superman costume and gets shit faced. When he's good and drunk he goes out into the garden and starts jumping on the bouncy castle. The neighbours can see him bouncing about all over the place, cape flapping about, making a right racket. They threatened to call the police, but he just told them to fuck off.
"After a bit he gets knackered from all the bouncing and he falls asleep. Everyone's glad of the peace and quiet. What they didn't know is that the bouncy castle had sprung a leak against a nail in his fence and it deflated while Superdad was asleep inside it. He suffocated to death."
"No!"
"Yeah."
I shake my head.
"That is a really shitty way to go. Suffocated in a bouncy castle wearing a superman outfit."
"Yeah. It's not high on my list of ways to die either. Thing is, it was really warm that week. The blokes came to take it away and as no-one answered the door they just rolled up the deflated castle and

carried it off with him inside. Didn't know he was there."
"Shit!"
"Yeah. Stuck it in a hot storage unit all week, and didn't get it out again till the weekend after. By then he'd turned to soup."
"That's pretty grim. Poor Superdad. Are you collecting for his funeral then? Flowers and stuff?"
"Not really. We want to buy the bouncy castle and have it burnt. The mercenary fuckers who own it want to just hose it off, patch it up and rent it out again. Didn't seem right, really."
"God no. You'd never get the smell out of it. And to think of kids bouncing about all over where Superdad died..."
We both shudder.
I take out my wallet, pull out the tenner.
"Here you go, Buster."
"Ta Lucifer. I don't like to tap the lads for cash, but it's a good cause."
"I don't mind this once. It's not like he's going to be doing it again, is it? Tell you what. Why don't you go collecting round the offices. They're always keen on giving to a good cause. Start with Dimples. Tell her I sent you."
"I'll do that. Cheers Lucifer."
"No problem, Buster."

Do You Like Sausages?

I used to work with a plate maker called Weasel.
He was really strange.
He lived in Leeds but had a fetish for York, for some reason.
He used to have the York papers saved for him at WH Smiths in Leeds station, and he'd go collect them on a Friday.
When York City Football team were in financial trouble he gave them £3000.
He's on ordinary Yorkshire wages, but gave his team £3000.
After that, they let him go to away games on the team bus.
I'm not lying.
Anyway, I'd decided to go for a day trip to York on the coming weekend, so I mentioned it to Weasel.
'I'm up your neck of the woods on Saturday, Weasel!"
"Are you?"
Yes, me and my girlfriend are off to York!"
"Do you like sausages?"
"?"
"I said, do you like sausages?"
"Err.... I suppose so, yes."
"Right! I'll tell you where there's a great butcher in York. His sausages are ace."
"Well.. we're not really going shopping for meat..."
"Whatever. Do you know Smith Street?"
Not really Weasel. I don't know York."
"Ok. Well, you know opposite Wellington Lane? The Black Swan on Wellington Lane?"
"Erm, no, I don't really..."
"ok, ok. Well, you know the Shambles?
"Kind of..."
"Good! Opposite there is Peach Street, well you go along there, take the third left next to the undertakers, keep going to the end..."
"I'm not really sure.."
"AT THE END you take a right, past The Victoria pub, the one that's just re-opened, and just down there, next to grocers, you'll find the

butchers. Best sausages in York."
"Well, thanks Weasel. Thanks."
"Are you going to get some sausages then?"
"Yeah, I suppose..."

We had a top time in York, saw all the good stuff, went to the Jorvik museum, had a pub lunch, loads of beers, saw the Minster, went down the Shambles, the lot.
Really good time.

Next Monday, I'm walking through the platemaking department.
"Hey, Lucifer!"
"Hi Weasel. How you doing?"
"Never mind. Did you get to York on Saturday?"
"Yes! It was great! We went to the Jorvik museum, saw the Shambles, had a great pub lunch..."
"Yeah, yeah yeah. Did you get any sausages?"
"Well, no... I.."
"Fuck you, FUCK YOU!! For fuck's sake, just FUCK OFF, LUCIFER!! I don't know why I fucking bother, you fucker..."
"Ok. Bye then."

A Shadow of his Former Self.

ring ring
"Hello? No, Cheryl, I've not got time to see him. He's in reception? I don't care if he's in bed with the wife, I haven't got time."
ring ring
"Hello. Look, the office furniture is being delivered on Thursday, I told you that. I realise he hasn't got a chair, but that's because he broke it. You know why he broke it? Because he's such a fat cunt. Tell him he can sit down on Thursday."
ring ring
"What is it!? No, I can't come and take a look at the air conditioning. It's too cold? The rest of the factory is sweating like Michael Barrymore at a pool party and you say you're too cold? Put a fucking jumper on then. No-one wants to see your tits anyway. Oh, stop crying!"
ring ring
"Grrr. The canteens on fire? How many people are in the queue? Ten? Well you can bet that if they're in the canteen at this time they're a bunch of piss-takers. Ask them to give a little back, and piss on the fire. It might improve the taste of your God-awful cooking. Shit! Was that an explosion? Hello? Look, there's a fire extinguisher by the door, I'll send someone up in an hour or so to asses the damage."
ring ring
"Oh, fuck off, will you?"
Bear was trying to get some work done.
He wasn't getting very far.
The Maintenance Department was bit like the 999 switchboard.
For some reason, many workers in a factory are utterly incapable of sorting out the slightest problem for themselves.
Bins not emptied?
Ring maintenance.
Bulb blown in the toilet?
Ring maintenance.
Eek! Spider!

Ring maintenance.

In between sorting out the mundane, tedious crap handed down from feckless, dull-witted office workers and mentally sub-normal factory folk, Bear had to organize larger projects, such as machine installation, building extensions and redecorating.

Right then, he was trying to plan the refit of the board room.

It was God's little pet project.

God owned the factory.

God paid the wages.

God called the shots.

Bear did as God asked.

Furniture, walnut.

Carpets, burgundy.

Walls, pale ivory.

Lighting, soft.

Everything was on order, the work would start at the weekend.

Bear frowned.

Something was wrong.

The phone had stopped ringing.

He shivered.

He didn't usually feel the cold, but the temperature in the room had dipped.

His hackles raised.

"Hello Bear."

"Fucking hell!"

The Shadow sat in the chair on the other side of his desk.

The Shadow was on the board of directors.

He was a nasty, cold-hearted fucker.

Think the bastard love child of Peter Mandleson and Joseph Goebbels.

Bear waited until the pain in his chest subsided before he spoke.

"Don't... don't sneak up like that."

"I didn't sneak anywhere. You were busy when I walked in. You simply didn't notice."

He was playing with the phone lead.

It had been removed from the back of Bear's phone.

Bear growled.

"Don't fuck with my things, Shadow. I don't like it!"

The Shadow laughed.
It sounded like sandpaper on a coffin lid.
"No need to be aggressive, Bear. It doesn't wash with me. I'll get to the point. I hear you are re-decorating the board room."
"That's right. We start work on Saturday. Everything's ordered."
The Shadow's fingers crept inquisitively across the desk, stroking a pen, picking up a paperweight, fondling a broken machine part. His eyes never left Bear, never blinked.
"Saturday? Excellent, excellent! I might have a little drive over, see how you things progress. I look forward to seeing the walls in a lovely shade of Soft Truffle."
"Pale Ivory. The walls are going to be in Pale Ivory."
"Hmm? Oh, I'm sure Soft Truffle would be a much wiser choice."
"God wants Pale Ivory. God's going to get Pale Ivory."
The Shadow laughed, shaking his head.
Cracking sounds came from the pen in Bear's fist. He glowered.
"Come now, Bear, God won't notice. I'd like it to be in Soft Truffle. Won't you do that for me?"
Bear snatched a note pad from The Shadows roving fingers.
"Pale Ivory."
The Shadow leant forward, staring intently at Bear, a whiff of menace drifting across the desk.
"Soft Truffle, I think. You'd be wise to change your mind, Bear. We are debating departmental budgets this week in the Board Meeting. Yours is under very close scrutiny. Very close scrutiny indeed. We wonder if you might be able to run a tighter ship in here, with a more... frugal crew, perhaps."
Bear's chair scraped across the concrete floor as he began to rise, the pen finally splintering in his grip.
"You snivelling..."
"Tut tut, Bear. Let's not resort to name calling! Why don't we just say that Soft Truffle is the colour for the boardroom, and leave it at that? Perhaps you'll order a little extra, just in case. Let's say, four tins? Mrs Shadow is fancying a change in the dining room, and Soft Truffle would go wonderfully with our new dining table. You keep your budget, I get my paint. Understand?"
Bear slowly lowered himself into his chair. Shards of shattered pen fell from his hand. He didn't speak, only nodded.

"Excellent! I'll be here at ten thirty sharp on Saturday morning. Have that paint ready, won't you?"
The Shadow clicked the lead into the back of Bears phone.
It instantly began to ring.
Bear glanced down at it, but when he looked up, The Shadow had gone.
ring ring
ring ring
ring ring
-
Saturday morning.
Bear was at his desk.
The phone was silent.
That was the only good thing about working Saturday mornings.
A quiet phone.
Even without looking up from his work, Bear knew that The Shadow had entered the room.
"Good morning, Bear!"
"It was. You'll be wanting your paint, then."
"How perceptive of you! Soft Truffle, I trust?"
"Soft Truffle. Are you parked out front?"
"No, round the side. Thought it better to be... discreet."
"I'll send someone out with the tins. Wait in the car."
"Will do. Thanks so very, Bear. Sorry for any... misunderstanding over the colour. I do hope this will not spoil our excellent working relationship?"
"I'll send someone out with the tins, Shadow."
"Of course, of course. See you on Monday!"
Bear watched him leave, then called for Jock.
"Jock. The Shadow's parked round back. A black Jag. Do me a favour and put these tins of paint in his boot."
"Will do, Bear."
Jock picked up the tins, turned to leave.
"Oh, and Jock?"
"Yeah?"
Bear slapped a large screwdriver onto the desk.
"Make sure the lids are down nice and tight. Wouldn't want them coming loose in the car, would we?"

Jock slipped the screwdriver into the pocket of his overalls and winked.
"That would be terrible, Bear. I'll be extra careful."

-

The car boot slammed.
Jock walked around to the driver's side window.
"All safely stowed away, Mister S. Nice car, this. Is it yours, or the companies?"
"It's the companies, so get your hands of the fucking paintwork, you ape!"
The Shadow stamped on the accelerator and roared out of the car park.
Jock shielded his eyes from flying gravel.
"Might want to take it steady, Mister S," he murmured. "Don't want that paint falling over, do we?"

-

Monday.
Bear was working.
Answering phones.
Shouting at people.
Jabbing a keyboard.
The Shadow burst in.
No sinister materialisations today.
He looked desperate.
"Bear! I need your help. That paint you gave me. It's all over the car boot!"
"That's where I said I'd put it. In the car boot."
"No! I mean the tins fell over on my way home! I've got twenty litres of Soft fucking Truffle swimming about in the back of my fucking car!! The stupid monkey who put them there can't have secured them properly!"
"Well he tells me he stowed them very securely, Shadow. He also said you drove out of the car park like a fucking maniac."
The Shadow squirmed.
"Yes, whatever. Look, it's a company car. The interior is fucked. I don't know what to do! If God sees the paint in the boot he'll know what we've been up to! He'll string us both up for taking company property and for ruining a company car!"

Bear shook his head.
"Don't know about this 'we' business, Shadow. I had to send Jock to the wholesalers on Saturday morning to buy twenty litres of Soft Truffle because four tins had mysteriously gone missing. Here's the receipt."
Bear waved it in the air.
The colour leeched from The Shadow's face.
He tried to snatch the receipt.
He failed.
He turned to leave.
"Wait."
Bear leant across the desk.
"I'll help you out, Shadow. Just this once."
The Shadow turned back. He looked desperate.
"Thank you, Bear! I'll make it up to you."
"Whatever. Listen. The garages are empty today. Take your car round and park it inside. Close the door. There are some overalls in that cupboard."
He pulled a large plastic container out from beneath the desk.
"This stuff is called Varn. It's roller cleaner. It's designed to get shit off shit. It'll clean your boot, but you'll have to scrub it hard. Got it?"
"Got it. I don't suppose you've got anyone free who might..."
"Shadow. Don't take the piss, ok? Get your fucking car round to the garage, pronto, before I change my mind."
"Yes, Bear. Sorry, Bear. Oh, and thank you, Bear!"
"Whatever."
Bear carried on working.
The Shadow disappeared.
-
An hour went by, then another.
Bear looked at his watch.
He called for Jock.
"What is it, Bear?"
"Get a wheelbarrow, Jock. You'll find The Shadow unconscious in the garage."
"Unconscious? How come?"
"Because he's been shut in there for two hours scrubbing paint out of his boot with Varn, that's how come. The fumes will have fucked

him."
Jock started giggling.
"He's going to have one fuck of a headache! Where do you want me to dump him?"
"In the board room. With this."
He passed Jock an empty vodka bottle.
Jock's eyes widened.
"Fuck!"
"That'll teach the cunt to threaten me. Keep it to yourself, Jock, and keep your weekends free. I've got lots of overtime for you. Got it?"
Jock liked overtime. Overtime was big money to him.
"Got it."
He left.
Bear went back to work.
An hour later he checked his watch again.
Yep.
God said he'd be taking a tour of the newly decorated boardroom about now.
Bear smiled.
ring ring
"Good morning, this is Bear speaking. How can I help you today?"

Dead Head

Morning, barely light, I wandered across the car park from school to church.

Black Clarke's shoes, scuffed toes crunching through early frost, cold wind slithering up half mast hand me downs, cutting thin legs.

I was alone.

Alter boys weren't supposed to unlock the church alone, but no-one else would come.

When I think about the reasons why we weren't meant to be in church alone, what happened to a lot of other catholic alter boys in the seventies and eighties, caught in a church alone, it makes me shudder.

Through the gate, along the mossy wall, picking off petrified lumps of fuzzy green with bitten fingernails, humming the themes to last night's telly.

I unlocked the vast sacristy door of black oak and black iron with a black key the size of my white scrawny forearm.

The door swung open like the gob of Jonah's whale, it's breath heavy with stale incense and alter wine, my own breath billowing in the frigid musty air.

I hurried inside and closed the door with a mouldy thud.

Crossed red threadbare carpet, pulled back a curtain of heavy velvet on a shiny brass rail, picked out vestments in my size.

Small.

Black cassock with a hundred black buttons and a big white tablecloth over the top.

At other schools you'd have been lynched for wearing clobber like that, but us Catholic kids didn't know any better.

We thought everyone did that.

Didn't know it was odd.

I wasn't an altar boy because I believed God or Jesus or Mary.

I became an altar boy for the same two reasons every other altar boy became an altar boy:

Because you got out of ordinary school lessons for a couple of mornings a week.

Because the families of dead people sometimes coughed up hard cash if you looked particularly angelic during funerals.

Sloth and Greed.

Two of the seven deadly sins right there, and I wasn't even ten years old.

What hope did I have?

With penguin robes in place I fetched tapers, matches, another big key.

I unlocked the door leading to the church.

Dry crypt air billowed from the dark chasm beyond.

I stepped into that darkness.

Rows after row of pews glazed in dark toffee varnish were on my left, but I didn't look at them.

I kept my eyes right.

On the altar.

This wasn't out of reverence.

It was because I didn't want to look at what lurked between the pews.

Not yet.

I climbed the steps to the altar, to the place where I was supposed to kneel

I didn't kneel.

I never did when I was on my own.

For a greedy sloth, failing to kneel was a minor digression.

With the matches and the tapers I lit the huge candles on the altar.

I let them burn for a minute, then slowly tipped one of the candles until the glowing wax dribbled onto my fingers.

It was something I had done countless times before, but the shock of the hot wax hitting my skin never failed to thrill me.

It didn't burn.

I knew it wouldn't.

It cooled quickly, leaving a heavy shell of wax on each finger in turn, until all my fingers were covered in a numb, warm shell.

As I looked up at the craggy features of a giant stone Jesus I gently clacked each waxy finger against my waxy thumb, one, two three, four, one, two, three, four...

The instant urge was to pick the wax off, feel the warm shell tearing delicately, deliciously from my skin.

I resisted.

I turned away from Stone Jesus, and tapping my fingers, walked down the steps away from the altar, keeping my head down.

Averting my gaze, not from the religious icons, but from the dark pews and what lay between.

At the bottom of the steps I turned and looked up.

The candles had failed to illuminate the grey church but the darkness had changed.

The gloom moved with the flickering flames, like ripples after a half brick is tossed into a polluted pond.

I stood at the front of the church, bottom of the steps, right before the altar, the most important place to bow, to kneel.

I stood straight, tapping my armoured fingers, one, two, three, four...

Greedy sloth didn't kneel, didn't bow.

I closed my eyes.

He was right behind me.

I knew he was.

The man who lurked between the pews was waiting, three feet behind my back.

I'd been frightened of him before, terrified, in fact.

Frightened enough to piss my hand-me-down pants.

But not now.

I smiled.

One, two, three, four... Peter Pointer, Toby Tall, Ruby Ring, Baby Small... all banging waxy heads with Tommy Thumb.

I turned.

My eyes opened.

My smile widened.

There he was!

Right in front of me.

Between the toffee pews.

Dead.

In a box.

With brass handles.

And flowers on top.

I walked around the coffin.

I'd seen coffins before, lots of times.

But this was the first time that I knew the person inside.

I inspected the flowers, their little labels of handwritten sorrow.

I read the shiny brass plate on the polished wood that said who he was and when he'd died.

Then I snorted once, twice, spat, and a big pool of snot and saliva dribbled onto the top of the coffin.

It sat there, glistening, reflecting candle fire.

I'd learned a new word at school recently.

I didn't know what it meant, but knew it was bad.

I'd been saving it up.

"Bastard."

The word echoed from the stone, from the pews, from the altar.

I looked up.

Stone Jesus didn't say anything.

When I looked down the blob of mucus had oozed to the side of the coffin and had begun to drip down it's side, just as the wax had dripped onto my fingers.

I watched, fascinated, then reluctantly wiped the saliva away with the corner of my cassock.

I headed back to the sacristy to prepare for the Requiem Mass.

-

There was a ginger kid in my class at school called Glenn.

He started school at the same time as me, in 1977.

We were four.

Apart from being ginger, there were two other things that made Glenn stick out in class.

   1. He was the grandson of the Headmaster.

   2. He made noises. Squeaks, grunts, oinks, whistles and moos. Constantly.

I realise now that he had Tourettes Syndrome, and that he really couldn't help himself, but back then we just thought he was a naughty kid.

The teachers thought he was a naughty kid.

The Headmaster thought he was a naughty kid.

And no grandson of his would get away with being naughty.

Glenn was made to sit at a desk at the front of class every day, away from everyone else.

He was treated like a leper.

He'd sit there on his own, whistling, twitching, oinking and squawking until the teacher could handle it no longer, and sent him to the Headmaster.

And off he'd go.

With fear in his eyes.

He'd be gone a while.

Then come back crying.

Now, the Headmaster wasn't molesting him or anything.

No, he was hitting him.

Smacking his little arse until he couldn't sit down.

And every day, in spite of himself, and no matter how he tried, Glenn would go moo.

And get hit.

And oink.

And get hit.

And quack quack quack.

And get hit.

Poor little sod.

This went on for three years.

Three years.

The Headmaster would stand in for teachers who were sick.

When he took over our class, we knew what was coming.

It was bad enough that Glenn made these noises in front of the teacher, but when he made them in front of the Headmaster, The Headmaster would go berserk.

The Headmaster had a favourite phrase.

Fathead.

He would bellow it at any kid who didn't measure up, didn't look tidy enough, didn't answer the question correctly.

Fathead.

What a lovely thing to call a five year old child who is trying their hardest.

Glenn would be biting his lips, almost going purple from the strain of keeping quiet.

It couldn't last.

"Oink."

"Silence, Fathead!"

"Moo moo."

"Silence I said, you idiot!"

"Quack."

And that was it.

The little ginger kid would be dragged from his chair, hauled to the front of class, have his trousers and underpants hauled down and the Headmaster would crack his little arse until he howled.

The rotten, black-hearted bastard.

Like I said, it went on for three years.

Then one day, Glenn was taken away.

No-one said why, nobody explained.

He was taken away, and I never heard another thing about him.

-

My younger brother is three years younger than me.

We're of similar intelligence, but he struggled with school.

I didn't do great, but I got by.

Just.

My brother didn't get by.

He became very quiet.

We didn't know why.

After a while we discovered what it was.

With Glenn spirited away, the Headmaster needed a new whipping boy.

My brother.

He was giving my younger brother the same treatment he gave Glenn.

It would have carried on too, except my mother marched into his office one day and told him that if he ever laid another finger on her son's head then my father would come down and bray him.

He stopped hitting my brother.

He still hit everyone else though.

Still bellowed 'Fathead' at little kids.

Still struck utter fear into young hearts.

Then he died.

Secret smiles in the playground.

Giggles in classrooms.

Ding dong the witch is dead.

The funeral was to be in the church next to school.

I volunteered to be altar boy.

-

I knelt by the altar, ready with my bells and candles and incense burner and little chrome holy water sprinkler, listening to the priest say Mass.

I could kneel like a good boy when I wanted to, when people were watching.

I pretended to pray, but through slitted eyes I watched the congregation.

No tears.

Pale faces and black clothes.

Not as big a turn out as you'd expect for a headmaster.

No kids.

Funny that.

I looked, but I didn't see Glenn.

I wondered if the mourners would think I was being angelic enough, if they'd give me money.

If they did, I'd spend it on sweets for me and my brother at the newsagents on the way home.

We all sat down as the priest began his eulogy.

I don't remember all of it.

It was a long time ago.

But one line sticks out in my mind.

The priest said:

"Every child at the school knew that if they had a problem, were frightened or unhappy, then they could go to the Headmaster and he would be there for them, to listen to them, to help them."

I remember screwing my fists up inside my cassock, the fragile shells of wax that coated my fingers cracking and crumbling, my fingertips feeling sensitive after being covered by the protective shell for so long, the bitten nails biting into my palms and looking at the priest in profile, and thinking:

"You are a priest, but you are lying. You bloody liar. The Headmaster was a horrible bastard. Everyone knew it. He was a bastard, and you are a liar."

Service over.

I got no money from the mourners.

Perhaps they guessed what I had been thinking.

Perhaps they had seen hate on my face.

Perhaps they had seen a stain on the coffin.

I didn't care.

I was just glad he was dead.

Oracle of the Follicle

I was in the toilet.
Again.
Maybe I should set up a little stall selling aftershave and rubber johnnies.
I might as well make some extra money from all the time I spend in there.
Can't see Soulless Boss liking that.
"Lucifer! Where's the proof copies for Spazda that you're meant to be working on?"
"Sorry Soulless Boss. I've not done them. How about a french tickler and a squirt of Sex Panther instead?"
No, it might be better to keep my toilet time a bit more low-key.
I was in the toilet looking in the mirror.
I get these weird hairs in my beard sometimes.
Hulk hairs.
Like normal hairs, only bigger and more gnarly.
Hurt like fuck as well.
I'll find what I think is a spot on my jaw line, fuck about with it relentlessly until it gets a bit infected, then suddenly a beanstalk erupts from my chin, hideous and wiry, and I pluck it out.
I hope I'm not the only person who gets this.
Maybe it's beard cancer and I don't know it yet.
Maybe I was accidentally irradiated as a child by a faulty microwave oven and my beard was mutating into a new species of beard, a beard that would take over the world.
Or maybe most blokes get them.
Anyway, I picked away at my chin, tears springing in my eyes.
"Ow! You horrible fucker..."
"What are you doing, Lucifer?"
"Fuck a duck! Don't do that, Scorcher! I nearly shat myself!"
"You'd be in the right place if you did."
"What?"
"Shit yourself. You know, if you're gonna shit yourself, the bog is the place to be."

"I suppose so..."
"I've shat myself in some odd places, Lucifer."
"I haven't. I don't make a habit of that kind of thing."
"Did it in the barber's once."
"What? Why did you do that?"
"I didn't mean to. He was giving me a shave, he plucked out a nose hair, it made me sneeze, when I sneezed I shat myself."
"Oh. Bet that didn't go down too well."
"No, it didn't. I go to a different barber now."
"I bet you do, Scorcher."
Anyway, Lucifer. What you doing?"
"Funnily enough, I'm pulling out a hair on my chin."
"You're making a right fucking mess of it."
"I know. It's one of them Hulk hairs."
"A hulk hair? What's that?"
"Like a normal hair only bigger and meaner and it fucks up my chin. Do you get them?"
"Yeah, I get them. You should leave them alone, though."
"I'm glad I'm not the only one who get's them. I was a bit worried, to be honest."
"Yeah, I get them, but you should leave them alone, don't fuck about with them."
"Why not? If I leave this thing alone it might take over my face. It's like copper wire. I'm going to pull it out."
"Don't do that! It's the worst thing you can do!"
"How come?"
"I did it once, Lucifer. It was terrible."
"Fuck. What happened, Scorcher?"
"I was doing just what you're doing. I found lump on my chin, fucked about with it, felt this stiff hair and started pulling it."
"Did it come out?"
"Yeah, and then some. I pulled it out, but it kept coming. Longer and longer. Hurt like a bastard, but I kept pulling. I couldn't stop."
"Shit! How long was it?"
"Three feet long."
"Fuck off."
"No, really! It were three feet long. With one big tug it finally came out of my face, and do you know what happened?"

"No..."
"My ear fell off."
"Jesus wept."
"Yeah. Had to go to A & E with my ear in a matchbox. Surgeon said it happened all the time. Blokes find a funny hair somewhere, fuck about with it, pluck it out and a bit something off. Got to be careful."
"Yeah, well your ear looks alright to me."
"It were my other ear."
"Scorcher, there's nothing wrong with that ear either."
"I know. The surgeon was fucking ace."
"See you later, Scorcher."
"Yeah, see you around, Lucifer. I'm busting for a crap."
"Nice."
I left him to it.
I looked in the mirror.
I could see the hair now, poking out.
I grabbed it, pulled.
It came out.
Just an ugly, gnarly hulk hair.
But for just a second, as I pulled it, I wondered...
And glanced at my ear.

The Big Man

For some people, size matters.
For some people it's the only thing that matters.
If it's not XL, XXL or XXXL then it's not worth having.
These people are usually men, usually big men.
They can't drive a Fiesta.
No, a puny Fiesta would simply crumple beneath the power and strength of the Big Man.
It has to be a Shogun, a Barbarian, a Ram, a Nitro.
Big names for big cars for Big Men.
They can't have a dog.
It has to be a big dog.
It has to be the size of a brown bear, wear a collar that would give a gimp a hard-on, have the bite strength of a hyena on speed.
A spaniel just won't do.
Not big enough for a Big Man.
It has to be a Ridgeback, a Doberman Pinscher, a Rottweiler, a Pitbull.
Big names for big dogs for Big Men.
Life must be pretty difficult for the Big Man.
All those keys on his belt must get heavy.
There are days when you fancy a nice salad, but you have to order the mixed grill.
Having to put seventy quids worth of fuel in the tank every week.
No, life isn't straight forward for the Big Man.
Maintaining your Big Man credentials is a full time job.
-
There's lots of Big Men in a factory.
It seems to breed them.
The biggest of the Big Men in our factory was Mule.
Six foot seven inches tall, at least twenty two stone, maybe more.
Big boots, big belt, big gut, big moustache.
What a wanker.
I couldn't bear to be in the same room as the cunt, honestly.
I'm six foot three.

Not small, but I'm no Big Man.
Whenever Mule saw me he'd get as close as possible, close enough for me to smell him, a reek like a dog, meaty and sour.
He'd stand close enough for his gut to brush against me, and he would look down at me.
Not say anything, just look down at me.
He let his body do the talking.
It said, I'm a Big Man.
It said, you are big, Lucifer, but you are not a Big Man, therefore I am vastly superior to you.
I let my body do some talking of it's own.
I would yawn.
If I had food in my mouth, I'd let him see it.
If his belly touched me I would rub my crotch, roll my eyes and groan.
Big Men can't understand that type of thing.
After a while he would generally get the message and fuck off.
On the List of People In The Factory Who I Like To Talk Bollocks With, Mule was just about at the bottom, number two hundred and seventy three.
Coming in at number ten on the List of People In The Factory Who I Like To Talk Bollocks With was The Duck of Death.
The Duck of Death is an engineer, a good bloke who's good at his job.
I was chatting to him one lunchtime.
"Hey duck! I'm after a favour. I need a little metal bracket making. It's to fit a light to a pannier rack on my bike."
"Hmmm. Let's have a look at the light. Hmmm... what about...."
Saw!
Drill!
Whirr!
Clang!
Ping!
"...this?"
"Fucking magic, Duck! That's perfect!"
"No problem Lucifer. Don't mind doing stuff like that for a mate. You get some blokes coming in here wanting stuff even though they blank you most days. Not so much as a good fucking morning or a

how do you fucking do."
The Duck of Death leaned over.
"Do us a favour, Lucifer."
"Yeah, what do you want?"
QUACK
"Pick the bones out of that, will you?"
"Fucking Hell, man! That stinks!"
The Duck of Death had struck again. He fell about in fits of giggles, tears streaming down his fat cheeks.
He had the worst farts in the world. He had a shit diet, ate shit food, drank shit beer.
It made his farts reek of death and decay.
The Duck of Death would shit himself on a regular basis.
God only knows what his wife thought on when she did the laundry.
At the end of a long hot day in the factory, his pants looked like a coprophile's napkin.
I know because he showed me them one time.
It made me do a sick-burp.
The door opened behind me.
A new smell fought for supremacy over the Duck's dinner ghosts.
Something meaty and sour.
His gut brushed against my lower back.
It was Mule.
The Duck of Death stopped laughing.
So did I.
I stepped away from Mule, wiping my back where he'd touched me.
It felt dirty.
Mule stood there, making himself as big as possible, breathing down through his moustache.
"I've got a job for you, Duck."
The duck raised an eyebrow, didn't say anything.
"This is what I'm after."
Mule slammed a grubby sheet of paper down onto the workbench.
It was a drawing of a metal frame, covered in scribbles and measurements.
Brown sauce and tea stains almost obscured the writing.
The Duck frowned.
"What the fuck is it?"

Mule tried to look superior.
"I've just bought a new caravan, Duck. It's real beauty. Sleeps eight."
"Eight? There's only you and the wife, isn't there?"
"And the kids, And the dog."
"The kids? They're in their fucking twenties aren't they?"
"Oh yes. They still come on holiday with us."
The Duck gave me a knowing look.
I didn't know what he was getting at.
"Anyway, Mule. What's this thing you want me to build?"
"It's a tow bar. For my new caravan."
"A tow bar? Haven't you already got on on your motor?"
"Yes, but this one is bigger. And stronger. My new caravan is very, very big, so I'll need a very very big tow bar."
The Duck rolled his eyes.
Mule continued: "It's my own design. It dawned on me that the best way to get double the strength would be to have two tow bars, side by side!"
Mule looked smug.
I looked perplexed.
The Duck looked thoughtful.
"Interesting concept, Mule..."
Mule put his huge paw on the back of The Duck's neck, and squeezed, supposedly friendly but just too hard.
"I'm taking the caravan on it's maiden voyage this weekend, Duck, so you'd better crack on. You don't want to make me angry, do you?"
"Oh no, Mule. I wouldn't want to do that. Come back Thursday. I'll have it ready."
Mule slapped the Duck's back. It almost knocked him off his chair.
"Good lad. I'll see you later."
Mule lumbered out looking very smug.
"What a cunt! What. A. Cunt. Man, he shouldn't talk to you like that, Duck. Now way should you build that thing for him!"
But The Duck of Death was grinning.
"Oh, I'm going to make it, Lucifer. It'll be my pleasure."
The Duck got to work.
As he worked he talked.
"He's a freak, is Mule. A right oddball. He's got two kids, a lad and a lass. Rumour has it that he still baths them."

"What? No!"
"Yeah. He's a control freak. Doesn't let them do anything without his say so. His daughter, she's just had a baby. Nobody knows who the dad is."
He gave me that knowing look he'd used earlier.
I understood this time.
"Fucking Hell! do you reckon he..."
"I'm not saying owt, Lucifer. But let's put it this way, he filmed the birth."
"No fucking way! He filmed his own daughter giving birth?"
"Yeah. He told me that himself. Straight from the horse's mouth. Or the Mule's. Ha!"
"Weird bastard."
"Tell me about it. Ever meet Barnaby, his glove puppet?"
I shuddered.
"I've had the pleasure. It really creeped me out."
"I know! What kind of bloke walks around campsites with a glove puppet, talking to kids in that stupid voice?"
"A paedo."
"Dead right. Definitely a fiddler."
"So why are you going to do that job for him? You should have said you were too busy!"
All the while we were talking, the Duck of Death was busy sawing and drilling.
"Take another look at Mule's design. See the flaw?"
I frowned at the grubby paper for a minute.
Then it dawned on me.
"Fucking Hell!"
The Duck giggled.
"It's going to be very strong, Lucifer. Two tow balls next to each other is bound to be. But there's no way on Earth it'll go around a corner."
-

The pictures appeared in the local papers, and Mule even made it onto the regional news.
It was one of those, 'and finally, let's look at what this fucking idiot has gone and done..." pieces.
He'd hitched up the caravan on the roadside and set off.

It was going so well, but then a roundabout appeared.
Caravans don't roll very well.
They're just not designed for it.
Neither are Mitsubishi Shoguns.
If something is designed to do a job, then you shouldn't mess about with it.
It's not big and it definitely isn't clever.
It's funny, but the policeman talking to Mule in the news report looks about average height, average weight, but he looks an awful lot bigger than Mule.
Or maybe it was just Mule looking small.
Whichever it was, Mule definitely didn't look like a Big Man.
Not big and definitely not clever.

One Night Stand

I woke up one Sunday morning in a room I didn't recognize.
I didn't have a fucking clue where I was.
Then I heard snoring.
I looked to my left, and saw the widest back I've ever seen, covered in spots.
Oh fuck.
I could not tell the gender.
The massive back was between me and the door.
A wall was on my other side.
I was trapped.
Hungover and trapped.
The snoring stopped and the back moved.
Oh fuck oh fuck oh fuck.
Luckily it was a girl.
A girl Honey Monster.
She seemed pleased to see me.
I tried to pretend to be happy to see her.
She really was massive.
I didn't have a clue what her name was or where I'd met her or where I was now.
She wanted morning sex.
I wanted a painless death.
I said that I needed a piss first, and squeezed past her bulk to the bathroom.
I pissed and panicked at the same time.
Who says men can't multi-task?
My clothes were in the bedroom, my boots were in the bedroom, my wallet was in the bedroom.
I went back into the bedroom.
And yes, I had sex with her.
Horrible, horrible sex.
The sight of that massive spotty back heaving around in front of me will stay with me forever.
I finished up, got out of bed, got dressed, walked downstairs.

She thundered after me.
"Where are you going, Lucifer?"
"Er... Home. I'm going home."
"Don't you want some breakfast?"
Don't fancy it."
"Will you phone me?"
"Yeah, yeah. Course I will."
"Do you want my number then?"
"Oh. Yeah. Write it down for me."
She gave me the pen and paper.
She told me her number.
She didn't tell me her name.
I wrote the first thing that came into my mind and thrust the paper into my pocket.
"Can I have your number, Lucifer?"
"Yeah, I suppose so. Get another piece of paper and you can write it down."
"I'll use half the paper I've just given you."
"Er... I'd rather not..."
"Just tear it in half."
I took the paper out of my pocket, tore it in half, passed a piece to her.
I gave her the wrong piece.
I gave her the piece that said 'Fatty 0113 1234567'
She looked gutted.
I said, "Sorry mate."
Then I ran away.

Blog Roll

Tap tap tap.
Send.
The printer sprang to life, spewing out sheet after sheet of fresh A4. OfficeDrone approached.
"You're looking busy today, Lucifer."
"Yes. I am looking busy today, OfficeDrone. I'm looking very busy indeed."
"Good to see, Lucifer. I thought that there wasn't much work at the moment! What project are you working on?"
"It's a project that I call, 'printing off things from the internet to read while I take a massive crap.'
"Oh."
"Now get out of my way, OfficeDrone, or I'll shit on your shoes."
"Oh, yes, of course."
I gathered my papers and went to the bog.
-
My bog, the one I consider to be my own, is at the end of a deserted corridor.
It once was the office toilets, but someone, in their wisdom, moved the offices about two hundred meters away to the far side of the factory.
The toilets were abandoned.
I claimed them.
Just as I gripped the handle of the toilet door, it gets kicked open from the inside.
The door slammed into my chest, knocking the air from my lungs and the sheaf of A4 from my hands.
I knelt on the floor, A4 drifting around me.
"Fffffuuu..ffffffffffuuuu..."
"What you doin' on the floor, Lucy?"
It was Cyclops, eighteen stones of shit thick, wonky eyed printer.
"Fffffuuu....ck... What am I doing on the floor, Cyclops? Oh, nothing, just..."
The first thing that hit was the door.

The second thing that hit me was the smell.
I fell backwards, retching.
"Holy shit, Cyclops! What have you done in there?"
"What do you think I done in there? I done a crap, of course. That's what bogs are for."
"That doesn't smell like human crap. What the fuck have you been eating?"
"Lot's of stuff. I got a very varied diet, me."
"Varied? It smells like pig shit and mustard gas in there. Is that what you call varied? It burns my fucking throat!"
"I don't eat nowt like that, Lucifer. I eat stuff like vindaloos, beef madras, chicken biryani,..."
"Curries? Is that all you eat? Curries?"
"Nah. I like bacon sarnies too."
Cyclops held up a half eaten bacon sandwich.
I can't quite believe it.
"Cyclops, were you just eating a bacon sandwich on the toilet?"
"Yeah."
"Where did you put it when you wiped your arse?"
"I sort of rested it in my undies."
"Let's just get things straight. You put a bacon sarnie in your underpants while you wiped your arse?"
"Yeah. My undies are like a little hammock for my sarnie."
"You dirty bastard."
I looked past him, to the toilets.
The bogs were a scene of devastation.
Both toilets were blocked, one overflowing.
Water and inky boot prints cover the floor.
Ink was smeared over the taps, paper towels are scattered everywhere.
And there's that smell, that gut twisting, bile-curdling smell.
"For fuck's sake, Cyclops! Look at it in there! Which toilet did you block?"
"Both of them."
"What? How?"
"Well, I crapped in that one and it got full and it got blocked, so I crapped in the other, and the same thing happened. These toilets are rubbish."

"Wait a minute. How did you get to the other bog after you'd filled the first one?"
"How the fuck do you think I did it? I just shuffled around!"
"You didn't wipe your arse though, did you, Cyclops."
"How do you know?"
"Because you've left a lump of crap in the middle of the floor."
"Could have been worse."
"How could it possibly be worse??"
"It could have landed on my bacon sandwich! Hur hur hur!"
"Hur hur fucking Hur. You need to be shitting outdoors, you fucking animal."
"You're a fucking snob, Lucifer. It's not like your shit don't stink, you know!"
"It doesn't smell like that! Nothing, nothing smells like that! You've got something wrong with you, Cyclops, you really have. I'd suggest a colonoscopy but you'd melt any camera that gets near your stinking hole."
"Oh, just fuck off, you big puff."
Cyclops stomped away, gnawing on his sandwich and scratching his arse.
"What's making your arse itch, Cyclops? Bread crumbs?"
He ignored me.
I turned my attention back to the toilet.
It really made me mad.
I know that sounds petty, but it really made me mad.
I failed to understand the mentality of someone who can leave a toilet in that kind of state.
I spend a lot of time in the toilets, some truly quality time, but there was no way I could go in there.
Unfortunately, I still had business to take care of.
Business that was becoming increasingly urgent.
My gaze drifted to the other door, the door to the forbidden land, the ladies toilet.
Should I?
I glanced around.
The corridor was deserted.
My mind said no.
My guts said go.

I crept into the ladies toilet for the first time ever.
I switched on the light.
Entered another world.
Delicate perfume drifted in the air.
Jars and bottles of pink and pale blue nestled by the beautifully polished sink, while pretty little soaps dressed in crisp tissue languished by the gleaming taps.
Dispensers of various feminine products hung on the pastel painted walls alongside a paper towel dispenser that actually worked, and even contained paper towels.
Over the radiator... can it be?.... an ACTUAL white fluffy towel! A real one!
Paper towels AND a fluffy white towel.
I had entered Nirvana.
I wandered around the fragrant room, stroking the towel, inspecting thte small feminine nick-nacks, utterly charmed by the stark contrast to the abattoir next door.
I could get used to this.
I really could.
I decide to use the ladies toilets more often.
I decided to use them all the time.
They were lovely.
If I'm careful, I thought, I won't get caught.
I didn't want to ruin a good thing.
It would be my little secret.
Just then, something caught my eye.
Hello, what's this?
A strange white egg perched by a small pile of pink cotton flannels. There was a button on the front of the egg, and a bright green light that flickered each time I moved.
The egg puzzled me, intrigued me.
As I looked closer I saw a little circular opening on the top of the egg.
I peeped inside...
PSSSST
A powerful jet of lavender agony fired directly into my eye.
The strange egg was an automatic air freshener dispenser and it had blinded me.

284

"My...my eye! My FUCKING EYE!!! AYEEEEEEE!!!! MYYYYYY EYEEEEE!!!" I screamed.
I panicked a bit.
In fact, I panicked quite a lot.
I stumbled backwards away from the vicious egg and my shoulder blade connected with the light switch.
The room was plunged into utter darkness.
There was much wailing and gnashing of teeth.
The blazing pain in my eye escalated, became too much to bear, and I was suddenly terrified that I would lose my sight forever.
An embarrassing, thrashing frenzy followed.
Bottle and jars scattered and shattered, soap and lotion splattered across tile and mirror as I screamed and sobbed in the pitch black toilet.
I ricocheted off the walls, inevitably slipped on a puddle of peony hand cream, pitched forwards and my head connected heavily against a hard object with a sickening crack.
I slumped to the floor, unconscious.
Time passed.
-
When I awoke, I found that I could see again.
Not much, but I could see.
Out of the darkness, a small green light flickered.
PSSSST
I could smell lavender.
Lavender and shit.
I had shat my pants.
I groped my way groggily to the wall, fumble upwards, found the light switch.
Oh God, what have I done?
I was covered in Tampax™.
The Tampax™ dispenser on the wall was dented and gaping open, a smear of blood showing where my head connected with it.
The floor was a pastel rainbow swirl of fragrant glop, oozing from shattered pump dispensers and cracked jars.
The only dark colour was red.
Red from my blood.
I shuffled to the mirror, acutely aware of a hot, heavy weight in the

back of my pants.
The face looking back from the cracked glass was smeared with bright blood and pink liquid soap, a cut in my eyebrow.
Strangely, my eye didn't hurt anymore.
The tears of panic and terror had washed away the agonizing lavender air freshener.
It was at that point that it dawned on me.
Somebody could walk in at any moment.
A second wave of panic seized me.
Got to clean up!
Into a cubicle, whipped off my shit filled undies, looked for a way of disposing of them.
Nothing.
They went down the toilet.
Cleaned myself up, paper followed the undies.
I flushed.
The toilet belched up the paper and pants then flooded the floor.
Oh fuck.
I left it.
I fumble the Tampax™ that weren't covered in goo back into the machine and pressed the door closed, then scooped as much of the crap off the floor as I could using paper towels.
I quickly ran out of paper towels.
I looked at the radiator.
I couldn't.
I had to.
I snatched the clean, white, fluffy towel and started trying to scoop up glass and blood and moisturizer from the floor.
I heard a pop.
Tampax™ rained down on my head again.
Stifling a panicked sob, I reached an important conclusion.
It was time to flee.
I tried to flush away as much evidence as possible, but the other toilet began to bubble and froth, overdosing on liquid soap and paper towels.
I slammed the cubicle door.
Foam gushed under the door.
I quickly washed the blood from my face, dried with a corner of the

ruined fluffy towel, and turned off the lights as I left.
The door clicked shut on my guilt, on the sound of water cascading over porcelain... and a sharp noise... *PSSSST*
As I shuffled away with my stack of soggy, unread sheets of A4 paper, I noticed the foul odour leaking out from under the other door.
I took solace in the fact that at least my carnage was fresh scented.
Up ahead, at the end of the long, long corridor, I could see a small sign.
Executive Toilets.
I shrugged, and walked towards them...

Three's a Crowd.

Once upon a time, I *almost* had a threesome.
Not the wildest sexual claim, I'll grant you.
It's like claiming I *almost* won the lottery, only the numbers I had were different to the ones being shat out by Guinevere or Lancelot.
I *almost* had a threesome with my mate Genuflect and a girl he met in a nightclub.
He was off snogging in the corner while I was chatting to a girl by the bar.
Doing alright, too.
I was well in, if I say so myself.
Genuflect hurries over, grabs my arm.
"Come on, Lucifer! We're leaving!"
"Are we?"
"Yeah! This lass I'm with is well game! She says she fancies a threesome!"
"That's very generous of her, but I haven't got a fucking clue what her name is or what she looks like."
"Her name is Elvira, and she's a goth!"
"Fuck off she's called Elvira. Her real name is probably Doris and she'll be on the pick 'n' mix in Woolies during daylight hours."
"Who fucking cares? She'll suck us both off!"
"Good point, Genuflect. Still, I'm not sure. I'm doing all right with this lass..."
"What's her name then?"
"erm... Magenta."
"Magenta? And you're taking piss out of Elvira?"
"Fair do's. Still..."
"Oh, come on, Lucifer! Do me a favour! Take one for the team!"
"*sigh* Alright. I'll come and have sex with you and Necrosis."
"Elvira. Her name's Elvira."
"Yeah, whatever..."

We went back to Elvira's.
Had a drink.
Had a fumble on the couch.

She got cold feet and called it off.
I guess she wasn't as freaky as she liked to think she was.
Genuflect was really pissed off. He stomped off to the kitchen and raided the fridge for booze.
Then he fell asleep on the couch.
I looked at Elvira over my snoring mate.
She looked at me.
I ended up fucking her on the living room floor.
Almost a threesome, but not quite...

-

Tuesday.
8.am.
I was thinking about doing work, but I was drinking tea and reading the paper instead.
Genuflect bustled in looking very excited.
"Morning Genuflect. You're looking all happy and dapper today."
"Yes I am, Lucifer!"
"Why? It's Tuesday. Tuesday's are shit."
"I'm looking very happy and dapper because we're going out tonight!"
"Good for you. Who are you going out with?"
"You."
"Are you?"
"Yes I am!"
"Where are we supposed to be going?"
"We're going to Gregg's Bar!"
"What? Oh, come on, Genuflect! I'm not going to Gregg's Bar! It's as rough as arseholes in there!"
"It's not so bad, Lucifer! Anyyway, that's where the girls are going to meet us."
"Girls? What girls?"
"My sister's mate has got a friend who knows this lass. I'm off on a blind date with her!"
"Where do I come into this beautiful relationship?"
"She's bringing a mate!"
"Wonderful. Any idea what they look like?"
"Tracy sounds nice. I've no idea what Sandra looks like."
"And the girl I'll be palmed off with is...?"

"Sandra."
"Thought so. I'm not going."
"Oh, come on, Lucifer! Do me a favour!"
"No. Anyway, I'm in my work clothes, I didn't have a shave this morning, I've no money..."
I'll buy the drinks!"
-
We went to Gregg's Bar.
Genuflect got the beers in.
After a bit, the girls arrived.
I knew it was them instantly.
I almost left.
Genuflect only let go of my sleeve when the girls came over.
"Hello ladies!"
"Hiya!" They cackled in unison.
We got acquainted.
Genuflect got the prettiest one.
The one with the missing teeth.
Sandra was no looker, but there was no escape.
I drank fast and made sure Genuflect kept the beers coming.
"You want another pint, Lucifer?"
"Please."
I whispered into his ear:
"I'm catching the last bus home at eleven. Got it?"
"Well, we'll see how it goes, Lucifer..."
-
Wednesday. 1am.
We fell out of the taxi.
Tracy's house looked new, but the garden was a bomb site.
You could just make out a rotting sofa in the long grass.
Nice.
Tracy and Genuflect stumbled into the house, shushing and giggling.
I followed them.
Reluctantly holding Sandra's hand.
"You want a Foster's, Lucifer?"
"Thank you, Tracy. That would be lovely."
Tracy and Genuflect stumbled into the kitchen.
The door slammed.

I could here moaning.
I sat on the couch with Sandra.
Planning my escape.
"Lucifer?"
"Yes, Sandra?"
"You gonna fuck me then, or what?"
Oh dear.
I didn't have any money.
Genuflect had the cash, and he was busy.
I was miles from home.
I had no other place to sleep.
sigh
"Go on then, Sandra. Get your kit off."
-
Twenty minutes later.
"You want to do it again, Lucifer?"
"No thank you."
"You got a girlfriend?"
"Well, no one serious. I go out sometimes with a girl who..."
"Bastard!"
"Excuse me, Sandra?"
"Bastard! I thought we were going out!"
"Well you thought wrong. I don't really know you, and.."
"Bastard! If I saw you with another woman I'd fucking blind her!"
"Right, I'd better be going..."
Sandra beat me too it.
She got up, spat in my face and stormed out of the house.
I was left alone with the couch and the groans drifting from the kitchen.
I tried to sleep.
-
My eyes clicked open when I heard her scream:
"Jesus Christ! You're not putting that monster in me!"
I sat bolt upright.
Monster?
I strained to hear what was going on.
She started wailing, like an animal in pain.
He was quite obviously putting 'that monster' into her.

I squeezed my eyes shut and wrapped my coat around my ears, wishing the noise would end.
It didn't.
It went on and on.
It seemed to go on for ever.
After a while I heard a loud banging.
I jumped off the couch and stumbled to the door.
Oh fuck.
It was the police.
They looked a bit cross.
The one with the sergeant's hat spoke first.
"Excuse me, sir, but we've had a report that somebody is being murdered on the premises. Or sounds like it, at least."
Oh fuck oh fuck.
What do you say to a copper in a situation like this?
"Sorry."
The policemen exchanged glances.
"Sorry for what, sir? Murdering somebody?"
"No no no! I'm sorry about the noise, even though it's not me making the noise, it's not even my house! Ha ha ha! No, the people making the noise are in the kitchen. I'll tell them to quieten down a bit."
I sounded like a right dick head.
The policemen looked at me like I was a right dick head.
Just then, the screaming started up again, worse than before.
The coppers looked shocked.
"Shall I call for backup, Sarge?"
"No, Constable Wilks, but draw your baton, we're going in..."
I panicked.
"No need for that, officers! It's not what you think!"
The sergeant's eyes narrowed. He was a man of experience, and he'd obviously seen a few things in his time.
"In the kitchen, are they, sir?"
"Yeah, that's right."
"Well, why don't we have a little nosey through the kitchen window then, Constable Wilks?"
"Good idea, Sarge."
The policemen crept around the side of the house.
I followed on.

We got to the kitchen window.
Peeped over the window ledge...
Genuflect had Tracy perched on the kitchen counter amongst the dirty dishes.
He had his strides around his ankles.
She was naked.
"Fucking Hell," muttered the constable.
"Shhh!" hissed the Sergeant.
We watched for a while in silence.
Genuflect was pounding away between her legs, and she was howling like a banshee.
"OWWOOOOOOO JESUSFUCKINGCHRIST!!!! AWOOOOOO!!!"
"Constable Wilks."
"Yes, Sarge?"
"Take your hand out of your pocket, you dirty little bastard."
"Oh, sorry Sarge."
Genuflect kept banging away.
A Breville toaster fell to the floor.
He hardly broke his rhythm.
"Do you want me to tazer him, Sarge?" whispered the constable.
"You'll do nothing of the sort, Wilks. You tazer him in that position and that young lady will get 5000 volts to her snatch. Can't have that. Imagine the paperwork."
Just then, Genuflect moved.
We saw something.
"Is that, is that a rolling pin, Sarge?"
"Rolling pins don't have veins, Wilks."
I couldn't believe what I was seeing.
It was as thick as my wrist.
A great, glistening, slithering... monster.
I looked at the policemen.
There mouths were wide open.
Experienced as they were, they'd never seen anything like that outside of a stable.
"Have you seen that thing, Sarge?"
"Aye, Wilks, but I can't believe it. It's like a Burmese python!"
"It's so..so.. angry looking!"

I used to know a police horse like that, only it weren't that impressive!"
"Shall I arrest him, Sarge?"
"Arrest him, Wilks? On what charge?"
"Assault with a deadly weapon."
"No, we'd better leave him to finish. We'd have to call the RSPCA to get that great ugly thing back into his trousers."
We walked around to the front of the house in silence.
The policemen gave me a look of kindly pity before they drove away.
I went back to the couch.
Tried to block out the noise.
As I lay there, my mind went back to that night when we *almost* had a threesome.
I realised what a lucky escape I'd had.
I mean, can you imagine trying to make an impression next to that thing?
I'd have been the hors d' oeuvre, while he would have been the main course.
Prawn cocktail versus a mixed grill.
I shuddered.
Listened to the screams.
That poor girl.
Eventually I drifted off to sleep.
-
I didn't sleep very well.
My dreams were plagued by throbbing gristle and screams.
Genuflect woke me just before dawn and we tip toed out of the house.
"Did you order a taxi?" I asked.
"No, she didn't have a phone."
"Brilliant. Where are we?"
"No idea. Let's just walk until we hit a main road."
Cold and aching from couch-sleep.
We walked for a long time.
As the sun came up we found ourselves in familiar territory.
Near the factory.
"No point going home now, Lucifer."

"Suppose not."
We shuffled inside, heard the tedious familiar clattering of the printing presses.
We clocked in.
Went to the canteen.
"Cheers for backing me up last night, Lucifer. Breakfast is on me."
"Good of you."
"What you having then? Bacon?"
"Yeah."
Tomato?"
"just a bit."
"Beans?"
"Two spoonfuls."
"Eggs?"
"Ooh, I fancy two of those."
"Sausage?"
"On second thoughts, I only fancy tea."

Weasily Forgotten.

Stepping into the plate room is like stepping into another dimension, similar to our own but somehow...flawed.
There's a subterranean feel to the place, a dark industrial grotto where nothing is quite right.
The faintly acrid odour of developer and fixer in the warm damp air, a constant hiss of idling compressors, the tartrazine light leeching colour, depth, life.
Stacks of wafer thin aluminium plates hide in brown paper packets, awaiting their exposure to the brilliant blue light that will change them forever, give them a brief few hours of glory on the presses before they are discarded, crushed, recycled, reborn.
Kegs of clear chemicals on the stained linoleum by the developing machines, a faint whiff of piss and and a strange brown fluid dribbling from a cracked tank lends a feeling of incontinence to the place.
A neglected abandonment.
One of the yellow fluorescent tubes flickers.
It has flickered for days.
Fading amber plastic covers to the windows, warding off the offending ultra violet side of the spectrum - only the infra red is welcome in the plate room.
Decades of dead flies on the window sills, carefully clipped articles from the York newspapers on the walls.
Press clippings of football glories that have been dead longer than the flies.
Parchment-like newspapers bearing dates from before my birth.
In the plate room the brightest colour is yellow, the darkest colour is black.
In between, in the sepia shadows, something moves.
A frail figure crouches over a murmuring radio.
A pair of rusty pliers are there to change the station, but they are never needed.
A twisted coat hanger for an aerial, picking up the results from York, Doncaster, Cheltenham, Aintree.

Weasel listens, then scribbles in the margins of his Racing Post.
His fingernails are bitten to stumps.
His handwriting is a beautiful flowing script, written in cheap biro.
Weasel's skin is the texture of his paper clippings, the colour of the plastic on the windows.
He puts down his pen and delves into a bag of broken biscuits from the market, pops one into his mouth, crunches carefully with weak teeth.
He picks up his pen and scribbles again; names, odds, riders, trainers.
The plate room is his world, but that battered radio brings him the thunder of hooves and screams of 'goal' from the Outside.
"Brought you a cup of tea, Weasel."
He ignores me.
"Three sugars and full fat milk, just how you wanted."
Weasel frowns, scribbles something about Haydock Park.
I leave him to his notes, the static murmurs, broken biscuits.
As the door closes behind me, I hear Weasel.
"Ta, lad."

-

Always the same.
Never changing.
Creeping through the stygian gloom with paper thin sheets of metal for the presses, squatting in the shadows, listening, scribbling.
But he did change.
He go thinner.
I brought Weasel his tea, saw his gaunt cheeks, more gaunt than usual.
Thin, sinewy wrists that reminded me of the dried reptilian ankles of overcooked poultry.
"Here's your tea, Weasel."
He wasn't writing in his paper.
The radio was on, the paper spread out.
But he wasn't writing.
"You alright, Weasel?"
"Tired. Just tired."
He looked more than tired.
He looked ill.

I sat next to him.
Thought of something to say.
"The pension bloke is in this week, Weasel. Why don't you see him? See what your options are?"
He shook his head.
"No point. I don't have a pension."
That shocked me.
Here's a man in his fifties, worked all his life, no pension.
"How come you don't have a pension?"
"I won't see retirement. None of my family have. I've got life insurance, you know, to make sure the wife is looked after, but I've no need for a pension."
He said it quietly, calmly.
"My old man, he used to drink in the club at the end of our street. He'd leave work, walk past our house and tap on the front window to let mi mother know she should put tea on. Tap tap tap. Just like that. Mi mother'd look out for him, listen for that tap, then she'd put the chops on and boil the spuds, ready for when he got in. One day, he tapped, and she got cooking, but he never come home. She sent me up the street to fetch him, but when I saw the copper and the ambulance I knew he were dead. He'd gone up to the bar in the club, ordered his pint, and the lass pulled it, but when she looked up he'd disappeared. She looked over the bar and there he was, laid out, dead."
"Bloody Hell, Weasel. That's hard."
He shrugged.
"It's how it is. I'd rather go like that than with something like cancer. That's what did mi mother, and mi brother went with a bad heart. It's in the family. We don't live long, our lot."
I didn't know what to say.
-
Six months later, Weasel put down his pen, switched off his radio and told Soulless Boss he was going home, he felt ill.
They ran the tests, took blood and urine.
Turns out it was cancer.
They put him on chemotherapy.
While Weasel got treatment, I made plates.
I entered his world.

Reprography is a fairly isolated job, but platemaking is like solitary confinement.
Hour after hour, day after day, the hiss of the compressor, the flash of blue light through the yellow air as plate after plate is exposed, developed, punched, stacked.
Cyan, magenta, yellow, black.
I turned to the radio for company.
Listened to the cryptic names of horses.
While the plates exposed and developed I'd sit in the shadows, listen to the click and whirr of machines, hear through static the hooves on turf.
I'd try not to look at his shoes.
Weasel always changed his shoes when he got to work.
Took off one pair of black shoes, put on an identical pair of black shoes.
The black shoes lurked by the desk, pining for they're owner.
Not knowing if they'd ever be worn again.
I wasn't going to try them on.
-
Weasel came in to visit.
He looked thin, weak, but fairly chipper.
The treatment was working.
Everyone was pleased.
They patted him on the back, speculated on when he might want to start work again.
I didn't say anything.
I remembered what he had told me, about his family, about his dad.
On his way home he passed through the plate room.
Nodded to me.
"See you later, Lucifer."
"Yeah, see you, Weasel."
I didn't see him again.
The cancer hadn't gone.
It had only been gathering it's forces inside his slight frame.
It always amazed me that something so powerful can be raging in such a feeble body.
The disease consumed him, stripped him to nothing, ate him from the inside.

It made me wish that he had died at a bar somewhere, waiting for a pint.
Eventually the word came round.
"Weasel's gone."
I went into the plate room, turned off the radio with the pliers, stared at those shoes.
I picked up the shoes, unplugged the radio.
I put them in the back a forgotten cupboard and locked the door.
Took the key.
Then I went to see Soulless Boss.
"I'm not doing plate making anymore."
I returned to my computer in the corner of the white painted studio, in the light, in the cold air conditioning, in the silence.
And started to type.

A Place in the Sun

The inkjet chatters quietly.
I sip my tea and yawn, while surreptitiously tapping away at the novel I'm writing, my ticket out of repro.
The printed copy clatters into the out tray, and I rapidly hide the document on screen.
Can't have anyone see what I'm working on.
There's some sneaky little bastards about.
I check the printed copy in the printer tray.
A shitty leaflet for a cheap shop selling tawdry clothing.
Print run: 150,000 copies.
And of these 150,000 copies, how many will be read?
About thirty seven, probably.
The other 149,963 will end up being shat on by cats and budgies, mauled by nervous terriers, or just shoved into the bin.
I like to think that I'm not bothered, but it's a lie.
I am bothered.
The waste grates on my nerves.
I try not to think about it.
I take the copy and the job ticket to Soulless Boss, plop it on his desk, and head back to my workstation.
"Lucifer."
I pull a face, roll my eyes, then turn back to Soulless Boss with my '1984-faintly-optimistic' expression on.
"Yes, Soulless Boss?"
"Did you get a reader to check this?"
"No, Soulless Boss. I checked it."
"Well get a reader to double check it."
My '1984-faintly-optimistic' expression starts to creak a little.
"It isn't a large correction, Soulless Boss. Look, that line of text there..."
"Get a reader to double check it."
My '2010-rather-antagonistic' expression gets the better of '1984-faintly-optimistic'.
"But..."

"Do it."
"Yes, Soulless Boss."
I stalk back to my desk.
Fuck.
I decide to wait a bit...
"Lucifer!"
"Just on my way, Soulless Boss."
I hustle out of the door.
To the Readers Room.
It wouldn't be so bad if Minty was working the shift.
I dislike Minty enormously, he offends me with his brittle fake jollity, his incontinence, his screaming panic attacks, but at least he's mostly harmless.
Unlike Hades.
I reluctantly approach the Reader's room, and through the sickly yellow light I can see the tideline of dry paper clinging to the windows.
Where the paper ends, a tangled matt of thick hair can be seen, like that on the back of an old border collie.
On hearing my approach, the hair twitches and lifts, revealing shaggy brows, a baleful eye.
Above the static murmur of an ancient radio, I hear one muttered word.
"Cunt."
Here we go.
I grit my teeth, ready for confrontation.
"Morning, Hades. Just got a little job for you to cast an eye over."
I try to sound breezy, nonchalant.
I sound fake.
Hades eyes glitter at me through his wiry brows.
He looks like the foul spawn of Jack Nicholson and Brian Blessed.
He looks from me, to the printed copy, to me again.
"What's this... this... shit?"
He sounds revolted.
"Erm... it's a job."
Hades growls; a low, dull rumble.
Jobs litter his tatty laminated desk, but spread over the top of them is the Daily Mail.

He looks back at the newspaper, his hands flat over the pages.
He is not looking at the print.
He is looking at his hands.
Hades has a skin condition, vitiligo.
He has a crazed network of pale blotches covering his entire body.
Where there are blotches, there is no pigment.
White streaks flash his wild black hair and beard, his face is a jigsaw of differing flesh tones.
His hands have a dappled quality, like the shadows left when sunlight filters through leaves.
It is those patterns that he is staring at.
His jaw muscles bulge.
He starts to pant.
The dappled hands clench and the newspaper crumples beneath their grip, a picture of the Duchess of York is twisted, a headline about immigrants is torn.
"You see... you see... that's the problem with this fucking place..."
Then he explodes.
What follows is a torrent of undiluted rage, a vicious unbridled assault on everyone, everything.
Hate belches forth in thick plumes; he is a volcano of vitriol, a Krakatoa of loathing.
I stand back and let the hatred waft over me.
He's always been like this.
Poison.
He's the first person to declare that the nights are drawing in, the days getting shorter, Winter is near.
He has a death hotline, and the news of the passing of a long retired employee is spread with grim pleasure, usually carrying the inference that it'll be us next, and if not next, then soon...
If anyone on the workforce is fortunate enough to get a promotion, Hades sees it as a bitter personal blow highlighting his own failed career, and the lucky devil who is on the rise will be savaged on the factory floor by him; any little past indiscretion will be dug up and dusted off by the 'grim reader', presented as proof that the lucky recipient of an office and a payrise is probably a bigamist, a philanderer, a thief, a buggerer.
A headline in the paper is enough justify his utter loathing of an

entire nation or ethnic group.
The slightest whiff of a colleagues happiness is enough to incur the full weight of his wrath.
He has always been like this.
Always.
I remember him delivering the news that someone we knew had cancer.
He walked away smiling.
It is the only time I've ever seen him genuinely smiling.
Hades has reduced good people to tears with his malicious gossip, backbiting and destructive lies.
He feeds on the unhappiness of others.
-
The thing is, this isn't the reason why I dread seeing him, talking to him, working with him.
No. It's because I'm terrified I will become like him.
Stuck among the churning, whirring cogs of a factory, watching all the other cogs happily spinning away, content with their lot, while inside the bitterness swells, the discontent, the impotent rage.
Who am I talking about? Me, or Hades?
I don't know. Maybe both.
He's been in the factory for nearly forty years, I've been here for twenty one.
I'm not there, yet.
Perhaps I should look out for the signs, the indicators of the black rot.
Hades does this thing; he collects all the page 3's out of The Sun and The Star.
He goes around the factory, quietly pilfering the pages out of newspapers and smuggles them back to his lair.
Then he puts all the pages together, creating a giant crumpled directory of cheesecake, a curious compilation of tanned tits and perky arses.
Once, I saw Hades sneaking to the toilets with this strange collection tucked under his shirt.
I waited a while, then I followed.
The toilets were quiet.
One cubicle door was locked.

I made a big show of washing my hands, pushed the toilet door open, pretended to leave, and let the door slam shut.
There was a long, silent pause.
Then I heard him.
Growling.
"Cunt. Fucking cunt. Fucking bitches."
Pages turned.
"Bloody fucking bitches. Slags. Bunch of fucking slags..."
Crumple crumple.
"Sluts...sluts...dirty...fucking...sluts..."
I'd heard enough.
I left him to swear at the page three girls.
God only knows what else he was doing in there.
Sitting in a toilet, swearing at pictures of teenage girls with their tits out just isn't normal.
But then again, standing quietly in a toilet, listening to a sixty year old man swearing at pictures of teenage girls with their tits out isn't normal either.
See what I mean?
I've got to be careful.
It's a slippery slope.

-

Soon, Hades loses steam.
He has been venting black bile for a good five minutes, and it seems to have worn him out.
The mauled Daily Mail is scattered across the desk in crumpled monotone rosettes, awards for Hades' display of hate.
And when I look at him, panting, angry about everything, about nothing, I feel sorry for him.
"Here, Hades. Don't you reckon it's time you packed it in? Why don't you fuck this place off and take early retirement?"
He turns his grizzled head to me, fixes me with a bleak expression.
"I retire at Christmas."
I'm shocked.
This is good news.
Not only does Hades get to escape, but I won't have to look at his grim features any more.
Result.

"Fantastic news, Hades! That's only, what, three months away! I bet you can't wait."
Hades shakes his head.
Those hands are tensing again.
"You don't understand. You don't...fucking...understand. The wife, she's made me do it. She's made me retire early. She's been taking Spanish lessons for the past two years. She can speak it like a fucking native. We're selling up, going to Spain. I don't want to go to Spain. Not with my fucking skin."
He holds up a tensed claw of a hand, the pale albino blotches livid against the curled brown paper on the walls.
"I'll fry in the sun. I can't spend more than a few minutes in direct sunlight before it itches, then it burns. But she won't have it. She said she's going there, with or without me. I've no fucking choice."
Hades falls silent, lowers his head, stares at the afflicted skin of his hands.
I have to say something.
"Look, if she's so set on going, and you'll be so unhappy, can't you .... can't you let her go? Can't you let her go to Spain, and you just stay here?"
He slowly shakes his head.
"I can't, Lucifer. I can't stand to be alone. If she leaves me, then I'll be alone, and I can't bear that. I'd rather burn..."
He keeps staring at his hands, at his pale skin, his dark skin, the pattern that curse him.
I put the job on the desk and leave.
There is nothing more to say.

-

Somewhere in Spain there is a villa with a pool, in a bustling resort. Children play and splash and scream, crickets sing in the bushes, swallows swoop low over the azure waters and steal sips from between the playing youngsters. Adults lounge in swimwear, drinking cold beers, reading paperbacks.
Life is good.
But in the villa, in the shadows, protected by glass and shutters and air conditioning and greasy layers of sunblock; tormented by the muffled screams and laughter, by the tan bodies slinking by, tan bodies impervious to ultra violet; in the cool of the darkness there

lurks rage, terrible, lonely rage.
Doomed to an indeterminate sentence in Costa del Purgatory...

Porn Free

"Lucifer, are you busy?"
It was Soulless Boss.
He knew I wasn't busy.
I'd done fuck all for three days.
That's just how it goes sometimes - there are busy days and slow days, lively weeks and dead weeks.
It was a dead week.
I glanced around at the paperback books, magazines, tea cups and crisp packets that littered my grubby desk.
"I've got quite a bit on at the moment, Soulless Boss. Maybe Thursday..."
"Don't get fucking smart. I want you to take this work ticket to the account executives, photocopy this stock order and fetch me three blue biros from the stores."
"That's a lot to remember, Soulless Boss. I'd better write it down. Have you got a pen?"
His piggy eyes narrowed as he tried to weigh up whether I was taking the piss.
Of course I was taking the piss.
"Just... go, Lucifer."
"Righto."
-
The account executives inhabit an ivory tower at the far end of the factory.
You need a pass key to enter their offices.
It keeps out the unwashed.
It keeps out the shambling Neanderthals who run machines and cut paper, sweep floors and grease cogs.
It keeps out the plebs with grubby desks littered with paperback books, magazines, tea cups and crisp packets.
It keeps the suits safe and clean.
I found my pass key and checked to see if it still worked.
It did.
I'll be fucked if I'm going to knock and wait for permission from a

suit.
I'd found the key in a door in an abandoned corridor about six months ago.
It became my key.
So I entered the offices.
The first thing that hit me was the smell.
Fresh coffee, new carpet, a whiff of perfume, a hint of pine forest.
It got me every time.
None of the usual smells you get in the factory.
Industrial solvent, microwaved leftovers, unwashed clothes, farts.
When the door clicked shut behind me I didn't want to open it again.
Row after row of desks stretched out along that long room.
Tapping keys, chatter into telephones, the hum of a photocopier.
The account executives really looked to be hustling.
As I walked silently by I saw the same green screen on every monitor:
two of diamonds, jack of clubs, eight of hearts, king of spades.
I heard the phone calls:
"Yes, I know you said the fridge was going to be delivered Tuesday, but I can't make it..."
"I really miss Timmy, mum. Can you put him on the phone? Please? Please? Mum, put the dog on the phone now! Timmy? It's mummy! I wuv you sooo much!"
"Hello? Yeah, it's Dave. Can you put fifty quid each way on Lavender Bandit at the 3.15 at Chepstow? Yeah, I'll hold..."
"...so I woke up, and he was in bed next to me... Cheryl, he was...wanking! I know! No, I just finished him off and called a taxi for him. Didn't get his name."
They looked busy.
Looks can be deceiving.
I slapped the job ticket down on a desk.
"Hi Dave. Soulless Boss sent this down for you."
Dave quickly switched off his monitor. He had been looking at tennis players showing their knickers.
"Lucifer! How did you get in here."
"The door, Dave. I came in through the door."
"Yes yes, but you need a pass key!"
"Door was open."

"Oh. I'd better ring maintenance. Can't have just anyone wandering in."
"No. We can't have that."
I went to the photocopier.
Dave went back to drooling over teenagers with tennis rackets.
As the machine whirred and buzzed and flashed I heard a laugh that set my teeth on edge.
"Haheeheeheeheeha!"
It had a deranged ring to it, like a rapist on helium.
I glanced across the room.
It was Burrows.
I shuddered.
Burrows is five feet tall, with strange thinning hair greased to his domed head. He's mid twenties but get's I.D'd when he's buying a pint of fucking milk.
He was talking to a secretary, whispering rapidly into her ear as his eyes darted around the office, taking it all in.
The secretary blushed and tittered.
Burrows took the opportunity to run a finger over her bare arm.
She didn't notice.
He whispered again, she laughed, but walked away with a worried expression.
He watched her go, his bulging eyes scurrying all over her retreating body.
Then he licked his finger.
I looked away.
My flesh crawled.
I jabbed the buttons on the photocopier and it burped out more paper.
The novelty of the office had worn off pretty quick.
I preferred the more honest dirt of my own desk.
Whirr buzz flash.
Whirr buzz flash.
Whirr buzz...
"Hello Lucifer."
A finger touched my bare arm.
"Jesusfuckingchrist!"
Burrows withdrew his hand quickly.

"Ooh! You're jumpy! You must have a guilty conscience!"
Only guilty of wanting to wring your creepy, rapey neck, you little...
"No, Burrows. You just... surprised me."
"A pleasant surprise, I hope! Haheeheeheeheeha!"
I didn't say anything.
He leant closer to me.
"I've got some new stuff, Lucifer. Stuff you might... like!"
He grinned at me.
His teeth were like a child's, tiny and wide spaced.
He squashed his tongue against the tiny teeth and the pink flesh bulged between the gaps.
I could have puked.
"I'm not interested, Burrows."
Burrows had a sideline in pornography.
He spent his evenings downloading every kind of hardcore filth you can imagine (and a lot you've can never imagine).
He burned DVDs and printed out lists for pervs to peruse.
I'm no saint, but I have certain standards.
I didn't want to have anything to do with Burrows.
"Do you like anal, Lucifer?"
"Fucking Hell. Shut up, will you? I've got work to do."
Burrows came closer, and started talking fast, really fast, in the same whisper he'd used on the secretary.
"I've got some great stuff where a bloke with a massive dick rams it down this young girl's throat and she gags and she pukes and she starts to cry and he doesn't stop and he grabs her throat and her make up runs and he fucks her skull and she pukes again but it's like snot and he slaps her and she screams and..."
"Shut up, just shut up you horrible runt."
A couple of account executives looked up from their screens, blinking owlishly.
I grabbed my photocopies and made for the stock room.
Three biros.
I slammed the door, fumbled for the light and let out a ragged sigh.
Burrows really creeped me out.
He was always talking about which blokes ordered what porn.
Ramjet likes gang bangs.
Dogsbody likes dwarves.

Boon likes then barely legal.
The Major was hooked on violent bumming.
Borstal likes shitting films.
In my opinion there are some things I really don't want to know.
Men's wanking preferences are high on that list.
"Biro's, biro's, where are the fucking biro's..."
I just wanted to get the pens and get out.
"Looking for the biro's Lucifer?"
"Jesusfuckingchrist!"
Burrows was next to me, wagging a pen.
I hadn't heard the door open.
I reckon the slimy gimp had slithered underneath it.
"Yes, Burrows. I'm looking for the biro's."
He pointed to an unmarked box.
"Biro's are in here, Lucifer."
I grabbed a handful and made for the door.
Burrows didn't move.
"Lucifer, I wanted to apologise about earlier. I didn't mean to be offensive..."
He was reaching out to me with that finger, making a bee-line for a bare patch of skin.
"Burrows, no offence, but if you touch me I'll snap your fucking finger off."
He withdrew his hand, and showed those horrible little teeth.
"Haheeheeheeheeha! You are funny, Lucifer! Look, I've got something for you. A present."
He slipped a disk into my hands.
A DVD.
It didn't have anything written on it.
"Not interested, Burrows."
I tried to give him it back, but he put his hands behind his back.
"It's nothing nasty, Lucifer! Trust me! Haheeheeheeheeha!"
He slipped out of the stock room and scampered away.
By the time I'd grabbed the biro's and left the stock room Burrows was already whispering to Dave.
I was about to throw the disk he'd given me into the bin, but then I stopped.
It looked innocuous enough, but what was on it?

What if I threw it in the bin, and somebody saw me, and picked it up, and loaded it into their computer for a look...
I thrust the disk into my pocket.
From across the room I heard that laugh:
"Haheeheeheeheeha!"
I hurried away.

-

I had the house to myself.
Early afternoon, my shift over, a few hours before the wife finished work.
The devil makes work for idle hands.
I'd forgotten about the disk, but when I rummaged in my work bag for my phone, I felt the cool shiny plastic of the CD.
What was on it?
I pushed the thought from my mind and went to throw the disk in the bin.
What was on it?
I decided to snap it into pieces and shove the bits to the bottom of the bin.
What was on it?
The disk bent...
I pressed the button on the DVD player, the drawer slid open and I popped the disk in.
I closed the curtains, just in case.
Pressed 'Play'.
The screen was a bit blurry at first, then the porn started.
Normal porn.
Tits cocks fannies.
Bit dull, fairly standard filth.
Not bad actually.
I was just starting to get into it, when the screen suddenly changed.
There was a load of ugly women scampering around a garden.
They were giggling and talking Spanish.
The ugly women started kissing.
I wasn't so keen.
The ugly women suddenly took their knickers off to reveal massive cocks, which they proceeded to suck vigorously.
Oh dear.

I fumbled for the remote control.
I managed to switch it off just as the big cocked ugly women began to fondle a small pony in a very inappropriate way that made the pony look alarmed...
Burrows.
I was going to kill him.
-
Next day I'd half forgotten about the seedy film.
It was fifty pieces of shiny plastic at the bottom of the bin.
I was working, minding my own business, when Dogsbody scuttled over.
"Hi Lucifer."
"Hello Dogsbody. What are you doing in here?"
"I hear you like the... unusual stuff too."
"What?"
"You know, the more, exotic material."
"Dogsbody, I haven't got a fucking clue what you are talking about."
He sighed.
"Well, to put it bluntly, I hear you're a fan of big cocked ladyboys. What's the new film like? The one with the little horse. Is it any good?"
I wanted to puke.
"Who the fuck has been saying I like big cocked ladyboy films??"
"Burrows. He's been telling everybody that you've put a special order in."
Burrows.
Burrows was a dead man.
I ran up the corridor as fast as I could.
Got to the door to the offices.
Fumbled for my pass key.
Put it in the lock.
Nothing.
The key didn't work.
Fuck.
I calmed down, took a deep breath, and knocked.
After an age, the door opened a crack.
It was Dave.
"Hello Dave. Can I come in?"

Dave looked disgusted.

"If you're looking for Burrows, Lucifer, he's not here. He told me to tell you he's not willing to supply that filth to you again."

"What?? The little fucker thrust that shit on me, Dave! Anyway, don't preach to me! I saw you perving at tennis players knickers on the net yesterday!"

"There's a world of difference between Anna Kournikova and big cocked ladyboys, Lucifer. A world of difference. Don't even go there."

He closed the door.

Muffled, almost too quiet to hear, from deep within the pine scented sanctuary of the office, I heard:

"Haheeheeheeheeha!"

I shuffled back to the studio.

Local Bike

dingaling
I pushed open the battered door and wheeled my bike into the shop. I stood on the carpet in a small puddle of my own making, squelching cold toes in waterlogged cycling shoes, eyes crossed as I watched the rain water drip from the peak of my cap.
"Hello?"
No answer.
I knew that the shop, my local bike shop, was doing pretty well. Business was good.
Appearances can be deceptive.
"Hello?"
The retail Marie Celeste wasn't giving anything away.
I always found the tired interior of the shop a faintly depressing place.
It had an air of neglect, a forlorn, Eastern Bloc emptiness that many shops once held back in the seventies but was now extinct.
Except for here, the local bike shop.
Drilled hardboard sheets coated in yellowing white gloss covered some of the walls, supporting chipped chipboard shelves in sagging rows that were in turn laden with haphazard cycling paraphernalia. Elsewhere, faded posters of track stars in leather hairnet helmets tore themselves from rusty drawing pins after decades of crucifixion on the cracked, rotten plaster.
The obligatory fluorescent light blinked madly over a garish of huddle children's bicycles, creepily incongruous amongst the sallow shades that surrounded them.
"Hello?"
Outside, peering through the rivulets of water meandering down the plate glass window, a tired looking prostitute tried to catch my eye. She looked pleadingly as she mimed a wanking action.
I mouthed the words, 'no thank you' and looked away.
The rainwater that leaked from my clothes darkened the dilapidated carpet beneath my feet.
Worn paths in the carpet lead in three directions.

To the counter, to the back office, to the workshop.
The counter was deserted, it's cracked glass offering a peek into another world of shiny metal componentry and slick black carbon fibre.
Gleaming baubles every bit as out of place as the children's bikes. In place of an office door there hung a soiled curtain, frayed and ominous, the sort of curtain you would instantly regret peeking through for fear of what there might be beyond...
"Hello?" I didn't expect an answer, but I got one.
"For fuck's sake..."
It came from the workshop.
I followed the worn carpet trail in that direction.
Another grim curtain hid the workshop.
"Erm...anyone home?"
"Who the fuck wants to know?"
"Lucifer."
Exasperated sighs and tuts came from behind the curtain.
"You'd better come in then, I suppose."
I held back the greasy material and stepped into the workshop.
Benches scattered with battered tools, ancient workstands and vices of differing sizes, a concrete floor blackened by decades of oil and grime.
On the wall, sepia stunners from long gone page 3's smiled cheekily over the detritus of the workshop.
Teflon, Dazzle and Saul were hunched in the stygian gloom, biting into giant sandwiches and slurping from chipped mugs of tea.
"Hello lads."
"Now then, you cunt."
All three started laughing, spitting crumbs and slopping tea over a very expensive looking Colnago racer.
The owner of the shop, Teflon, stopped laughing first.
"Sorry Luci, it's just that we're having a competition to see who can call customers a cunt without them knowing. Dazzle's just taken the lead with that beauty."
"That's nice. I'm glad to see customer service hasn't lapsed in any way."
"Yeah, Saul got a beauty yesterday. Some knob-head wanted to know if you could put a Shimano derrailleur with Campagnolo

shifters, and he says, 'You cunt really get away with that!"
More laughter. Milky tea and chewed ham dripped from the
glittering paint of the Colnago.
"What can we do for you, then, Luci?" asked Teflon.
"I got a puncture. Some glass has slit the sidewall of my tyre, and..."
Saul sighed.
"Fucking Hell... give it here."
Through muttered curses, Saul set to work. He's a miserable fucker,
but he's magic with a bike. I didn't respond to his insults, I just let
him crack on with what he had to do.
Dazzle was sat in the corner, munching his sandwich with his left
hand whilst slowly pumping a track pump with his right. His skinny
arms were knotted with rock hard muscles.
Here, Teflon!" called Dazzle. "Luci's a know-all. Why don't you ask
him?"
"Yeah, Teflon. Ask Luci," muttered Saul.
"Ask me what?"
Teflon gargled a mouthful of tea. "Right then, Luci. You're a smart
arse. Tell me this. Where does all the milk come from?"
Was it a trick question? I didn't know, but I played along.
"Cows, Teflon. All the milk comes from cows."
"Ah, yes! But where are all the cows?"
"Erm... in the fields. The cows are in the fields."
Teflon waggled his eyebrows, and the strip lighting reflected off his
tanned bald head.
"Hah! But there's not enough of them! Think about it! There's
fucking tens of millions of us in England, and we're all having milk
on our cereal, milk in our tea, cheese in our sarnies, yoghurt for the
women and the puffs, ice cream for the kids! That is a fuck of a lot
of milk, by anyone's guessing. So where's it coming from? By rights,
all the fields should be over flowing with fucking cows, and every
other wagon on the road should be a dairy tanker! But it's not! So
where... is... the...milk... coming...from?"
"Hang about. Where does it say you have to be wither a woman or
gay to like yoghurt?"
"Be honest, Luci. When did you last have a yoghurt?"
"Erm.. yesterday."
"Exactly. You fucking puff."

As they all laughed and Saul fettled and Dazzle pumped, I got to thinking; where does all the milk come from?
To be honest, Teflon had a point.
There's not THAT many dairy farms about, not that many cows about.
I know that Yorkshire doesn't have that many dairy farms compared to, say, Devon, but I'd been to Devon before, and the fields weren't heaving with cows. I can't honestly remember seeing that many at all.
Where DOES all the milk come from?
The thought of it kind of disturbed me.
I shrugged. "Maybe it's rat milk. Maybe they've got these underground farms filled with millions and millions of rats like battery chickens and they're all fitted with tiny milking machines and all the milk we're drinking isn't really cows milk but is rat milk, and the cows in the fields are just for show."
The workshop went silent.
Saul stopped fettling.
Dazzle stopped pumping.
Teflon slowly spat his tea back into his mug.
They all stared at me.
"Fucking Hell, Luci." Teflon got up and walked away, shaking his head. He left his tea on the work bench.
"Here, your bike's fixed."
"Erm.. thanks Saul. You've done a smashing job. What do I owe you?"
"Pay us next time."
"Ok. ta."
Saul disappeared through the dirty curtain.
Only me and Dazzle remained.
Dazzle was laughing quietly to himself, and he'd resumed his pumping.
"Rats! hehehehe! Did you see their faces, Luci! I thought Saul was gonna puke! Rats! Hehehe!"
Dazzle's arms were really straining now. He had both hands on the pump, grinding it down as he forced more air into...
Into what?
"Dazzle, what the fuck are you pumping up there?"

He grinned back at me, and nodded at a closed door.
A valve poked through the keyhole.
The pump was attached to the valve.
Shiny black rubber protruded obscenely from the gaps around the door, and faint struggles could be heard from within.
"Holy shit, Dazzle. What's in there??"
Dazzle's grin grew wider, and he started to giggle.
"A shoplifter!"
I was going to ask if that was a bit dangerous, but at that moment the world ended.
It's hard to describe the noise, or the wave of pressure, or the dark rain of shredded rubber that flitted down around us. Dazzle rolled on the floor, screaming with laughter, laughter I couldn't hear.
All I could hear was a high whining.
Fuck. I was deaf.
The door that had held back the overinflated tyre was hanging open to reveal a filthy toilet. A scrawny teenager staggered out with wild hair and a nose bleed.
Like a silent movie, I watched as Dazzle grabbed him by the collar and frog marched him through the curtain, into the shop.
I followed.
The hapless scrote was flung into the street, where he sat for a while in a small stream of rainwater, cigarette ends and jauntily floating crisp packets. After a short while he stumbled to his feet and wandered away.
The prostitute was no longer there.
The rain had begun to ease.
I turned to thank the lads for repairing my bike, but the shop was deserted. I couldn't hear anyone, but then again, I couldn't hear fuck all thanks to Dazzle's theft deterrent.
I left the shop.
Climbed aboard my bike, rode away.
On a deserted patch of scrub land, a mournful horse grazed on grass and litter and watched as I rode past.
I looked at him, and he looked at me.
Where were all the cows?

Help The Aged.

I've been thinking about Albert a lot recently.
I'm worried that I might be the only person who remembers him, who knows him.
You've got to look out for old people in the community, you know. Stuff can happen. We've all heard about backlogs of letters and rain bloated newspapers; bottles of neglected silvertop on leaf strewn doorsteps, quietly curdling; a flickering telly behind thin curtains that are always drawn, day and night, night and day, day and night...
You've got to keep a weather eye out for those warning signs, those cries for help and attention from the aged citizens.
You don't want to look out one morning and see an ambulance at number fifty three, green clad paramedics carrying out the desiccated mummy of Mrs Ducundiano who you've not seen since August '08 and who would sometimes give you a coconut macaroon of dubious vintage if you happened to be passing.
The guilt would haunt you, torment you, tighten like a cheap plastic belt on your very soul until you could stand it no longer and you felt compelled to seek out a sympathetic priest to hear your confession as a true earpiece of the Almighty Triumvirate, and berate you, absolve you, cleanse you in the quiet, cool waters of the confessional...
Or you could just watch half of Songs of Praise while you eat your tea.
Same fucking difference.
Anyway, I'm worried about Albert.
I slouch to the toilets, go into the cubicle on the left, drop my trousers, sit down. I don't know why I bothered dropping my trousers - I need neither a crap or a piss. Force of habit, I suppose. The right thing to do.
I have brought nothing to read. A schoolboy error, you might think, perhaps I'm losing my edge. But wait. I reach behind the cistern, locate glossy paper misted with condensation, and Hey Presto! A copy of Fiesta from around 1987.
Quality.
It's not in bad condition, considering it's resting place in a gent's

lavvy, but there is a little warping to the pages, a light whiff of mildew about it's puckered leaves.
I slowly thumb through the pages.
I don't get aroused, you understand. Pornography has come a long way since this particular magazine was first plucked excitedly from the top shelf of a newsagents by a randy punter. Back then, it was quite acceptable to wank like a madman over the knicker section of a Kay's catalogue. In fact it was actively encouraged.
Pornography was deliciously rare, a product that had to be sought out with considerable effort. If you wanted to see tits and fannies you would have to put on your coat, leave the house, got to a newsagents, make sure the shop was reasonably empty, wander in and peruse the choice of magazines, pretend to consider buying Auto Trader or National Geographic, allow your gaze to wander upwards, discretely ogle the strumpets on display, carefully choose your favourite according to brand loyalty and budgetary constraints, take your sweaty selection to the counter, realise it's a woman behind the counter, and FLEE! FLEE! ABORT MISSION! drop the magazine behind a stack of Happy Bread and spend your money bitterly on unwanted confectionary under the withering gaze of a thoroughly disapproving propietoress who saw exactly what you had just done with that copy of Razzle.
If you wanted a publication of richer content, something... meatier, then you would be forced into that most bleak and chilling of establishments - the sex shop. For a tenner you could acquire a small, stout publication with a leering European crack whore on the front, sealed in heavy duty polythene.
You could only check the content for strength once you were safe at home, partly because you wouldn't want to be seen outside Morrison's desperately wrestling your way into German pornography, and partly because you would need half the sharp utensils in the kitchen to actually pierce the stubborn plastic coating. It was always, always disappointing. The British editors would have been busy covering all the interesting bits with solid, cock shaped blocks of black ink, veiling all points of contact between Helga and Fritz with maddening diligence. Not that I craved cock, you understand, but as my cock wasn't getting any action, it was always cheering to know that some cock somewhere was getting a proper

sorting out, and that a photographer had been on hand to commemorate the event.
You, with your super fast broadband, your bookmarks of alarmingly specific niche pornography, your instantly erasable internet history...
You don't know you're fucking born.
Anyway, back to the toilet, the copy of Fiesta, my concerns for Albert.
I'd read this magazine from cover to cover many times before, was on nodding acquaintance with each girl, Mandy, Trudy, Beryl, Ruby, I knew their strengths and weaknesses, from pert breast to spotty arse, frizzy perm to graceful neck.
We were not lovers; more than that, we were friends.
The stories in the magazine fascinated me.
To think that this era was quite naive, pornographically speaking, they were certainly imaginative. One bloke had written in about how he used to fuck his landlady. She was older than him, and it turned him on when she would flip her legs up, hold his face to her arse and smother him with an immense fart. Another bloke liked to get lads round to the house to shag his wife, and then he'd creep up a ladder outside, peek in the bedroom window and wank over them. I mean, he's up a ladder. Wanking.
Rich stuff.
After the girls, my girls, and after the stories of ladder wanking and landlady farting there were the Reader's Wives.
These creeped me out, and I never lingered. They looked like crime scene photos, toothless crones and pouch-bellied housewives gurning reluctantly for a deluded husband who misguidedly though it a good idea to splay his missus over the pages of a soft core porno mag.
No, no, no.
I would carefully hold this part of the magazine closed, and leaf the edges of the pages past without witnessing the horror.
And now we come to the interesting bit.
A part of the publication called, 'One for the Ladies'.
This consisted of a single page in the whole magazine devoted to blokes showing us their cocks.
Blurry polaroids of men grinning reluctantly at the camera as the

missus decides what's good for the goose is good for the gander, snapping away at Derek from Doncaster with his tackle flapping around in the living room in front of a three bar fire.
And here he is.
Albert.
Albert is stood forlornly in his own living room, a popular spot for male exhibitionism, it seems. Better than the front garden, I suppose. The difference with Albert is, he's alone. There is no-one on hand to instruct Albert to say 'cheese', and he does not say 'cheese', he does not smile. Albert stares into the camera lens with a strange intensity, a puzzled, lost expression on his grizzled features. He is, of course, bollock naked; it goes without saying. He is naked, his flaccid penis hanging loosely against his sagging ball-bag, a slight pot belly casting a vague shadow over the aforementioned region.
I know that Albert is alone because he has been forced to use a long stick to operate the camera mechanism, a device he uses with surprising dexterity, but it still seems rather alarming as it looms into shot on the far right of the screen.
Albert is alone, he looks sad and puzzled, he uses a stick to operate a camera to take pictures of his own cock.
If that isn't a cry for help, I don't know what is.
Guessing from the age Albert seems to be in the picture, and from the age of the magazine, I reckon Albert is no longer with us.
Albert is almost definitely dead.
Yet, strangely, he lives on.
There he is, staring at me with his funny stick and his sagging genitalia, a sad face and a wall clock forever frozen at one twenty seven.
Like Stonehenge and the great pyramids of Giza, I haven't got a fucking clue what message Albert wanted to leave behind on those crumpled pages of a popular wank mag, but I hope it's a comfort to him, wherever he is, that somebody saw him and remembered him. After all, who will remember me?
Maybe I should crack out the old Olympus Trip and a garden cane and recreate that famous pose, in the hope that, in twenty odd years time someone will stare into the pages of an old magazine, and think, 'what the fuck was that crazy bastard up to?'

I carefully fold up the copy of Fiesta, slip it behind the cistern, pull up my trousers, and go back to work.

What's The Big Flap?

I walked in off the hot street for a cold beer.
I knew they sold cold beer. The sign, written in faded chalk, said "COLD BEER".
It also said, "WORK WEAR WELCOME". I wasn't wearing work wear, but it was good to know.
It was dark inside the pub. I stood in the doorway and allowed my eyes to adjust to the gloom, to the sour beer smell, to The Eagles on the jukebox.
Dull shapes moved slowly in the perpetual twilight.
Gradually the dull shapes turned into people, and some were actually wearing work wear. The advertising was obviously effective. Other people looked like they'd never done a day's work in their lives.
I say I wasn't wearing work wear, but that's not strictly true, as I was on my way home from work and I had been wearing the same clothes that day.
My clothes didn't count. Grimy overalls, scuffed rigger boots and jeans thick with plaster dust constitute work wear.
My clothing was conspicuously clean and fresh.
I walked to the bar, ignoring a few side on glances, and ordered one of those famous cold beers. Like I said, the advertising was effective.
Someone further down the bar called out:
"Aye up, our kid!"
It was my brother, Devil.
I wasn't really surprised to see him there as it was his kind of pub. He used to work at the same factory as me, but he jacked it in and tried being a barfly instead.
It was a career change that suited him, perhaps a little to well.
He moved down the bar and sat on the stool next to me. He was grinning from ear to ear, looking like he didn't have a care in the world.
It made me think about quitting my job and becoming barfly too.
I said, "Now then Devil. Keeping busy?"
"This and that, Luci. This and that." He caught the bartender's

attention. "Deano! Get my brother a beer, will you?"
Devil talked to Deano like he was a friend. Deano didn't look like he was friends with anyone.
Deano dumped my beer in front of me. He said, "You're too late, Devil."
Devil winked. "Better get me one then, Deano!"
Deano glowered, and slouched back to the pump.
I said, "So what are you so happy about, Devil? Been getting your end away?"
"Ha! Just the opposite, our kid! I've got shut of that crazy cunt, Scarlet!"
"Scarlet? I don't know a Scarlet..."
"What? Come, on, man! Scarlet! That mad bird I've been banging!"
I shook my head. "Nope. You've not told me about her. Remember, I've not seen you in a few months."
"Shit, I could have sworn I told you about her..."
An old man with no teeth nursing a half of mild leaned across to me. "He's told every other bastard in this place about her!" he cackled.
Deano came back with a beer. He dead eyed me. "That'll be four sixty."
I looked at Devil.
Devil looked preoccupied.
I paid for the beer.
Devil sprang back to life. "Anyhow, this Scarlet lass. I started seeing her a few months back. Can't remember where I met her, it just sort of happened. She's a bit posh but lives in a block of flats. I don't know how that works, but that's how it is. Bit of a student type. Really dramatic about everything, you know? Anyhow, I starts seeing her. We go out for summat to eat, like for a pizza or something, and she'd say, "Devil, oh Devil, I'm not wearing any panties!" and I'd think, 'fucking hell! Randy bitch!' and I'd take a look under the table, and I wouldn't want mi dinner anymore."
"Why didn't you want your dinner anymore?"
"Coz of her fanny, that's why. See, Scarlet's a ging, so she's got ginger eyebrows and ginger eyelashes and ginger hair and ginger pubes..."
"I get the picture."
"Right, well, she doesn't like the ginger pubes so she always shaves

the lot off, which is all right, you know? But what's not alright is that her fanny is bright red and she has this one massive big flap."
I snorted, and beer came out of my nose.
"Don't laugh, y'bastard!" laughed Devil. "It was horrible! Flapping around down their while I'm trying to tuck into my pepperoni! It put me right off!"
I composed myself, wiped beer from my nose onto the beer towel. Deano looked disgusted, but I didn't care.
"Two more beers, Deano. One massive big flap and a bright red fanny, Devil? That sounds bleak."
"Bleak it was, our kid. Bleak it was."
"I'm interested, just how big was this massive big flap? I mean, compared to normal flaps, that is."
Devil took a drink. "Ok. Do you remember when we used to queue for the school bus?"
"Yeah, I remember."
"Right, well you'll remember that on Tuesdays the Special Bus would go past at twenty five past eight and everyone in the school queue would go quiet and look away?"
"Yeah..."
"And do you remember why everyone would go quiet and look away?"
"Yeah, because there was a that old bloke on the Special Bus with no teeth and a red face who would always lick the window and he had a massive tongue... oh fucking hell no..."
Devil nodded, drank his beer.
I shook my head in stunned silence.
The old man leaned across to me again. "Disgusting, isn't it?"
"Fuck off, Tommy!" yelled Devil. "You're not much better looking than he was, than that fanny was!"
Tommy went back to his beer.
"Any road," continued Devil, keeping one eye on old Tommy, "I tried to break up with Scarlet. I really tried! I was really put off because of the... you know..."
"Massive big flap?"
"Yeah, that. But I'd have a few beers, then she'd ring me, begging for a fucking, and before I knew where I was I'd be round there banging her! You know what my problem is, Luci? I'm weak, that's what it

is. Just plain weak..."
I didn't know what to say, so I said, "Yeah, you're really fucking weak, mate." It didn't help.
"It wasn't just the massive big flap though. She was really kinky! You know what she had me do? She had me tie her up with nowt on and put tape over her mouth, sling her in the boot of my Ford Fiesta then drive around for miles and miles before pulling into a lay-by, open the boot, roll her over and bang her right there, in the boot, in a lay-by in the middle of fucking nowhere! If that's not fucking kinky then I don't know what is!"
I said, "Yeah, that's pretty kinky."
"And then this other time she phoned me and says for me to come over to pick her up. I got to her flat and she's waiting in the lobby, wearing this mad robe. You know, like a king's? All red with this big furry trim! So she gets i the car and tells me to drive. We go out into the countryside, miles from anywhere, and she tells me to pull over by this gate. I stops the car and she suddenly leaps out of the car and throws off this robe! Underneath she's got nowt on! Totally in the nuddy! And she goes belting off across this field, waving her arms about screaming 'Rape! Rape!' "
"Fucking hell! That's mental!"
"I know! I had to go after her to try shut her up! I was bloody knackered by the time I caught up with her!"
"What did you do?"
"I gave her a slap then bummed her in the woods."
"Oh."
"Yeah, I wasn't proud."
I ordered two more beers. It looked like I was paying.
I said, "So how did you get rid of her then?"
"Well, last night, enough was enough. She wanted to try that trick again with the daft robe and the rape fantasy thing. It's just not my cup of tea. Honest. So off we go to the arse end of nowhere in my Fiesta, but this time she's in the boot. I mean, I ask you. What kind of lass likes to be driven round in the boot of twelve year old Fiesta? So off we go to the woods and out she leaps and goes scampering off into the woods, and I noticed that she's got a really red arse."
"A red arse? What, like sore or something?"
"Nah, just bright fucking red! You know how her fanny is bright red,

well, so's her arse. So she's running off into the woods with naff all on and her bright red arse wobbling about like fucking baboon's, and I thought, 'Fuck that for a game of soldiers' so I chucked her daft cape over a fence, put the old Fiesta in gear and fucked off."
I was shocked. "You left her?? You just drove off and left her? A girl on her own in the fucking *nude* in the back of beyond and you drove off and left her?"
"I chucked her daft robe on the fence, mate. She wouldn't technically be nudey if she had that."
"That's not the point! If she goes and get's raped and killed then you look like the prime fucking suspect! What if she dies of hypothermia or something? Or falls and breaks her leg? Jesus Christ, didn't you think it through? Why didn't you just phone her and tell her 'Sorry love, you're chucked' rather than leaving her for the badgers??"
Tommy leaned over again. "That's just what I said to him, kid. The foxes and rats will be gnawing that poor girl now..."
"Rather them than me, Tommy," Devil said into his glass. "They've got enough to feed 'em for a week just with that massive big flap."
I shook my head. I felt like I should do something, alert the police. What if she was injured out there, lost and alone in the woods?
Then Devil's phone started ringing.
He checked it.
"Shit. It's her."
A said, "What, her...as in, *her*?"
"Yeah. It's 'The Flap'."
"Well at least she's not dead..."
Devil took the call. I tried not to listen, but I couldn't help it.
"Oh, hi babe! Listen I'm sorry.... yeah... yeah? You *liked* it? It actually turned you *on*? What's that? You're doing *what* right now? You dirty little... Ok. Yeah, ok. I'll be right over."
I looked down. Devil was absent mindedly rubbing his hard on through his pants. I looked away.
Old Tommy sipped gently at his half. "Some people," he mumbled, "have no moral fibre."
I said, "Tommy, I've noticed that you've been topping up your glass from the drip tray. You're in no position to judge, mate."
I saw Devil heading for the door.
"Where the fuck are you going, mate? I guess she's not dead then!"

Devil looked sheepish. "Nah, man. She fucking loved it, the crazy bitch. A van driver picked her up and offered to take her to the coppers, but she ended up wanking him off in a truck stop, you know, as a thank you. She wants me to go over and fuck her, then drive her across to Doncaster."

"Why, what's at Doncaster?"

"Nothing, that's why she wants me to kick her out of the car there." Devil disappeared, and a minute later I heard a shitty little car speed out of the car park before fading into the muffled rumble of the afternoon traffic.

I ordered another beer, and when it came I slid it across to Tommy. "Have a pint of moral fibre on me, Tommy."

I walked out into the shimmering heat of a dusty Friday afternoon, and headed for home.

Office Politics

I have moved.
After nearly twenty years in the same shitty space, the same off white walls and scuffed linoleum, the same fucked chairs and knackered desks and flickering fluorescents, I have finally picked up my keyboard and computer and moved.
From one end of the factory to the other.
I am now in a bright, breezy office that feels like an airport terminal.
I have a new desk and a new chair and fluorescent tubes that do not flicker.
Gone are the stuttering whirr of dying cooling fans in the back of ancient, dust-clogged PCs. Gone are the vacant, staring faces of inquisitive morons peering through fly shit-speckled glass at us, gawping in wonder at a job they perceive as exotic and aspirational simply because it doesn't involve getting covered in ink or listening to the deafening clatter of aging print presses.
No, in the airport terminal it is deathly quiet. All sounds are magnified to an excruciating level. I found myself actually sucking crisps the other day, because the crunching was exquisite agony and people looked up owlishly from their desks to find the source of the hideous din.
I am not alone in this cavernous office.
Curious creatures dwell here, have dwelt here for decades. People who have never, ever set foot on the factory floor, have never seen a printer or a print press or reams of paper or squat tubs of dark ink. These be-suited bovines shuffle slowly to work through quiet corridors that avoid noise, dirt, sweat, work. There are stairs to the office, but they drift upwards in a shiny steel lift, jostling into the metal box on one level, belched out on the next carrying tupperware and biscuit tins, cake boxes and pie. They arrive at nine, yawning and bleary, meander towards their twee-cluttered terminals and fire up the blinking screens.
I have already been working for three hours.
As their computers come to life the office workers fill an over worked fridge with their wares, and begin to boil gallons of water for

the onslaught of endless tea breaks to come.
They always arrive at work at the same time, move around at work together, murmuring reassurances to each other, repeated phrases that induce polite laughter or resigned sighs. They are an odd shoal, a troop of shaved and nervous apes wearing expensive spectacles and crisp shirts, smelling of lovely cologne and a hint of red wine from the night before.
My new desk is clean and flawless, empty of everything except a screen, a phone, a keyboard and mouse, a pen, a ruler, a cup.
I have been sterilised.
I now wear a dinky little uniform consisting of blue polo shirt with a cheeky gold logo, blue stay-pressed pants, a blue jumper for when I get chilly, and if I turn up without any part of this uniform on I get told to fuck off home and I'm not allowed to return unless I'm dressed like everybody else.
The office bovines do not have to wear the dinky little uniform.
They can wear whatever they like, as long as it is officey and smart. The male of the species wear shirts of various hues and ties ranging from 'sober' to 'wacky'.
Smart trousers of grey, black or brown sheathe their weak lower limbs, shiny shoes finish off the ensemble.
The females are more flamboyant. Bright swathes of aquamarine and azure waft around their sagging, bulging forms; arms that flap with excess fat are caressed by pastel chiffon; goiters and scrotum-necks are coyly draped in crushed silk scarves.
The currency of this curious community is food. They arrive every morning rich, they leave each evening poor. I can honestly say that I have never seen such unashamed gluttony in all my life. It never stops, never ends, they never get full, they never tire. The mornings are crammed with an orgy of conspicuous gluttony, from trips to the canteen for pale, quivering bacon in bland baps, to the microwave ping of porridge, scrambled eggs, beans on toast, pastries.
Wednesday is pork pie day. An especially rotund woman takes a list for pies on the Tuesday.
"How many pies do you want, love?"
"Sorry, pies?"
"Yes, pies. How many?"
"Erm... what sort of pies do you mean?"

"Pork pies, love, baked fresh. Wednesday is Pork Pie Day. Every Wednesday is Pork Pie Day. I fetch pork pies in, fresh from the butchers, still hot. How many would you like?"
I like pork pies, but it's a slippery slope. I like scotch, but I try to avoid it at breakfast time.
"No pies, thanks."
"No pies?? But Wednesday is Pork Pie Day! Every Wednesday is Pork Pie Day! Now don't be silly love, how many pies?"
"No pies."
She scowls at me with undisguised suspicion, then waddles away to the far end of the office.
I can hear her muttering with her clan:
"Mumble mumble... no pies!...mumble.. but it's Wednesday!...mumble... bit strange...mumble... ooh, bit of brown sauce..."
They are staring at me over an ocean of monitors and blue partitions. They look shocked and afraid, as though I have rattled their belief in religion, questioned their faith and found them without an answer.
I stare back at them.
They look away.
I go back to my work.
-
The next day Pork Pie Wednesday goes ahead, as it does every Wednesday.
All the great traditions are observed.
The Passing of the Brown Sauce. The Drinking of the Salty Liquor from the Bitten Pie. The Consuming of the Second Pie then the Third Pie, The Rapturous Enthusing over All Things Pie...
The clan are comforted by their rituals, the Gods of Pastry and Mechanically Recovered Meat are appeased.
My own liking for pork pies has diminished quite considerably through witnessing the tragic spectacle that is Pork Pie Wednesday.
-
The clearing of a throat in this silent world is like a gun shot. To cough is to sin. Laughter is sacrilege.
But there is one who wallows in the discomfort of others, one who has taken the art of throat clearing to a new rarefied plateau, one who clears his throat with the ostentation of a judge attempting to

quieten an unruly courtroom.
I don't believe that silence should necessarily be observed in silent places; quiet should not demand quiet. We should be able to talk, cough, fart, sneeze, laugh and curse as we see fit, as long as it does not offend others too greatly. This cough, however, this throat-clearing that drifts on the air conditioned breeze of the deathly silent office is too much. It is a throat clearing that demands attention, a throat clearing of the sort you might make if you were trying to draw a friends attention to their open trouser fly, accompanied by a subtle downwards glance to their pants.
And who is this Craftsman of the Cough, this Pharaoh of Phlegm? The Bog Wanker, that's who.
Not satisfied with flagrantly masturbating in the toilet cubicles of the factory, this utter fuckwit takes his antisocial behaviour out of the bathroom and adjusts it for the consumption of a wider community. His curious tred is accompanied by that attention demanding 'aHEM', triggering something deep in the subconscious to involuntarily swivel the head around in his direction, and feast your eyes on The Bog Wanker.
He is portly and balding, hunch shouldered as though he doesn't want the gazes and attention his 'aHEM' demands. He walks in a very strange way, as if he is wearing skis. Little steps, lifting each foot with care and effort before placing it carefully on the ground a little way ahead, moving his torso with the energy of one speed-walking, though he is in fact moving with painful slowness.
He is carrying either a cup to make tea, or a huge plate of random foodstuffs to place in the microwave.
I have on one occasion watched with teeth grinding irritation as he boiled a kettle, *aHEM* poured it into a Pot Noodle cup, *aHEM* and while it bubbled and festered he carefully chopped fresh mushrooms *aHEM* before lovingly garnishing that grim, rehydrated crap with them.
Why? Why why why??
I haven't had him wank next to me in these new toilets yet.
There is still time.
To think that he travels the long distances between toilets in this huge factory, propelling himself with that painfully slow, invisible-ski walk, all the while intending to have a wank when he eventually

reaches that distant destination, well it quite frankly boggles my mind.
-
The mad scramble of five o'clock has passed now, and it is quiet. It is always quiet, but now it is a very different quiet. This huge room is empty now, except for me. The silence is of my own making, to be broken as I see fit, not by the cough of a chronic masturbater or with the unwanted offer of pie.
The gaggle of chipper shirts and skirts waddled their merry way to the door at five-on-the-dot carrying empty sandwich boxes, flaccid carrier bags, vacant tupperware, full stomachs.
I watched them go with a flood of relief, glad to see the back of them, just as I'm sure they were glad to see the last of me.
Because this is their domain, not mine. I am the one shunning the Sacrament of the Pie, I have rejected their tentative, food-based offers to become one of them, to join them.

I'd rather fucking starve.

Coffin Todger

I saw Coffin Nail today.
This surprised me, because I thought he was dead.
By all rights he should be dead, but I saw him, so that means he's still ticking over.
I was riding my bike along a nice little lane, the kind of lane where you ride slowly so you can have a good nosey up the driveways to see what kind of car the rich people are driving, or what kind of wallpaper rich people hang on their walls, or with any luck, the kind of underwear rich women wear as they get changed by the bedroom window.
I didn't manage to quench my grubby voyeuristic thirsts, but I did notice something.
A crumpled shape, withered and bent, a fucked up old gargoyle of a man struggling to breathe, clinging to the gatepost of a fancy house like a drowning man clinging to a broken mast.
Coffin Nail.
I'd not seen him since they retired him from the factory on medical grounds. None of the managers wanted him to die at work because it would have cost them - death-in-service payments really piss off the managers.
I pulled my bike over to the kerb and waited politely for the old goat to stop coughing what was left of his lungs up and wipe his puckered mouth with a darkly stained handkerchief.
He stared at me with runny eyes, gasping and fighting to get a trickle of clean air into his raddled lungs.
I decided to open the conversation.
"Hi Coffin Nail. You're looking well."
His lips curled back to reveal long, stained teeth protruding from withered gums.
"Fuck off, you sarcastic little arsehole."
"I'm not being sarcastic!"
"Yeah, not much..."
"Really I'm not. See, I heard you were dead. You look a lot healthier than dead."

I don't know if the noise he made was a laugh or a wheeze.
He nodded at my bike.
"What's that silly fucking thing you're playing on there?"
"It's called a bicycle, Coffin Nail. It's a wonderful new invention."
"Once a sarcastic arsehole, always a sarcastic arsehole. Take piss again and I'll knock your fucking teeth out!"
He held up a shaky clenched fist of parchment and liver spots.
"What I mean is, what the fuck are you doing on that thing? A bloke doesn't fuck around on a kid's toy like that! A bloke should have a motor!"
I shrugged. "I've got a car, I just let my wife use it."
"Wife? WIFE? Fucking Hell, lad, you dress up like a ponce and piss about on a push iron, whilst your missus swans around in your fucking motor? You want to have your fucking head examined!"
He pointed a bony finger at me.
"There's a term for blokes like you, lad. Cunt whipped! You're cunt whipped, that's what you are! Your missus get's the car and you get a fucking kid's toy!"
I thought about that. I didn't feel particularly cunt whipped. If I'm honest, I get whipped from so many other directions I wouldn't notice if I was cunt whipped or not.
Maybe I'm just plain whipped.
"I don't mind the bike," I replied. Cuts down on pollution..."
"Pollution's a fucking myth. Never been proven. I've worked in all kinds of places that are supposed to be bad for your health. Never did me any fucking harm."
I couldn't quite believe what he was saying.
Coffin Nail quickly looked up and down the road, those rheumy eyes full of shifty intent.
"Listen, lad, you wouldn't have any smokes on you, would you?"
I shook my head. "Sorry, Coffin Nail. Can't help you. I don't... oh, wait a minute!"
I rummaged in my bag, found a tin of small cigars and a mauled book of matches. Christ knows how long they'd been there, but they were there.
Coffin Nail raised an eyebrow.
"Cigars, eh? Lah-dee-fucking-dah. You couldn't have just had a packet of Benson's like a normal bloke, could you?"

"You'd have felt let down if I had. Are you sure smoking's a good idea, you know, in your condition?"
Coffin Nail lit up and pulled smoke deep into his diseased lungs. He had chronic emphysema. It was so bad he had no right being alive now, but he was. Fair play to him.
"I haven't had a good idea in forty years, lad," he murmured as smoke curled out of his mouth like dragon fire. "I'm not going to start having any now."
There were two bags of shopping on the pavement. I hooked one bag over each of my bike's handlebars, and we set off walking slowly towards Coffin Nail's house.
I thought, what the fuck, and I fired up a little cigar of my own. It felt good to be ambling along, smoking a cigar.
I fired a quick glance at Coffin Nail. He looked bad. His face looked like it had been folded up a dozen times and kept in the loft for fifty years. I felt a bit guilty about giving him a smoke.
"Here, you've got your medicine on you, haven't you?"
Coffin Nail patted his pocket.
"Full inhaler. Brand new. Don't worry lad, I promise not to die on you."
He frowned.
"What you said earlier, about thinking I was dead. What gave you that fucking daft idea?"
"I saw your missus walking up the road with a black armband on. I thought you'd snuffed it."
"Nah, that wasn't for me. It were for the dog. It were getting old and it's back legs were fucked and it couldn't see much any more."
"Oh. Sorry to hear that. You take it down the vet?"
"Nah. I drowned it in a bucket in the garage."
"Oh."
As we smoked and walked I noticed two crossed knives tattooed on his forearm. It was an old tattoo, blurred and blue, but they were unmistakably Gurkha knives.
I nodded at his ink. "What are they, Coffin Nail? They're Gurkha knives, aren't they? Kukri. That's what the proper name is, isn't it? Were you in the Gurkhas?"
He yanked his sleeve down and scowled at me. "Bit fucking nosey, aren't you?"

"Sorry. Just wondered."
"Aye, well don't wonder. It's not something I like to talk about."
I decided to leave that particular subject alone.
If a man has a something he doesn't want to talk about, but he's happy to let you know about drowning the family pet in a bucket, then it's best not to delve too deeply.
I blew some smoke. "So, if you don't like to talk about that, what do you like to talk about?"
Coffin Nail thought for a minute.
"Cunt. I like to talk about cunt."
I coughed on my cigar. "Well, I don't reckon you'll get on Mastermind with that chosen specialised subject, but I'm ok with that."
"I've just come back from the hospital, lad. Been to get this new medicine, and all my other medicine, for that matter. Fuck me, there's some fit nurses there. Gagging for it, all of them. Tits bursting out of those uniforms, arses tight as drums in those blue strides they wear. It even got a twitch out of me, lad, and that's saying summat, nowadays. Well this young nurse tells me the name of the medicine I was getting and I misheard her, coz I was looking down her top, so I looks up and says, 'What's that new stuff you're giving me? Viagra?' And she laughs her head of and says it's Valium, they're giving me Valium, so I shrugs and says, 'I'd rather have the Viagra!'
"Well, these nurse are all laughing so this female doctor comes out and says, 'What's all this? what's all the laughing?' So these nurses tell her what's been said and that doctor gives me this right dirty look! She says, 'I don't think Viagra will do you any good!'
This got right on my fucking wick! I grabs myself by the tackle and gives it a right good shake at her, and says, 'give us a couple of those blueys and I'll see if I can do *you* any good!' She says that she doubts it, so I says, 'Try me! I'll provide the donkey derby if you'll provide the jockey!'"
Old Coffin Nail really had me laughing. He was stood in the street with a cigar in one hand and the saggy crotch of his trousers in the other. When he let go of his crotch a small wet patch started to spread across the fabric. I pretended not to notice and carried on laughing.

"Shit," he muttered, and pulled down his shirt to cover the piss patch.
At the top of his street an old woman shuffled towards us. She was fat, really fat, and gripped onto one of those four wheeled tartan shopping carts for dear life.
"That's more like it," muttered Coffin Nail, eying her up. "Look at that, lad. Gagging for it, she is."
"What, Mrs Frobisher?" I asked in disbelief. "She's well into her seventies, Coffin Nail. The only thing she's gagging for is a pot of tea and a fig roll."
"I've got a fig roll she can have!" His bony hand strayed towards his crotch again, then slipped into his pocket. He must have remembered the damp patch.
We stepped off the pavement to let Mrs Frobisher get by. There wasn't room enough for us all. To be fair, there wasn't enough room on the pavement for anyone except Mrs Frobisher.
as she passed, Coffin Nail mentally undressed her with his runny eyes. I mentally dressed her again as quickly as I could.
"Look at the fucking rig on that, lad! A bloke could have some fun on that!"
"Jesus. No, I don't really see it, Coffin Nail. She's not my type..."
"Fuck off! With a couple of those Viagra in me it would take half of West Yorkshire Police Force to get me off of her..."
"It would take the other half to get her off of you if she rolled over. She's fucking massive!"
Coffin Nail wouldn't have it. He watched her limp away down the street with an expression of raw lust on his haggard features.
"The thing is with you young 'uns, lad, is that you want something you can't have. When he's hungry, a poor man doesn't dream about caviar, does he? Nah, he's never tasted it! He wants summat he likes." Coffin Nail nodded after Mrs Frobisher. "He dreams about that."
"If Mrs Frobisher isn't caviar, then what is she?"
"She's Spam."
We finished our cigars and walked to Coffin Nail's gate. I gave him his shopping bags. He leant close to me.
"Here, lad. You haven't got any mints on you, have you? It's just that if the wife smells cigars on my breath she'll go fucking scatty."

I got a pack of gum from my pocket and gave him a couple of sticks. I decided to needle him again. "So I'm cunt whipped, am I? Who's the one scared of his wife catching him smoking?"
Coffin Nail chewed the gum carefully. He didn't want to lose the few teeth left in his head.
"You're a bloke, I'm a bloke, every bloke who's ever lived - we're all cunt whipped, lad. That's what it is to be a bloke. Cunt whipped. It's why we die first and they live for ever."
He took his shopping, nodded at me and shuffled to his front door.
I made sure he got his key in ok.
Maybe a Viagra would help him with that.
He shut the door.
I went home.

Yosser Hughes Eat your Heart Out.

Christ, fiction is so much harder than the truth.

I've spent three days working on the biggest load of bullshit I've ever written.

Two pages of lies, fabrications, grandiose exaggerations and utter bollocks.

I have sweated, I have cursed, I have stared blankly at the screen until a fine layer of dust has settled on my eyeballs and they have dried like the eyes of a fish in the sun.

Every word had to be dragged out of me like a diseased molar from an abscessed jaw.

No flow, no skipping sentences dancing across the page, no playful double entendres or bleak flashes of painfully remembered horror.

And the title of this masterpiece?

What could be worthy of such pain, such tortured creation, this literary golum molded from naught but my own sweat and sacrificed hours and the very writhing of my tormented soul?

Two letters:

C.V.

Yes, that's right.

I am trying to escape.

Like a downed pilot ensconced behind the grey walls of Colditz Castle, I am quietly making plans.

My hair is short and it is smart and my face is cleanly shaved.

My suit is pressed and my shirt is fresh and my tie is confident yet conservative.

I have a number of days leave squirrelled away should I need to attend an interview.

I have vacuumed the crap from the insides of the family car and I have paid six pounds for Eastern European men to wash and wax the exterior until it gleams.

I have cut down on the booze.

I am prepared.

All I need now are the necessary faked documents and I will be ready to flee for the border.

And this is where I come unstuck.

The C.V.

It is pitiful, it really is.

When I list my professional achievements with brutal honesty it is enough to make me weep.

Twenty two years of doing the same job, in one guise or another.

There are only so many ways you can fluff up the sentence 'career history: reprographics, from 1989 until 2011'.

Fuck me. I've just realised that my working life spans four decades.

That's a long time using an NT cutter - surely by now I'm adept enough to painlessly open up my fucking wrists?

An old college mate has contacted me.

He runs a studio, a slick professional outfit.

He wanted to know if I was still in the trade, if I was interested in applying for a job.

I said yes and yes.

But when I got to my C.V., dusted off an old mac that still had a fucking floppy drive, and I looked at what I had listed as my great achievements in this most prestigious of career choices, I realised there was only one thing I could add to it.

Years.

All I did was press tap...tab...tab... until I got to the part about years-in-service and changed the number from 14 to 22.

22 years.

In eight years I've achieved the princely sum of FUCK ALL.

The years before that are not much better.

And as those years sneak past, my urge to leave is slowly overwhelmed by the bleak fact of my increasing unemployability.

Any employer worth his salt is going to look at a C.V. that reads '22 years in reprographics' and think 'what the fuck is wrong with this bloke??'

It's a question I've asked myself many, many times.

So what do you do if your C.V. is a perfect study of minimalism?

You lie.

Everyone lies on their C..V., of course, to one extent or another, but nothing compared to what I've got to do.

So I've been inventing lies for three days and now I have a horrible taste in my mouth, the taste of concentrated bullshit.

I look at what I've written and I gag.

Am I writing about me? What happens when I get asked a question in an interview, and my mask slips to reveal my real face pulling spaz faces at my prospective employer?

I'm fucked, that's what.

So I've decided to write an honest C.V., a C.V. I can put out there and honestly claim it to be mine, a C.V. packed full of achievements and life experience.

Here it is.

Name: General Lucifer

Address: The City of Dis,

Fifth Circle,
South of Heaven.
email: g.lucifer@rocketship.com

I have been employed as a reprographic mac operator at The Factory for twenty two years now, and in that time I have achieved naff all. I have shown great consistency and diligence in irritating my supervisors to the point of complete nervous breakdown, and I have successfully avoided a much deserved sacking on any number of occasions.

My wealth of knowledge and experience will prove beneficial to any prospective employer, as long as that employer is in the business of having sex with drunk women, hiding in the toilet for prolonged periods of time, drinking vast quantities of tea and seven different styles of malingering.

I can also offer a broad range of other skills, such as Eating Bacon, drawing cruel cartoons of fellow employees, griping, talking rubbish and tossing-it-off.

CAREER HISTORY

Four colour planner (1989-1996)

I started work at sixteen on a five year apprenticeship that took seven years to complete and by this time I was already drinking quite a bit. I had not started fucking anyone yet, apart from myself, but I was a very keen learner and considered fucking to be a skill that I had a very great desire to master.

At work I was making tea, cutting up film and shit, and using paint the colour dog crap to spot out negatives.

An old man shoved his cock in my ear.

I consider this to be the moment I lost my virginity.

It was disappointing.

I grew my hair really long and started listening to rock music.

I started drinking a lot.

A girl finally let me fuck her but it was quite a let down. When I tried to massage her clitoris she said, 'Ow, give over, your trying to frig me, not remove a fucking stain.'

I shot my bolt too fast.

I realised I'd need a lot of practice to get good at this.

At work I was sleeping in the darkroom and lusting over a girl in accounts. I took her on a date but made the mistake of treating her with respect so she dumped me. It turns out she was wanking off all the printers in their cars after work.

I didn't have a car so I never got wanked off.

It is against the law to be wanked off on a bus, I think.

the seven years of my apprenticeship finished and I was finally a fully qualified four colour planner.

Everyone in the factory gathered round and cheered as they stripped me naked and threw me in a massive vat filled with cold water, piss, glue, ink, rotting food and mashed paper.

After I got clean I discovered that they were getting rid of film planning and were buying Apple Macs.

Seven years wasted.

Fucking typical.

Apple Mac Operator (1996-present day)

I trained to be a mac operator under the expert tutelage of a man in his fifties who had messed about with a mac for a few weeks and who now considered himself an expert.

He had a big moustache and he picked his arse and sniffed his fingers and he didn't wash and he thought that the only thing you needed to disguise the smell of shitty fingers and body odour was the sweet smell of a sucked fruit Polo.

I used to like fruit Polos.

Now the smell makes me dry retch.

The man with the moustache used to say, 'One of the things I really hate about you Lucifer, is...'

Insert what you like. He really hated me.

I bought a house and fucked girls in it.

I started getting pretty good at it, and even started fucking other men's wives, I got that good.

I was drinking more by now and I'd also started smoking cigars the size and colour of Linford Christie's cock. I'm guessing.

By now I had A Reputation, both at work and locally.

Locally I had A Reputation for being drunk and for fucking.

At work I had A Reputation for being hung over and for being fucked.

Both were true, after a fashion, but not as bad as people made out.

Not that I can remember.

I was pretty drunk, after all.

Then I met a girl and settled down a bit and got thrown out of America and went to Italy and got drunk and got engaged then got married then had some kids.

I happened just like that.

It's all rather a blur.

And with a house and a wife and some kids I couldn't afford to fuck about so much.

I actually started to try.

At about this time I started writing.

So I put the hours in, worked hard, lost a bit of the reputation as a drunk trouble causer and got a couple of breaks.

I was given a nice little design role, and at the same time I was made a kind of assistant studio manager.

I liked the design part because I've always been a bit artsy craftsy glue and bits of paper. I liked the managing bit because I got to chat to the office girls and dress a bit dapper and I got a good wage by taking the piss with the overtime.

The skills I can bring to a management role are the an ability to laugh loudly at shit jokes, to nod seriously like I have heard important information when I'm actually listening to music in my head, and I am also very good at prioritizing work according to the amount of thigh or tit the account executive has flashed at me.

The skills I can bring to a design role are the ability to dress up a crappy piece of direct mail like the cheap whore it is, make it tacky and gaudy and appealing to the sort of person who chooses to advertise their product with something as hideously ugly and crass as a direct mail marketing campaign.

I am no longer a designer, and I am no longer an assistant manager.

I got rather good at laughing loudly and whoring my art and ogling tits and thighs and nodding seriously, so good in fact that people made noises about giving me a permanent job.

So my boss got cross and demoted me.

I lost a lot of money, and I lost my house, but I was allowed to keep my wife and kids.

So I'm just a reprographic mac operator again.

I'd rather be a writer, but I'm not.

Yet.

Now are you going to give me a fucking job or what?

Dead Wood

"Don't worry, Lucifer, you'll get used to it."

"I'm not getting used to it. I've worked in this office for weeks now and I'm no nearer to getting used to it."

"I'm telling you, you'll acclimatise. It might feel a little strange at first..."

"Strange? Getting used to this shit is like getting used to a chronic debilitating disease. Getting used to it is like getting used to... I don't know... cock tumours or something."

"Cock tumours? What are cock tumours? I didn't know you could get tumours on your cock!"

Billy wriggled his hand nervously down the front of his work issue stay-pressed pants and fumbled carefully with his cock.

"Jesus..." I looked away. I had no desire to sit there watching a workmate massaging his cock in search of cancerous growths.

I stabbed some keys and blinked at the monitor.

I'd made a mistake. I'd taken my eye of the screen for one fucking second, suffered one momentary lapse of concentration, and I'd made a mistake.

Again.

The tab keys and delete keys on my keyboard are fucked, worn away, illegible.

It happened all the time. Not big mistakes, just stupid little errors that would be easy to spot if I wasn't so fucking jaded.

I never felt fresh and ready for work, keen as mustard. I always felt tired and my stomach lurched whenever a new job flopped onto my desk with the wet slap of a heavy plastic wallet filled with some deluded fool's idea of what might deliriously excite Joe Public when it drifted onto his doormat on a Tuesday morning.

Junk mail is never welcome. Ever. The jobs I work on are shit, the printed product is shit, the dinky little envelopes that leave the factory filled to the brim with impersonal personalisation are shit.

"Dear Keith Ringworm we are delighted to inform you that you have been chosen out of the billions of writhing nobodies on the planet to qualify for a grand prize of £50,000 (or an Elvis tea cosy)..."

A waste of trees, a waste of ink, a waste of fucking time.

Job after job, day after day, year after year, relentless piles of direct mail.

I couldn't see an end.

"Do you think Amoxicillin will prevent cock tumours, Luci?"

I looked up.

Billy still had one hand rummaging around inside his pants while the other fumbled with scores of foil covered blister packs of pills inside his rucksack.

"Jesus Christ, Billy! Don't let any fucker in this office catch you doing either of those things. Wanking and popping pills are not considered suitable occupations for an office worker."

Billy gasped in panic as he realised what he was doing. He pulled his hand from out of his pants too quickly and caught his watch strap on something delicate. He let out a shrill whimper and crumpled to the floor in a glittering rainbow of anti-inflammatories, anti-depressants, anti-biotics.

I carried on punching the keyboard. "Good work, Billy. You're the only bloke I know who can start out giving himself a preventative medical examination for cock tumours only to end up accidentally circumcising himself with a Sekonda. Well done."

Billy scrambled on the floor, desperately shovelling prescription medication back into his rucksack before anyone noticed.

I saw that I'd made another mistake. I swore, jabbed delete.

Billy hauled himself painfully back into his seat, washed down a mouthful of various pills with cold decaffeinated tea sweetened with Canderel.

"I'm already circumcised."

I looked up again.

"What? I really didn't need to know that, Billy."

"My mother thought it would be best if I was circumcised. You know, for hygiene. I didn't need it doing for any medical reason, but my mother thought it would be more hygienic."

"Hygienic? What's wrong with just giving it a scrub with a flannel like everyone else does? Anyway, how old were you when she got you circumcised?"

"Twenty seven."

"Fucking Hell. I don't even want to know why your mum has an opinion about your dick when you're that kind of age, never mind why you listened to her."

"She's a nurse. She gets me my medicines."

"I see. So your mother plies you with medication that isn't even prescribed to you, then she wants to look at your cock. That's quite a relationship you've got going on with your mum, Billy."

"It's nothing weird! She's a health professional!"

"Health professional my arse. Remember those pills you took the other month? They were so powerful we all thought you'd had a fucking stroke. You couldn't talk and you slobbered on your keyboard and your left eye went all droopy. It was only the fact we found that packet of horse tranquilizers, or whatever they were, that we didn't ship you off to Leeds General Infirmary fucking pronto. I still think we should have sent you anyway!"

We lapsed into silence, me struggling to focus on a job, him struggling to get eye drops in.

Billy was obviously uncomfortable with silences.

"What do you reckon the big meeting's about, Luci?"

Sigh.

"Fuck knows. It won't be good news though."

"It might be."

"It won't be."

There's always meetings. All the little supervisors and managers are regularly summoned around a big desk behind closed doors to discuss new and improved ways of kicking our arses. One time it was a big reduction in overtime pay, another time it was a ban on mobile phones, yet another time they decided to dress us up as clones in itchy little uniforms. The Holy Grail was to find a way of sacking people without paying them a fortune in redundancy. They hadn't found a way of doing it legally yet. It was the only thing that saved my sorry hide.

"But it might be good news, Luci. Maybe they're gonna give us our overtime rate back!"

He wouldn't give up!

"Christ, are those eye drops rose-tinted or something? Those bastards take, they don't give, Billy. You can forget them giving us any overtime money back, you can forget them giving us a long overdue pay rise and you can most definitely forget a thank you for all your hard work at Christmas. You wait. The news will be shitty."

Billy shook his head, pulled a sad face.

"I feel sorry for you, Luci. I mean, how can you go through life being so negative? Everyone's got to come here and do their job, get on with it, so why can't you do your job with a smile instead of a scowl?"

I stabbed the keyboard harder, trying to get the job to do something that it clearly did not want to do.

"Maybe it's because I've usually got a massive fucking hangover, Billy. Maybe that's why I scowl."

"Well maybe you shouldn't drink quite so much then..."

My screen froze, keyboard and mouse became useless. I pushed away from the desk and grabbed hold of the partition that separated me from Billy.

"What? What did you just say? That I shouldn't drink so much? That's fucking rich coming from you! At least I'm honest about what I use to numb the grim tedium of everyday life, but you hide your poison in shiny foil packets and call it medicine! I'll show you medicine..."

"Luci, your shouting!"

"Fuck it Billy, I don't care! None of these fuckers can hear me! Just look at him!"

I pointed across the room at Soulless Boss.

"Look at him! That black-hearted bastard used to be ambitious, driven, a real go-getter! See him staring at that laptop? Know what's on the screen? A flower. A picture of a flower! He's been staring at that picture for nearly two hours! He's fucked! Know what's made him fucked? Medicine! He's ripped off his tits on medicine! He's staring at that flower but for all I know he's got Jesus Christ and a choir of fucking angels singing to him!"

I waved an arm, taking in the rest of the office.

"Now look at the rest of these drones, Billy. Just you stand up and take a look at them. What do you see? Tell me what they are doing."

Billy half stood up and looked around the room furtively. He sat back down with a shocked expression on his face.

"Most of them are asleep, Luci! Why are they all asleep?"

"Medicine, Billy. They've taken their medicine. Look at that weird little fuck downstairs, Burrows. Off on permanent sick with stress. What about Mallett, hiding in his office all day? Check out his desk. You'll see a box of tissues. Why? Because he can burst out crying at the drop of a fucking hat and he doesn't know why! And there's a reason why every single bloke on the night shift goes home at six in the morning and starts drinking, and keeps drinking while their wife and kids get up for work and school, and they wave them off at the door with a tin of Kestrel Super Strength in their hand. That's not normal behaviour, Billy. It's fucking wrong."

Billy looked shell shocked. I felt like a bit of a cunt for ranting at him.

I felt tired all of a sudden.

I needed a drink.

"Look, Billy, the bottom line is, this place is no Center of

Excellence. The cream of the crop do not aspire to work in a Northern factory producing junk mail. Those guys are working for NASA, or finding out the breeding habits of octopi on the reefs around the Galapagos Islands, or discovering a miracle cure for cock tumours. It doesn't take a genius to blanket bomb the nation with cheap pamphlets selling double glazing, Sky television deals and life insurance. The reason why everyone here is on industrial strength booze and tranquilizers is because they woke up one day and realised they were in a hole, a deep, shitty hole, and they couldn't find a way out so they started to panic, and the easiest thing to stop the panic is to go back to sleep again, numb the pain, pop a pill, crack a beer. They all knew they were never going to do that dream job on the Galapagos Islands, or in space, or cure the sick. That kind of realisation comes as a shock, a disappointment. Sometimes the only cure for disappointment is to get all fucked up."

I pressed the restart button on my computer.

It made a happy little pinging noise.

Billy looked up at me with fear in his eyes and a Vicks inhaler up his nose.

"Luci, is everyone like that? Everyone in the factory, I mean? Are they all on drugs and booze to shut out how they really feel?"

I shook my head.

"Not all of us, Billy boy. Some people actually love this shit. It's all they've ever wanted. You've got to be a cold hearted fucker to thrive here though, with zero imagination. Someone like Jekyll."

Jekyll was my new boss.

He was ten years younger than me, about four stone lighter and eight inches shorter.

You wouldn't look twice at the little cunt if he passed you in the street, but that was his secret weapon. He slipped under the radar. He was fucking brilliant at his job, he had a photographic memory for every little detail that passed under his nose and he never, ever made a mistake.

Oh, and he was also a total fucking sociopath.

His capacity for cruelty knew no bounds. He genuinely seemed to relish humiliating his staff in front of others. He was notorious for being incredibly rude and arrogant with everyone, regardless of rank, and he suffered from a monstrous vanity. In his creepy world every woman who spoke to him was desperate to fuck him, every man was in awe of him.

Truly a wanker of the highest order.

Credit where credit is due, he'd managed to topple Soulless Boss from his perch. I had been glad to see that bastard get his comeuppance, but Jekyll made Soulless Boss look cute and cuddly in comparison.

He had it in for me. Mistakes offended him, and in his eyes I was one big mistake. He'd been turning the screw on me for weeks, letting me know that he was the boss at every opportunity, trying to grind me down to the point where I snapped. Nothing would have given him greater pleasure than to see me just fold, go on sick with depression or stress.

I wouldn't give him the satisfaction.

Twenty two years of getting trodden on toughens you up. Not always in a good way, but you find strength where others might crack.

I could take it.

The door opened and Jekyll glided in.

Billy scurried to yank the Vicks from out of his snout and look busy.

I kept prodding the keyboard, shoving the mouse.

Jekyll was smirking. I didn't like that.

"Gentlemen, I've just come from the board meeting. I have some good news..."

Billy's jaw dropped, then his face lit up. He shot me a look.

I didn't react.

"It seems that the factory is thriving! While other print works are going into administration we are going from strength to strength."

I still didn't react.

"But we can't afford to relax. We still have room for improvement..."

Jekyll was staring right at me. This was the crunch.

"We are introducing a new system. Any mistakes, no matter how small, will result in a ticket. You get three tickets and we all have a little meeting to find out what's going wrong, and how you can be helped."

Me and Jekyll were in a staring contest now.

"The company line is that this is being introduced to help you boys, to find out where training is needed, but I think I can let you in on the real meaning of this. You see, there's a lot of lads out there in the trade who are looking for work. Good lads, with experience. We get dozens of C.V.s a day. Dozens. This got the bosses thinking. If we can get rid of the people we don't need, the dead wood, then we can get some of these experienced lads in on a cheap rate. They've looked into it. This ticket system is fail safe. You get too many tickets and we start writing warnings. Three warnings, and you're sacked. Simple!"

Jekyll grinned at me. I'd seen a grin like that before, on the faces of kids who liked setting fire to cats or kicking dogs to death. It was the grin of seeing someone in a bad situation, relishing the misfortune of others.

I knew that I was fucked.

He did too.

They'd found the Holy Grail.

While me and Jekyll stared each other out, Billy was quietly going to pieces. He blubbered and gibbered, babbled about how much he needed that job and how nobody was perfect and mistakes were going to happen.

Then he grabbed his bag and ran for the door.

He'd gone.

Jekyll watched him go, amused and puzzled by his reaction.

"Why's that pussy getting worked up? He's got nothing to worry about. The only people who need to worry are those that make mistakes, the dead wood."

He was staring at me again.

I felt my heart thump a bit harder. I forced myself not to grip my pen too tightly.

"The reason why he reacted like that, Jekyll, is because you've just told him that if he makes the slightest mistake he's going to get the fucking boot! Billy's a bit of a fragile character, threats like that get to him!"

"That wasn't a threat, Lucifer. You'd know about it if I was threatening you, believe me. Like I said, Billy need not be worried, he's not dead wood."

He smirked at me.

The pen snapped in my hand.

I smiled at Jekyll.

I could hear the blood rushing in my head. It sounded like the sea.

"Just supposing I were to kick off right now, Jekyll. I mean, really kick off. Do you think there's anything you could do?"

Jekyll blinked, stepped backwards.

"What?"

"Theoretically, I could twist your fucking head of like a bottle cap, you know. Your neck isn't much thicker than my wrist. I reckon if I got a good hold on you I could twist it clean off. Now, how might you stop me doing that?"

Thump thump thump, the blood was really pounding now. It felt pretty good, to be honest.

Wait to get sacked, or blaze of glory.

Heads or tails.

Jekyll glanced around.

"Well. Lucifer, first thing I'd do is smash that monitor into your face.

Then I'd throw as many things as I could at you to buy some time."

"These new monitors don't have much weight behind them, Jekyll. A couple of keyboards and a desk tidy are not going to slow me down a significant amount. And besides, take look around the office. Do you really think any of these lot could help you, even if they wanted to?"

"No, I suppose not."

Jekyll stepped closer.

But it doesn't matter, does it Luci? Because we both know you're going to do precisely fuck all, aren't you?"

And that blood sounded louder in my head, and little bits of shattered yellow plastic crunched together in my fist, slippery in the sudden sweat, and I chose the fastest point to clear the desk and get a grip, brushing aside computer and screen and tea mug and telephone, moving quick with the weight of my body bearing down on that thin neck, being careful not to let him gouge at my eyes with anything like a pen or his fingernails which I noticed were quite long, and the thump thump thump of my heart in my chest changed gear, and I felt a strange elation, a feeling of 'fuck it, just do it' flooding my system, and I could actually feel the sensation of gristle and muscle and cartilage and larynx collapsing beneath my fist, cracking and clicking and snapping like the ruined remains of the pen...

"No, you're not going to do anything."

Jekyll smiled his shitty smile and walked away.

"Jekyll."

"Yes?"

"This place can get rid of all the dead wood it likes, but all that will happen is that it will collapse. Dead wood is what's holding this place together. Dead wood is all it can get. Without dead wood, this place would be fucked."

Jekyll chose to ignore me.

He left me alone at the desk in the corner, left me to make mistakes, one at a time, until I earned my first cozy chat with the management.

I stabbed the delete key until it broke.

A Strife Aquatic

"Watcha doin', Lucifer?"

"Holyfuckingshit! Don't creep up on me like that, Scorcher! I swear, you're going to kill me one of these days!"

"I can't help it, mate. Stealth is in my nature. They reckon I could have made an ace assassin, what with my stealth and that."

"They reckon, do they? Who are 'they', hmm?"

"You know. 'Them'."

"Ohh, them! Why didn't you say!"

I turned back to my computer.

"Yeah, they said I'd be a perfect killing machine, being a person naturally gifted wiv a silent approach and a steely calm."

I looked at him again.

Steely calm. He had a face like a bloodhound on morphine and he was picking his undies out of his arse.

"So how come you work in a shit hole like this, Scorcher, rather than swanning around Europe bumping off heads of state?"

"They said it would be irresponsible to put such power in the hands of a man of my potential. They were frightened that if I turned double agent, I could've killed the whole government within firty days. Tony Blair wouldn't know what fuckin' hit 'im."

"David Cameron."

"Wot?"

"David Cameron. He's prime minister now."

"Is he? Well 'im then."

Scorcher mimed creeping up on David Cameron and slitting his throat.

"I'm sure he's breathing a sigh of relief as we speak."

"Yeah, I espect so. So wotcha doin' then, Lucifer?"

"Funnily enough, I'm looking on the internet for a new job."

"Watcha wanna new job for? What's wrong wiv this one?"

"Because I hate it, because I'm rather shit at it, because they'll probably fire me soon."

"Fair enough, I suppose. What sort of job you want then, Luci?"

"I'm not sure Scorcher. I'm just looking, but I don't see anything I actually want to do. I've never known what I want to do, if I'm honest."

"Why not be a frogman?"

I didn't even bother looking at him this time.

"The list of reasons why I'm not going to be a frogman are endless, Scorcher. I'm not going to even try to list them. I've got a better idea. Why don't you fuck off and be a frogman?"

"I've tried it, Luci, but to be honest frogmanning is a young man's game."

Here we go.

"Are you honestly trying to tell me you were a frogman?"

"Yeah, fifteen years, man and boy."

"Go on then. Where were you a frogman? Bahamas? Great barrier reef? Galapagos?"

"North Sea Ferries."

"Oh. So you were a frogman for North Sea Ferries?"

"Not for them. Off them."

"What? You've lost me now, Scorcher."

"Well, y'see, we was part of this little treasure hunting team, but we reckoned we didn't need all that outlay on boats and shit, so what we'd do is board the North Sea Ferry to Rotterdam in Hull as a passenger..."

"In your frogman outfits?"

"Yeah, in our frogman outfits, then we'd wait until we were in the right place out in the North Sea and over the back we'd go."

"Off the back of the ferry. You just lobbed yourself off the back of the ferry."

"Yeah."

"And the captain and the crew weren't the slightest bit suspicious that the blokes in rubber who boarded the ferry in Hull had gone missing by the time they'd got to Rotterdam?"

Scorcher tapped the side of his nose.

"The skipper were in on the game. Owt we found we split with him and his crew. Besides, we needed them to slow up a bit when they were on there way back to Hull on the return leg."

"Why did you need him to slow up?"

"So's we could grab a hold of the anchor as the ferry went by, and get a tow back to shore."

"Fuck off."

"For real! Look, I found this on the last dive I did. I kept it as a memento. I always keep it wi' me as a reminder o' those days at sea."

Scorcher dug around in his pocket. Found something, dropped it in my hand.

I looked at it.

"Scorcher, this is a pound coin."

"Aye. But look at the date, it's an old'un."

"It says nineteen ninety one."

"Yup. They don't make them no more."

I gave him it back.

I put my fingers in my ears and closed my eyes tightly.

I stayed like that for a bit.

When I opened my eyes Scorcher had gone.

I carried on looking for a new job.

Double Drunk Friday

Friday morning.

5.57am.

It is cold, it is dark, the roads are greasy, the fallen leaves clogging the gutter in a rotting sludge.

I'm shivering outside the factory, under the buzzing tangerine glow of the sodium lamps, stood in thick dew sodden grass, plucking up the guts to walk in again, clock in again, jump on the conveyor and go through the same shit routine again.

it's times like this I wish I smoked.

Tear of the plastic, pop open the carton, rip off that foil and fire up a coffin nail.

Just stand there, smoking.

The thing is, if I had just one smoke out there in the dark, just paused long enough to take it down to the filter, I don't think I'd go into the factory. I'd just turn around and go home, crawl back into bed, lay in the dark with my eyes wide open, smoke on my lips, waiting for the world to come crashing round my ears.

The beginning of the end.

It would be the beginning of the end because I know I wouldn't go to work again, I just know it. Maybe that's how a breakdown begins. Maybe that was what leads to shuffling around the house in threadbare y-fronts and an egg stained dressing gown,

using final demands as coasters for cracked mugs of piss-weak tea,

shouting at Ken Bruce's Pop Master on Radio 2,

wanking mechanically at the sight of Lorraine Kelly on daytime telly, laughing at the tragic stories on the news,

crying at the happy stories on the news,

cowering on the stairs pretending to be out when the window cleaner comes around, getting the feeling you get on an airplane when you hit turbulence and drop a thousand feet but you're just sitting still on the sagging couch with cup-a-soup,

staring out of the window wishing a runaway juggernaut would plow across the front garden and smash right into the living room, just to relieve the dread-filled tedium...

No, maybe it was best I didn't smoke.

I trudge across the grass in sodden shoes, go into the factory.

Loud hissing of compressed air, strip lights, the chung chung chung of perpetual motion machinery churning out endless reams of flimsy personalised crap.

I walk to the scrum of workers surrounding the clock machine, struggle through to peg in.

There is a buzz of barely contained excitement, strangely jarring at such a grim hour, such a grim place.

Peel blunders into me, skipping from foot to foot, tittering like a loon. Peel is six feet six, wild eyed, built like a giant stray labrador, always on the edge of genuine madness. He worked long hours, twelve hour nights and weekends too, shoving palettes of paper around the factory, driving the forklifts like a maniac, striding around looking happily bemused.

"What's going on, Peel? You lot should be knackered after the week you've had. You've not had a break in three weeks."

"I know Luci! That's why we're giddy as bastards! no work this weekend, so you know what that means! Double Drunk Friday!"

A small cheer goes up in the mob.

"Double Drunk Friday? What's that about?"

Peel winked, tapped his nose, grinned a knowing grin, made a clicking noise.

"Ah, Double Drunk Friday is ace! It's the best! What you do, you go home, get parked on the couch and fire into the piss of your choice. Me, I like sherry, I do. I only drink for an hour though, any more than that and you're a fucking alky!"

He nodded knowingly before continuing.

"So I fire into the sherry as quick as fuck, get as much as I can down me in an hour. By seven thirty I'll be arseholed!"

"Sound like heavy going. So what happens when you're that fucked on a Friday morning? What do you do?"

Peel shrugged.

"Dunno. Watch telly, computer game, have a wank... then I go to bed."

"Sounds like a riot."

"Yeah! It's ace! So I goes to bed, sleep it off, get up in the afternoon, come round a bit, have a bite of summat, then..."

He looked at me with puppy like eagerness, urging me to finish it off for him.

"You get fucked up again?"

"BINGO! Another sherry hour! Double Drunk Friday!"

The bell rings.

A mad scrabble of clock cards and work boots and car keys, then they're gone.

Gone to get drunk.

I felt like joining them.

Nearly did.

But didn't.

I went to work.

Twinkle Twinkle Little Star...

I imagine office life is a bit like prison life.

Not the stuff about getting savagely bummed in the showers or buying porn with batteries and cigs or having to make a knife out of a toothbrush and a razor blade to stripe a nonce, nothing like that.

I'm on about getting shoved in a big room with a load of strangers for much of the day, people you'd never actually choose to associate with if you weren't forced to, and then having to get on with them, interact with them, avoid killing them.

Because office life is hopelessly inane.

I bet prison life is hopelessly inane as well, only you can brew your own hooch in a bucket under your bed in prison, or tattoo a tear drop onto your cellmate's face with a rusty pin, and there is always that potential for spontaneous violence to add a little spice to the day.

I don't think there's ever been an office in the history of offices that's had a lock down enforced after the staff kicked off because of a shortage of paperclips, resulting in a thirty six hour siege and shit smeared water coolers and a burnt out stationary cupboard and the work experience girl getting her throat cut in a bungled hostage situation.

don't get me wrong, if it ever does kick off I'll be the first on the roof with my shirt wrapped around my face lobbing tiles at the rozzers and demanding helicopters and pepperoni pizzas, but I can't see it happening any time soon.

Or ever.

Office types are a docile bunch, generally speaking.

They live in a world that is obvious, predictable, inane.

For example, I grew a moustache. A great big fuck off moustache. Not a Movember thing, this one was big porn star/European partisan/finch-perched-under-the-nose size moustache.

An office drone trundled past to the tea urn.

He stopped in his tracks, double taking the moustache nestled under my sneezer.

He took a couple of steps closer.

He smiled.

I ignored him.

He kept smiling.

I kept ignoring him.

He cleared his throat a bit, so I looked at him.

He smiled again, kind of raising his mug to point at my face, so I said,

"Yes?"

He said, "You've got a moustache."

I said, "Yes."

I ignored him again, but he kept staring, and he said, "Moustache," and I said "I know," and he eventually fucked off.

He must have informed the other drones about the wondrous news, because this incident happened twice more in the day, word for fucking word.

Then I finished for the day and clocked out and went home and I had a drink and I shaved of my moustache, then got angry for doing so because I felt like the drones had somehow won.

But just like prison, not everybody in an office is an utter cunt.

There's a bloke on my shift called Twinkle.

I've not worked with him before, he works in another department, but we all had a bit of a reshuffle so know I'm in a room with Twinkle.

Twinkle is gay. I mean really, really gay. I've met plenty of gay people, but Twinkle is by far the gayest. Everything he does gets that special sprinkle of magic gay dust, so that mundane things suddenly shimmer a bit.

What is it that makes one person gayer than another? If you know any gay people, or you're gay yourself, let me know.

I like Twinkle. He's really honest and open, not like the others. Maybe it's something to do with coming out. Once your honest about your sexuality, maybe it's easier to just be open about everything else.

Twinkle has a ruddy drinker's complexion and I like him for that too. He won't eat bread because he says it will make him fat, but he loves the vino tinto.

He calls everyone 'captain' in a way that suggests he's hailing a large ship from on board a small dinghy.

I don't really talk to him much, I don't really talk to anyone much lately, but he came over to me the other day while I was working.

"Evening captain!"

"Now then, Twinkle. How's it hanging?"

"Ooh, you know, little to the left and just North of the knee! Hee hee!"

"Nice. You busy?"

"No, Luci, dead quiet! Just been online, ordering a new collar for my little doggy."

"What kind of dog you got?"

"A Chihuahua!"

"Figures, I suppose. You won't have bought him one of those big studded collars then."

"Ooh, no! This one's lovely. Cost me over two hundred quid!"

"Two hundred! Fuck me, Twinkle, what's it made of? Solid gold? You'll break the little sod's neck!"

"No, silly! This one's got pearls on it. Real pearls!"

"Twinkle, does a dog really need a collar with pearls on it?"

"Whether he needs them or not, he almost got a pearl necklace last night when he jumped on the bed, so I thought I'd get him his own so we'd be matching! Hee hee!"

"Fucking hell, Twinkle, how come gay men are always so bloody randy? The chances of me getting my end away on Tuesday night are exactly zero, yet you and your bloke are giving each other facials with the fucking dog barking encouragement. I don't get it!"

"The thing is, Luci, we don't have any of that messing about like women do. I say to a bloke, 'fancy a fuck', he's says, 'go on then', we fuck, I cum, he cums, we both get dressed, have a glass of wine and watch telly. Simple as."

"Sounds ideal, putting it like that."

"Exactly! Never fancied giving it a go?"

"What, being gay? Not really, no. The life style sounds pretty good, but it's getting bummed that I'm not keen on."

"That's the best bit!"

"Each to his own."

"What I want to know, Luci, is if you're feeling horny and the wife's not putting out, what do you do?"

"I do what the vast majority of the male heterosexual married population do when they're randy. I have a wank."

"Oh! Does the wife not mind then?"

"Mind? She encourages it! She sees it as one less job for her to do. It's like her coming home and finding I've cleaned the oven. She's pleased she doesn't have to do it."

"Seems a shame!"

"It is a bit, I suppose. What about your bloke, then. Does he mind you having a crafty wank?"

"Ooh yes! He gets terribly jealous! If I've been wanking then there's nowt left for him, is there? Besides, I do get a bit... obsessive about it, when I start."

"Obsessive?"

"yeah, I can't stop myself! Hee hee!"

"Just out of interest, what are we talking about here? How many times are you doing it in a day then?"

"Fifteen or sixteen times."

"What?? Jesus, your cock must be a wreck after that kind of session!"

"It is a bit red, yeah."

"Red? I'll reckon it looks like your chihuahua has been gnawing it!"

"I think that's what pisses my boyfriend off most. He won't go near it when it looks like that, you know, all weepy..."

"I can't say I blame him. Seems like a sensible bloke."

"Oh he is, he is! I've got a picture of him on my phone, if you want to see what he looks like!"

"Well... go on then."

"Give me a minute.. on here some where... Here we go! This is Gary!"

Very nice. He keeps himself very neat and tidy, doesn't he."

Yes. I've always gone for the groomed look. Here he is on holiday in Marbella."

"Lovely. When did you go there?"

"Last Summer. Oh look! Here's Christmas! He's wearing a Santa hat, see?"

"Yeah, so he is. Look, Twinkle, have you got any pictures of Gary's face? These are all pictures of his cock, and while that's fine and everything, it's just not my thing. No offense."

Twinkle flicked through the pictures on his phone.

"Hmm.. I could have sworn there was at least one... Nope! It's all cocks I'm afraid! Heehee!"

"Oh well. I'm sure he's... very handsome, or something."

Twinkle was looking very intently at the phone.

His booze burnt face flushed and sweat beaded his shaved head.

His hand slipped into his trouser pocket, started to rummage.

I said, "Look, I've got some work to finish off here, Twinkle..."

"Oh. no problem!" he replied. "Listen, Luci, you're not needing the lavvies in the foreseeable, are you?"

I kept my gaze fixed on the monitor. "No. You get in there and have yourself a party mate. Don't leave an mess though, eh?"

"Cheers Luci, your a pal."

Twinkle scuttled off.

I was left alone in the office.

Twinkle was gone for two hours.

At home time he still hadn't surfaced.

I thought about knocking on the bog door, seeing if he was alright.

Then I thought about what I might see, decided to give it a miss.

I packed my things away, turned off the light, fucked off home.

-

I came in to work last Monday.

Where Twinkle should have been sitting there was a massive Christmas tree.

It was one of nasty silver tinsel plastic pieces of crap, dripping in neon baubles and lights, blinking dementedly at a frequency that would have given Stevie Wonder an epileptic fit.

I walked over to the nearest office drone, shielding my eyes to avoid spazzing out on the carpet.

"Here, drone, where's Twinkle?"

"Oh, hi Luci. Twinkle got the sack."

"Fuck! How come?"

"They said he wasn't working hard enough, that he was always tossing it off."

"Fair point, I suppose. What's this fucking monstrosity doing here then?" I asked, pointing at the tree.

"Well, we had a bit of a think, and we decided we didn't want anything quite as camp and glittery as Twinkle anymore, so we got that."

I looked at the tree, started to feel all swimmy and sick, looked away.

"Poor fucker. Nice time to sack a bloke that, isn't it? Right before Christmas!"

"Maybe he could get a part time job here Luci - we're looking for a fairy for the top of the tree! Ha ha ha! Ha ha ha!"

"Fuck off, drone."

"Oh."

Drone looked hurt.

I went back to my desk.

For some reason I couldn't help thinking of Gary's cock wearing a Santa hat.

Guilty Pleasures

When I make a pot of tea, I can look through the little window set into the door opposite and see the canteen.

The canteen appears framed, a moving picture filled with poor quality foodstuff and bloated, dyspeptic consumers. When I look back to my tea mug, cruelly crush the sodden bag against the side of my stolen Starbucks pint mug, then glance back at my moving canteen picture I find the scene has changed slightly, a different pouchy, paunchy man is at the greasy counter but the same girl is serving.

Stacey.

Big smile of slightly crooked teeth, tight jeans with a hint of love handle swelling over the top, a muffin top. She once fitted into those jeans, but not anymore, not quite.

Big tits in a bikini top, glittery jumper slung over carelessly, slipping off one shoulder, giving the lads a peek of aquamarine strap, a holiday hint of bargain beachwear.

Blonde Stacey, grilling bacon, toasting bread, blonde fringe flopping, big tits flopping, hands rough from cleaning jobs and catering jobs, voice rough from Berkley fags and pub white wine.

She was fit once, proper knockout, back when she was a cleaner, eighteen years earlier. Hoovering the offices and dusting the studio in denim shorts and tight tees, giving the lads hard-ons as she vigorously vacced the day's dust or wiped coffee spills from the desks. I used to spill coffee on purpose, just to watch Stacey scrub, watch Stacey jiggle.

It was magic.

But that was then and this is now. Poor Stacey, feigning happiness through the hangover, a hint of stale chardonnay through the counterfeit perfume, a black eye showing through thick make-up. Stacey is no longer fit enough for the blokes to hide their leers, age and hard living has made her attainable, dragged her into their league.

The glittery sweater slips a little more, showing some cleavage, showing some bloke's name in blurred blue ink, showing a love bite from a bloke she met in the pub.

A fat bloke at the counter says something to her as he stares a murderous stare down her top.

She laughs an uncomfortable laugh, and loads a bap with cheap, dried out sausages.

I return to my desk, put my mug down, spill a few drops for old time's sake.

Then I go through the door to the canteen.

"Hi Stacey."

"Oh, Hiya Luci love! What can I get ya?"

Everything she says sounds like an offer of sex. It's a nack, it's a curse.

I try not to stare at her tits, but I fail.

If there had been other people in the queue I'd have asked for beans, or tomatoes, or yoghurt and fruit.

But I'm alone with Stacey, alone with her tired smile and her sagging softness.

"Spam and egg, please."

I look guilty. Stacey winks at me with the eye that hasn't been punched recently.

"Nowt wrong with having a bit of what you fancy now and then, is there?" She says, loading a bap with greasy, quivering, pink meat.

"No, I suppose not." I give her a fiver, she gives me some change.

"Thanks Stacey. See you later."

"Yeah, see ya Luci!"

She winks again.

I want to tell her that I remember her in those denim shorts, I remember how she walked, how she laughed before she became hoarse, how blue her eyes were before they were black and blue, how men didn't dare to stare because she was just to good, just too hot.

But I don't.

Instead I take my sandwich and my hard-on back to my desk, and get on with my work.

Epilogue.

Rambling about the fading charms of a canteen worker doesn't seem a great way to finish a book, does it? It doesn't to me, at any rate, but that's just how it is.

You can only end a story well if the story is over, and for me it isn't. I'm still in the same crappy job, applying and failing to get similar crappy jobs in similar crappy factories.

People keep saying to me that I have to get out, that I have to try and do something different.

Well I have.

I've written this book.

It might not mean much, but at least it's something different.

And who knows? Maybe it will help me get out of the factory.

I'll keep you posted.